D1112096

Information Technology and Organizational Transformation

Wiley Series in Information Systems

PREVIOUS VOLUMES IN THE SERIES

Boland & Hirschheim: *Critical Issues in Information Systems Research*

Schäfer: *Functional Analysis of Office Requirements—A Multiperspective Approach*

Mumford & MacDonald: *XSEL's Progress—The Continuing Journey of an Expert System*

Swanson & Beath: *Maintaining Information Systems in Organizations*

Friedman: *Computer Systems Development—History, Organization and Implementation*

Huws, Korte & Robinson: *Telework—Towards the Elusive Office*

Lincoln: *Managing Information Systems for Profit*

Silver: *Systems that Support Decision Makers—Description and Analysis*

Irving & Higgins: *Office Information Systems—Management Issues and Methods*

Cotterman & Senn: *Challenges and Strategies for Research in Systems Development*

Walsham: *Interpreting Information Systems in Organizations*

Watkins & Eliot: *Expert Systems in Business and Finance—Issues and Applications*

Lacity & Hirschheim: *Information Systems Outsourcing—Myths, Metaphors and Realities*

Österle, Brenner & Hilbers: *Total Information Systems Management—A European Approach*

Ciborra & Jelassi: *Strategic Information Systems—A European Perspective*

Knights: *Managers Divided*

Krcmar: *EDI in Europe*

Lacity & Hirschheim: *Beyond the Information Systems Outsourcing Bandwagon — The Insourcing Response*

Ward: *Strategic Planning for Information Systems*

McKeen & Smith: *Management Challenges in IS—Successful Strategies and Appropriate Action*

Ciborra: *Groupware & Teamwork—Invisible Aid or Technical Hindrance?*

Remenyi, Sherwood-Smith with White: *Achieving Maximum Value from Information Systems—A Process Approach*

Wigand: *Information, Organization and Management—Expanding Markets and Corporate Boundaries*

Galliers and Baets: *Information Technology and Organizational transformation—Innovation for the 21st Century Organization*

Willcocks & Lacity: *Strategic Sourcing of Information Systems — Perspectives and Practices*

Information Technology and Organizational Transformation:

Innovation for the 21st Century Organization

Edited by

Robert D GALLIERS

Warwick Business School, UK

and

Walter R J BAETS

Euro-Arab Management School, Granada, SPAIN

JOHN WILEY & SONS

Chichester • New York • Weinheim • Brisbane • Singapore • Toronto

Copyright © 1998 by   John Wiley & Sons Ltd,
Baffins Lane, Chichester,
West Sussex PO19 1UD, England
The copyright to Chapter 4 has been retained by the original publishers as detailed on the chapter title page.

National   01243 779777
International (+44) 1243 779777
e-mail (for orders and customer service enquiries):
cs-books@wiley.co.uk
Visit our Home Page on http://www.wiley.co.uk
or http://www.wiley.com

Reprinted July 1998

Other Wiley Editorial Offices

John Wiley & Sons, Inc., 605 Third Avenue,
New York, NY 10158–0012, USA

WILEY-VCH Verlag GmbH, Pappelallee 3,
D-69469 Weinheim, Germany

Jacaranda Wiley Ltd, 33 Park Road, Milton,
Queensland 4064, Australia

John Wiley & Sons (Asia) Pte Ltd, 2 Clementi Loop #02–01,
Jin Xing Distripark, Singapore 129809

John Wiley & Sons (Canada) Ltd, 22 Worcester Road,
Rexdale, Ontario M9W 1L1, Canada

Library of Congress Cataloging-in-Publication Data
Information technology and organizational transformation : innovation for the 21st century organization / edited by R.D. Galliers and W.R.J. Baets.
    p.   cm. — (Wiley series in information systems)
Includes bibliographical references and index.
ISBN 0-471-97073-5 (cloth)
1. Information technology—Management. 2. Organizational change.
I. Galliers, Robert, 1947- .   II. Baets, W. R. J. (Walter R. J.)   III. Series: John Wiley series in information systems.
HD30.2.I5277   1997
8658.4'038—dc21
                                                                                97–25963
                                                                                CIP

British Library Cataloguing in Publication Data

A catalogue record for this book is available from the British Library

ISBN 0-471-97073-5

Typeset in 10/12pt Palatino from the authors' disks by York House Typographic, London.
Printed and bound in great Britain by Biddles Limited, Guildford and King's Lynn.
This book is printed on acid-free paper responsibly manufactured from sustainable forestation, for which at least two trees are planted for each one used for paper production.

Contents

Contributors   ix

Series Preface   xix

Introduction   Information Technology and Organizational
Transformation: The Holy Grail of IT?   1
Bob Galliers and Walter Baets

PART 1: STARTING AFRESH

1.   Linking Strategy and IT-based Innovation: The
Importance of the "Management of Expertise"   19
Harry Scarbrough

2.   Computer Supported Collaborative Working:
Challenging Perspectives on Work and Technology   37
Liam Bannon

3.   The Metamorphosis of Oticon   65
Niels Bjørn-Andersen and Jon Turner

PART 2: IT AND THE LEARNING ORGANIZATION

4.   Organizational Learning and Core Capabilities
Development: The Role of IT   87
Rafael Andreu and Claudio Ciborra

5.   The Corporate Mind Set as a Precursor for Business
Process Change: About Knowledge, Perceptions and
Learning   107
Walter Baets

6. **The Role of Learning in Information Systems Planning and Implementation**   133
    Tapio Reponen

PART 3: INNOVATION, NETWORKS AND CORPORATE IDENTITY

7. **Innovations as Precursors of Organizational Performance**   153
    Johannes Pennings

8. **EDI, Organizational Change and Flexibility Strategies**   179
    Ramon O'Callaghan

9. **An IT Architecture to Support Organizational Transformation**   195
    Walter Baets and V. Venugopal

PART 4: IT AND ORGANIZATIONAL CHANGE

10. **Reflections on BPR, IT and Organizational Change**   225
    Bob Galliers

11. **The Role of IT in Organizational Transformation**   245
    Jon Turner

12. **LUCIA Accelerates Service Delivery: A Case Study of Business Process Re-engineering**   261
    Peter Meester and Jan Post

PART 5: AFTERWORD

13. **Success and Failure in Corporate Transformation Initiatives**   271
    Andrew Pettigrew

Postscript   291
Bob Galliers and Walter Baets

Index   293

Contributors

Rafael Andreu

Rafael Andreu studied Industrial Engineering at the UPC (Barcelona), from where he graduated in 1969. He also holds a Doctor's degree from UPC and a PhD in Management from the Massachusetts Institute of Technology, where he specialized in Information Systems, awarded in 1978. Dr Andreu joined IESE in 1969 and is now Professor of Information Systems. He has taught Quantitative Methods and Finance, and he is currently Chairman of IESE's Information Systems Department. He was also Professor of Information Systems at UPC and Associate Director of the MBA Program at IESE.

He has written articles in leading business journals and is co-author of the book *Estragegia y Sistemas de Informacion* (McGraw-Hill, 1991). He has consulted extensively in the field of Information Systems for many companies in Spain, both public and private, including several multinational corporations. Dr Andreu's areas of interest include the role of Information Systems as one of the firm's resources and the implications of this particular view for IS planning; the IS relationship to business strategy and its balance with other management systems such as the control, planning and incentive systems, and the organizational structure of the firm.

Walter Baets

Walter Baets is Dean of Research at the Euro-Arab Management School, Granada, Spain. Previously, he was an Associate Professor in Information Management at Nijenrode University, The Netherlands Business School and Programme Director of its Executive MBA. He graduated in

Econometrics and Operations Research at the University of Antwerp and did postgraduate studies in Business Administration at Warwick Business School. He obtained his PhD at Warwick on the topic of IS strategy alignment in banking.

He had a career of more than ten years in strategic planning, decision support and IS consultancy before becoming Managing Director of the Management Development Centre of the Louvain Universities—an aspect of this role being the co-ordination of management development activities in Russia. Most of his professional experience was gathered in the telecommunications and banking sectors.

His research interests are: IT and organizational complexity; the impact of (new information) technology on business and organizations; knowledge, artificial intelligence and neural networks; and knowledge management and organizational learning.

He is a member of the International Editorial Boards of *The Journal of Strategic Information Systems* and *Information & Management*. He has acted as reviewer/evaluator for a number of international conferences and for the European Commission's RACE programme. He has published in a number of international journals, including *The Journal of Strategic Information Systems, European Journal of Operations Research, Business Change & Re-engineering, Marketing Intelligence and Planning, Journal of Systems Management* and *The Learning Organization*.

Liam Bannon

Liam Bannon is Director of the Computer Supported Cooperative Work (CSCW) Centre, Computer Science and Information Systems at the University of Limerick, Ireland.

Dr Bannon was trained in computer science and experimental psychology, in Ireland, Canada and the USA. He was one of the first pre-doctoral fellows at the Honeywell Systems & Research Center, Minneapolis, in the late 1970s and has worked in human factors-related areas since that time. He completed a post-doctoral fellowship on the Human-Machine Interaction project lead by Don Norman at the University of California, San Diego in 1985. More recently he has worked in Scandinavia, principally in Denmark, with the Universities of Aarhus and Copenhagen, as well as the Copenhagen Business School. He has been a visiting researcher in many countries, including Sweden, Finland and the Netherlands, and has consulted widely.

Dr Bannon has been involved for many years in industrial and academic research centres in the areas of design and evaluation of human-computer interfaces, computer-mediated communication systems, and CSCW or Groupware systems in North America and Europe, and has published widely on these topics. He is editor of three books in the area of social dimensions of IT and has been on the Programme Committees of several HCI and CSCW international conferences. He is one of the founding editors of the journal *Computer Supported Cooperative Work* published by Kluwer, and one of the instigators of the European CSCW Conferences, of which he has been a past Programme Chair. He has also worked as a consultant to a number of commercial organizations, including Xerox and Honeywell in the US and Rank Xerox in the UK, as well as a number of governmental science policy agencies. He is actively involved in European Union activity in this area, including an ESPRIT Basic Research Action on CSCW—COMIC, an EU DELTA project and a Human Capital and Mobility network.

Niels Bjørn-Andersen

Niels Bjørn-Andersen is Professor in Information Systems at the Copenhagen Business School. He holds an MSc and a PhD within the field of decision support systems, both from the Copenhagen Business School.

Niels Bjørn-Andersen is considered one of the leading European experts in the field of organizational and social issues of computing. Within his field he has published more than 100 books and articles, from the micro area of ergonomics to the strategic issues—from evaluation to actual implementation. He is on the editorial board of five international journals.

Professor Andersen has worked for governments and government institutions in a number of countries as well as for a number of private companies. Most recently he has been consulting in such areas as IT for competitive advantage, strategic planning for IT, and the use of IT in business process re-design.

Claudio Ciborra

Claudio Ciborra is Associate Professor of Organization at the University of Bologna, Italy, and Director of the Information Systems and Organization Department, Institut Theseus, Sophia Antipolis, France. He has also been Visiting Professor at the Stern School of Business, New York University. He has published widely in the fields of information technology and human resource management. He has acted as a consultant for numerous private companies including Olivetti, Unilever, British Airways and France Telecom, and has also worked for public sector bodies in Italy and the EU generally.

Bob Galliers

Bob Galliers is Chairman of Warwick Business School, Univerity of Warwick, England, having headed Warwick's Doctoral Programme in Information Systems, prior to taking up the Chairmanship in 1994. He was previously Foundation Professor and Head of the School of Information Systems at Curtin University, Perth, Western Australia, where he developed Australia's first Master's Programme to emphasize the management issues associated with the introduction and utilization of IT in organizations.

Professor Galliers was educated at Harvard University (where he was recipient of a Harvard College Scholarship), at Lancaster University (where he was awarded his Master's Degree in Systems with Distinction) and at the London School of Economics (where he obtained his Doctorate in Information Systems as a result of pioneering research into Information Systems Planning practice in Britain and Australia).

He has consulted in business and information systems strategy, the management of change, and executive information requirements determination on behalf of major multi-national corporations and public sector organizations in Europe and Australia. He has been invited to give keynote presentations on these topics in North America, Europe (East and West), South Africa and the Asia Pacific Region.

He has written many papers and articles on these topics and on information systems management issues generally. He is editor-in-chief of *The Journal of Strategic Information Systems*. He is also author of the book *Information Analysis* (Addison-Wesley, 1987), which discusses the problems and methods of determining management information requirements, and of *Information Systems Research: Issues, Methods and Practical Guidelines* (Blackwell Scientific, 1992). He is co-author of *Towards Strategic Information Systems* (Abacus Press, 1987), which plots the development of the commercial utilization of IT from the early days of data processing to more recent times when organizations have been able to use it as a lever for strategic advantage, and of *Strategic Information Management: Challenges and Strategies in Managing Information Systems* (Butterworth-Heinemann, 1994).

Peter Meester

Ing. Peter C. Meester graduated as a mechanical engineer in 1968 and joined the Dutch PTT in 1970. Since then he has held a number of positions in management consultancy, customer services management and financial control. In the latter position he advised the Telecoms chairman about investments in, and exploitation of, the telecom infrastructure.

His special interest is in the human factors in process engineering, which he distinguishes from systems engineering, viewing the former as a matter of management and implementation while linking the latter more with automation.

He is member of a Dutch group of managers studying the social/ psychological aspects of automation and organization. In recent years he has been member of a special task force of Dutch Telecom HQ, established to renew the customer service processes. In that position he was second in charge for the re-engineering of the consumer market processes and in particular responsible for the development of the LUCIA programme.

He is currently Operations Manager and one of the founders of Delta Business Engineers of Dutch Telecom. Delta BE now offers Business Process Re-engineering to the market, based on the expertise gained in the LUCIA programme.

Ramon O'Callaghan

Ramon O'Callaghan is Fortis Professor of Information Systems at the School of Economics and Business Administration, Tilburg University, The Netherlands and programme director of the MBA programme. He holds the degrees of Doctor of Business Administration (Harvard), MBA (IESE), and BSc/MSc Electrical Engineering (Polytechnic University of Barcelona). His education includes further courses on IS and telecommunications at MIT and a certificate in International Business from the Ecole Superieur de Commerce de Paris.

He has researched in the field of digital signal processing and has lectured on computer architectures. He joined the Systems Division of Texas Instruments and worked in both software support and sales engineering. After completing his MBA he worked as controller with the largest Spanish wine-producer. He spent five years at Harvard where his doctoral research examined the adoption and diffusion of EDI in the property-and-casualty insurance industry in the USA. Before joining Tilburg, he was Associate Professor of Information Systems at Nijenrode University. He has been involved in a number of European community projects within the ESPRIT and RACE research programmes and has acted as reviewer for the Commission. He has published on EDI and Inter-Organizational Systems in books and academic journals. He is active in international conferences on Information Systems (ICIS, ECIS, SISnet) and is case studies editor for *The Journal of Strategic Information Systems*.

Johannes Pennings

Dr Pennings is Associate Professor in Organizational Behavior at the Wharton School, University of Pennsylvania, USA. He holds BA and MA degrees in Sociology (Utrecht) and a PhD in Organizational Psychology from Michigan. Previously, he held positions in Alberta (Canada), Pittsburgh (Pennsylvania) and Columbia (New York).

His current research interest focuses on three areas: organizational effectiveness; organization-environment relationship; and organizational innovation.

He is a frequent publisher of articles, conference papers and contributions to books in these areas of interest. He co-authored *New Perspectives on Organizational Effectiveness* (Jossey-Bass, 1977) and *New Technology and Organizational Innovation: The Development and Diffusion of Micro-Electronics* (Ballinger Publishing Company, 1987). He authored *Interlocking Directorates: Origins and Consequences of Connections Among Organizations' Boards of Directors* (Jossey-Bass, 1980); *Decision Making: An Organizational Behavior Approach* (Wiener Publishing Company, 1983) and *Organizational Strategy and Change* (Jossey-Bass, 1985).

He has consulted on behalf of companies such as Royal Dutch Shell (UK), Hay Group (USA) and AT&T (USA), and KPMG—Peat Marwick and McKinsey & Company, in Europe.

Andrew Pettigrew

Andrew Pettigrew is Professor of Organisational Behaviour at Warwick Business School, the University of Warwick, England, where between 1985 and 1995 he founded and then directed the Centre for Corporate Strategy and Change.

Andrew Pettigrew has written, co-authored or edited 10 books. He has published many articles in international scholarly journals such as the *Administrative Science Quarterly, Organization Science, Organization Studies, Journal of Management Studies, Human Relations, International Journal of Human Resource Management*, the *Strategic Management Journal* and *Public Administration*.

Andrew Pettigrew was the first Chairman of the British Academy of Management (1987–1990) and was President of the British Academy of Management (1990–1993). In 1995 he was the recipient of the Distinguished Scholar Award by the Organization and Management Theory Division of the US Academy of Management.

Jan Post

Jan Post joined PTT Telecom (The Netherlands) after graduating in Engineering. After some years in engineering roles, he joined the headquarters team in different staff and planning functions. In 1990 he became the programme manager for the BPR programme for the domestic market and recently became the Director of PTT Telecom Delta Business Engineers, which is the BPR consultancy of PTT Telecom.

Tapio Reponen

Tapio Reponen is Professor of Information Systems and Rector of the Turku School of Economics and Business Administration (Finland), where he obtained his BS, MS and PhD in Economics. He has been visiting scholar in the European Institute for Advanced Studies in Management (Brussels), the Graduate School of Business Administration at Harvard and Electricité de France.

His main research interests are strategic information systems and the role of learning in IS planning. On these topics he has published widely and given numerous lectures, both at academic conferences and for the business community.

Harry Scarbrough

Dr Harry Scarbrough is a senior lecturer in Organizational Behaviour at Warwick Business School, the University of Warwick, England. He has many years' research and consultancy experience in the area of the organizational implications of new technology, and has published extensively on this topic. His most recent work focuses on the management of Information Systems expertise, with a particular emphasis on the financial services sector. He is editor of *The IT Challenge: Strategy and IT in Financial Services* (Prentice Hall, 1992) and co-author *of Technology and Organisation: Power, Meaning and Design* (Routledge, 1992). His most recent book is *The Management of Expertise*, published by Macmillan in 1996.

Jon Turner

Jon Turner is Director of the Center for Research on Information Systems at New York University and Associate Professor of Information Systems at the Stern School of Business, NYU, USA. He has been a Visiting Professor at the Copenhagen Business School on a number of occasions. Prior to joining NYU in 1978, he designed large computer and communications systems for ITT Corp and ran a major academic computer centre. Professor Turner has published over 50 articles, monographs and books in systems design, human-computer interaction, job design and the strategic use of technology. His undergraduate degree is from Yale University and his masters and PhD degrees are in computer and behavioral science from Columbia University He is The Americas Editor for *The Journal of Strategic Information Systems*.

V. Venugopal

V. Venugopal is Assistant Professor of Systems and Operations Management at Nijenrode University, The Netherlands Business School. He did his doctoral research in the area of Operations Management. His areas of interest include Decision Support Systems, Artificial Intelligence, Manufacturing Systems, Total Quality Management and Innovation Management. He has published in international journals such as *Decision Support Systems, Computers in Industry, Computers and Industrial Engineering, European Journal of Operational Research, The Learning Organization*, and the *International Journal of Production Research*. Before joining the academic world, Dr Venugopal worked in software engineering.

Wiley Series in Information Systems

Editors

Series Preface

The information systems community has grown considerably since 1984, when we began publishing the Wiley Series in Information Systems. We are pleased to be a part of the growth of the field, and believe that this series of books is playing an important role in the intellectual development of the discipline. The primary objective of the series is to publish scholarly works which reflect the best of research in the information systems community.

THE PRESENT VOLUME

As the information systems field matures, there is an increased need to carry the results of its growing body of research into practice. The series desires to publish research results that speak to important needs in the development and management of information systems, and our editorial mission recognizes explicitly the need for research to inform the practice and management of information systems. Bob Galliers and Walter Baets have produced *Information Technology and Organizational Transformation: Innovation for the 21st Century Organization* to serve just such a purpose. It blends empirical studies of the way information systems are implicated in organizational transformation with theoretical synthesis by leading scholars and lessons learned from practice. The promise that information technology will yield organizational (if not world and societal) transformation has almost become a cliché. The reality is full of unsuspected outcomes, unanticipated difficulties and unrealized dreams. The blending of theory, empirical studies and practical experience in this volume gives the kind of conceptual breadth that is increasingly required in approaching the complex issues of information technology and organizational transformation.

The contributors to this volume represent a wide range of disciplines and backgrounds. What they share is a long-standing concern with the way technology development, work practices, organization designs and corporate strategy mutually shape the changing field in which we seek change that is humanly and economically satisfying. The experience of the individual, the identity of the organization, the perspectives of the intervention leaders, the expectations of participants and public, the guiding images of design, and the unfolding rationality of situated action are all intertwined in the process of seeking organizational transformation with information technologies. The contributors explore these themes and their interactions in a way that blends the best of theory and practice. This volume will be of great interest to those charged with guiding organizational transformation today, as well as those preparing to do so in the future.

Introduction:
Information Technology and
Organizational Transformation:
The Holy Grail of IT?

BOB GALLIERS[1] AND WALTER BAETS[2]
[1]Warwick Business School, University of Warwick, UK and
[2]Euro-Arab Management School Granada, Spain

INTRODUCTION

The issue of information technology and organizational transformation is not entirely new; much has been written about various aspects of this subject. Why then, should another book appear on this, albeit key, issue? The reasons, as can be seen from the following, relate to the focus of attention and the prescriptive tone of much that has been written on the topic thus far. The focus of past research in this subject area has concentrated on key success factors and reasons for past failures. While making an important contribution, IT professionals and managers are interested to find out *what* can be done and *how* other companies went about the task. Furthermore, research thus far has been somewhat fragmented, with different disciplines approaching the subject in different ways, often with little heed being paid to what their academic "neighbours" are doing or saying. Of course, we could find a number of excuses for this, but we believed it could provide an interesting per-

Information Technology and Organizational Transformation. Edited by R.D. Galliers and W.R.J. Baets. © 1998 John Wiley & Sons Ltd

spective for us to gather together a number of scholars from different backgrounds as well as a number of managers in order to provide a multidisciplinary perspective on the subject.

This is what we have done in this book. Those who have contributed share the opinion that the subject of IT and organizational transformation is best perceived from such a multidisciplinary viewpoint rather than as a discipline in its own right or from a particular discipline base. We cannot claim to have located the holy grail of IT and organizational transformation, but we hope to have provided, in a Weickian sense, something of a map to aid the traveller on what can be a tortuous journey.

In this book we take as given that there is no such holy grail, no optimal state to which companies should aspire; no absolute best practice. We should not attempt to *copy* solutions in other words; rather, we can, and should, *learn* from them. The reader who is looking for cook-book solutions will be disappointed with this book. The reader who wants to learn from the experiences of other people is, however, likely to find some important lessons gleaned from the combined experiences and no small amount of expertise of the contributors.

We also accept implicitly the existence of what are called "positive feed-forward mechanisms" (Arthur, 1994). While the economies of Western Europe, North America and much of the Asia Pacific region have moved into the service sector, we still tend to use economic theory dating back to the industrial era in order to explain behaviour and to guide companies. These days, however, we are operating in a knowledge society, where research and development costs are high and each first version of a new product or service is very expensive. Subsequent versions, in most cases at least, become progressively cheaper. This puts burdens on entry strategies. Being the first player in the market can be a decisive move. Leveraging this move with supportive actions or products can cut off the competition. Arthur refers to this phenomenon as one of increasing returns in the economy. Until recently, we have tended not to pay a great deal of attention to this phenomenon. Recent examples of what has become known as "first mover advantage" have, however, focused the mind somewhat. Two such examples are the way Microsoft DOS became the industry standard for PCs and how Microsoft Windows, despite the earlier technical problems, gained its leading position in the PC operating system marketplace. Approaching managerial problems via feed-forward mechanisms leads to other managerial paradigms, and some of these are considered in this book.

In line with the cook-book syndrome of what has been called the "Heathrow School of Management" (i.e., the "becoming-an-excellent-manager-in-five-minutes", or "earning-your-MBA-in-five-hours" type of book) a large proportion of the popular management literature is not only rather prescriptive, but often trivialises complex management problems. The IS management subset of this literature has always been an easy victim to this disease. On the contrary, in this book we assume that managers learn more from descriptions and the actual experience of other people, rather than from prescriptive theories, superficial or otherwise. For that reason this book has been structured in a way to describe some of the evolution which has and probably will take place in the area of IT and organizational transformation. The book also provides examples which a manager can then relate to his or her business.

The last important assumption on which this book has been based is the ever changing interrelationship between, and interdependence of the fields of Information Systems, Organizational Behaviour, Corporate Strategy and Cognitive Psychology. The contributions in this book provide evidence of the benefits associated with adopting a multidisciplinary approach, incorporating lessons and concepts drawn from these disciplines, specifically in relation to gaining a better understanding of what IT can do for modern day organizations, and what modern day organizations need to take on board with respect to their use of IT. In this respect, we attempt to tackle the subject using a more holistic approach than has tended to be the case until now. We think that this enriches the book considerably, both for the practising manager and for the academic with interests in this subject domain, irrespective of his or her discipline base.

IT AND NEW ORGANIZATIONAL FORMS

Many aspects of IT and organizational transformation have been written about in the major information systems journals emanating from Western Europe and North America. Only a small proportion of this research attempts to be holistic and descriptive, however. Baskerville and Smithson (1995) suggest five reasons why and where we go wrong in this regard, *viz*:

1. *"IT professionals tend to elevate any single, highly successful practical experience instantly into an overarching paradigm for managerial success."* Novel approaches to information systems management may take on ideological textures. The wave of "total quality management" is a well known example, as is the "core competencies" idea. Closer to the IS area, we have been encouraged of late to adopt radical Business Process Re-engineering (BPR). The majority of such ideas are stated in rather strong language, using words like

"catastrophe", "dramatic", "here and now", "severe", "imperative", and so on. A lot of criticism can be made of these approaches (Jones, 1994): they often give a seductive message of a simple road to success to the unsuspecting manager who, as a result, too seems to accept this "cook-book" culture. A limited number of success stories complement the picture, suggesting that a solution for one company would automatically apply to any other. With complex organizational change this is certainly a risky, often misleading, message. In addition, a lot of organizational change where IT is involved is given the BPR label, often for the sake of fashion and status: even the labels tend to be misused at times.

2. *"IT researchers search for the single universal formula that will transform any type of organization in any situation from mediocrity to excellence."* Researchers are equally guilty of accepting the cook-book message in their search for the universal "correct formula". We have learned in the past that almost any introduction of IT in a company creates its own set of additional, often new, problems. Too readily, researchers simplify "reality" for the sake of comparability of research results and generalizability. Furthermore, the new types of IT which are becoming available (Groupware, EDI, neural networking, inter/intra net, etc.), may well create quite a new set of problems of which we are as yet only vaguely aware at best. An organization dealing with change in its business and technological environments faces a situation that is both complex and dynamic, in which linear and non-dynamic approaches can be outmoded by the time they are applied. Sometimes, researchers generalize too readily. In such cases failure in applying the proposed methodology is then related to poor application or implementation. As a consequence, IS researchers should be more modest in what they try to achieve—and regarding what they claim to have achieved! On the other hand, the multidisciplinary approach which we are advocating opens up a wider perspective which promises to be more complex, it is true, but is also likely to lead to more promising and interesting results.

3. *"IT researchers assign a pre-eminence to information technology in organizational transformation that neglects many other important social and environmental factors."* Though perhaps it is the role of the IT researcher to approach managerial problems with IT at the forefront of his or her thinking, the universe does not revolve around IT. Hence, even though IT is undoubtedly an important aspect, a number of other factors are just as, if not more critical. This is a point that those addressing the issue from a socio-technical perspective, for example, have long stressed. Physical and social

networks are only loosely coupled at the moment, although computer networks seem to bring these two a little closer, it is true. Communication theories used in IT only address formal information flows, and we need to remind ourselves that such flows are but a fragment of the complete picture. Due to these considerations, communications between IT executives and general managers tend not to be optimal—in other words there is a "culture gap". The consequence of this could be that IT research often misses the point, since it is so often overly focused on internal, technical issues.

4. *"Management theorists seem unable to cope with the unpredictability, the multivariate nature and 'messiness' of human organizations in a cultural context."* This finding brings us closer to problems associated with new (chaotic) organizational forms. Management apparently is becoming increasingly unpredictable. This influences the nature of the planning activities, but even more it changes the scope of the implementation of these plans. Organizations are seen as being biotic rather than mechanical. Organizational direction is then a flow or trend, emerging from the interaction of a number of individuals and their actions. Hence, if an organization is messy, this holds true, and to a greater extent for an electronically networked organization. IT amplifies in many respects the organizational mess. An emergent organization is not necessarily a machine-based organization. All this makes IT even more necessary to support management today, but it should certainly also reorient the kind of thinking regarding the kind of IT managers need. A new balance is therefore necessary in our thinking regarding IT and organizational transformation.

5. *"Several critical factors influence the interaction of changes in IT and emergent organizational forms: these include organizational learning, structural premise and power."* Though theories that deal with these issues are not new (e.g. Argyris and Schön, 1978), they have not received sufficient attention in the IS research community, the work of Andreu & Ciborra (1996) being a notable exception. IT has changed from merely a reporting medium to a tool which enables the organization to learn from itself and to create and foster a knowledge base. Richer communication via e-mail and Groupware, for example, are but two of the possibilities that can enhance single-loop learning. While such learning receives considerable attention in this book, so does the double-loop learning cycle. In this context, IT becomes an instrument to build knowledge and to communicate this knowledge throughout the organization. Not only is it necessary in this case to introduce additional IT tools, but also to foster a changed attitude towards their use—possibly also

an adapted and integrated information architecture will also be necessary to engender this kind of learning. IT needs to be designed in such a way that it is adaptive to the autogenously living organization of individuals. IT components should be easily reconfigured by individuals or sub-groups. In addition to the question of organizational learning, we should not forget issues of power and empowerment. An understanding of each of these factors can lead researchers and practitioners to a better understanding of the potential for leverage which IT can have in organizational transformation.

A CIRCLE OF FORCES

While we would have liked to have kept the scope of this book as wide and as open as possible, raising in so doing as many ideas as would be relevant to our topic, we have perforce had to limit the scope of this work. We have created an arena in which the contributors to this book could position the relevant trends which they have identified in their day-to-day work and research. We are perfectly aware that this is an artificial boundary and, as with any limitation, it reduces the value of the analysis. However, in delimiting our subject matter in this way, we have been able to provide coherence to our treatment of the topic, without which the utility of our analysis for both managers and academics could well have been compromised. Figure i.1 illustrates the scope of the work.

The four forces shown in the figure need some explanation. *Information Technology* has clearly undergone a series of tremendous changes itself over the past 40 years or so, particularly during the past decade. Advances in electronic networks are a particular case in point and these have had major implications for the way organizations conduct their business in both a local and global context. Two such technologies—the Internet and EDI—have been the subject of much recent research (e.g. Cavaye & Cragg, 1995; Krcmar, et al, 1995; Rao, et al, 1995; Swatman, et al, 1994; Webster, 1995). What emerges from this research is that these new network structures not only lead to major change within and between companies, but they are well on their way to restructure entire industries. Furthermore, the network issue has an important impact on the bargaining process and bargaining power, which directs us to the heart of the business. Within the context of this book, network technologies receive special consideration. From a software perspective we can add to this the evolution in Groupware and its impact on organizational decision making (Yellen, et al, 1995).

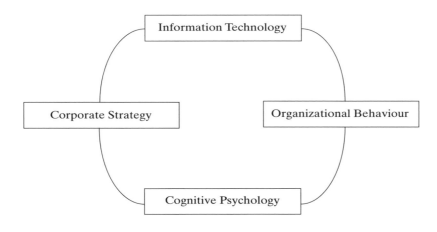

Figure i.1 *A circle of forces for the consideration of IT and organizational transformation*

We can observe two trends in *Corporate Strategy* theory which are relevant to our consideration of IT in this context. The first relates to the necessity and means of aligning an organization's IT strategy with its corporate strategy (e.g. Baets, 1992; Dutta & Doz, 1995; Galliers, 1991; Jordan & Tricker, 1995; Ward & Peppard, 1996). As argued in these papers, this alignment influences to a considerable degree the way IT strategy is considered. In many organizations the focus is still predominantly on technological issues and on strategy formulation. Less attention is paid to the wider organizational and implementation issues. We, among others (e.g. Earl, 1989; 1996), consider this to be too limited a view that compromises the ability of organizations to achieve the alignment they are looking for. One could easily repeat here the earlier criticism that IT is once again too inward looking in its focus. Having said that, we are beginning to see the results of research that is more outwardly focused (e.g. Atkins, 1994; Holland, 1995; Meier, 1995; Roche, 1996). We are also beginning to see case studies on the subject of IS strategy alignment, which, of course, consider both directions of the relationship (Ciborra & Jelassi, 1994; Loebbecke, et al, 1996; Ramani & Pavri, 1994).

Another aspect of corporate strategy research which is relevant here relates to two schools of thought in the wider business management research community, i.e. that which might be termed "the design school" (e.g. based on the work of Porter, 1980; 1985) as against the more eclectic and pluralistic approaches to strategy. Whittington (1993) terms the latter the "processual", "evolutionary" and "systemic" schools. While we shall not deal with this debate here, it will be seen that we favour those contributions that adhere to the systemic/emergent/pluralist school, rather than the deterministic/prescriptive or "design" school. We suggest that there is a mutual influence between the emergent character of corporate strategy and the role which IT (in its broad meaning, as discussed in this book) can play within a company.

Within *Organizational Behaviour* research, the learning organization concept has been paid considerable attention (Argyris & Schön, 1978; de Geus, 1988; Garvin, 1993; Pedler et al, 1991). A learning organization enables each of its members to learn continually and helps generate new ideas and thinking. By this process, organizations continuously learn from their own experience and that of others, and adapt themselves so as to improve the likelihood of achieving their goal(s). In a way, learning organizations aim at converting themselves into "knowledge-based" organizations by creating, acquiring and transferring knowledge so as to improve their planning and other activities.

In order to develop a learning capability, organizations need to develop systemic problem solving skills, learn from their own experience as well as others', disseminate knowledge quickly and efficiently throughout the organization, and be willing to experiment with new approaches (Garvin, 1993). Developments in IT can help enhance an organization's learning capability, for example, "intelligent" IT tools are capable of supporting certain aspects of learning processes and are commercially available, but there is considerably more to it than that. Hence, in addition to discussing how such tools can be integrated within a broader corporate context, other considerations from the field of organizational behaviour will also feature in the book. The role of social networks and information as a socially mediated construct are but two examples of such considerations (Galliers & Swan, 1997), which leads us into the fourth component to our circle of forces.

The fourth component is *Cognitive Psychology*, a field that has become increasingly relevant in the context of IT and organizational change and learning over recent years. Aspects of research in the field of artificial intelligence (Baets, 1995; de Callatay, 1992; Firebaugh, 1989; Rumelhart & McClelland, 1986) are of particular relevence here, particularly in relation to knowledge management, knowledge elicitation, "connectionist models" and neural networks. The potential which modern day artificial intelligence has within the day-to-day management of organizations is certainly considerably greater than was the case even just 10 years ago. Its promise for the future will also be considered in our treatment of the subject.

STRUCTURE IN THE CHAOS

The book is divided into four parts: *Starting Afresh; IT and the Learning Organization; Innovation, Networks and Corporate Identity; IT and Organizational Change*, followed by a fifth—an *Afterword*—which reflects on past successes and failures with transformation initiatives. For each of the first four parts, two research papers are included, together with one paper on an application or a case study. In this way, each part can be considered as being self-contained. However, each part gives only a limited view of the total canvas we are trying to assemble. Readers are therefore advised, in true systems thinking tradition, to read the whole rather than just the parts. In addition, and as is the case with any structure, this delimits the subject area and may suggest that the book's structure is in some way "optimum". This is not our claim. We could have structured the book quite differently, and this only goes to reinforce the earlier points regarding the non-prescriptive nature and multidisciplinary character of our story. In the last part we scan the future by reviewing the question of IT architectures and the future of organizations in the so-called Information Age. In some respects, this part synthesizes lessons drawn from the earlier chapters. Each chapter will now be summarised in order to give a flavour of our treatment of the subject.

1 Starting Afresh

1. Linking Strategy and IT-based Innovation: The Importance of the "Management of Expertise" (Harry Scarbrough)

This chapter serves as an introduction to our treatment of the subject of IT, its strategic applications and the management of organizational change. It also introduces us to the notion of the management of expertise. The empirical research cited here challenges the view that strategic information systems stem from a rational use of technology. It highlights the contested nature of strategic applications and shows how they emerge from processes of (internal) conflict and organizational learning. These processes involve the social construction of strategic IS. They are closely linked therefore to the distribution of knowledge and expertise within a company. Any attempt to develop truly strategic IS applications needs to take account of these factors.

2. Computer Supported Collaborative Working: Challenging Perspectives on Work and Technology (Liam Bannon)

This contribution concentrates on work processes and the importance IT plays in supporting these work processes "any time—any place". It challenges a number of current concepts on emerging change. It provides an introduction to the role of learning and knowledge and gives a new perspective on knowledge. This contribution sets the scene for much that follows in the book by challenging the received wisdom on the nature of knowledge and information.

3. The Metamorphosis of Oticon (Niels Bjørn-Andersen and Jon Turner)

This chapter describes a real life experience of how IT can be used to help reshape a company. The Oticon case illustrates a culture-driven change process in which an holistic view has been chosen in favour of a re-engineering view. The realities of organizational learning are brought into sharp focus and this perspective is used to show the limitations of the business process orientation. The concepts of a paperless desk, fast, flexible task forces and decision making in such an environment are interesting features.

2 IT and the Learning Organization

4. Organizational Learning and Core Capabilities Development: The Role of IT (Rafael Andreu and Claudio Ciborra)

This chapter links learning and IS explicitly. It presents a framework where resources, work practices and capabilities (knowledge) create in a dynamic way a means of learning. The role of IS/IT in the learning processes involved is then analyzed and a set of guidelines for action is proposed as a result.

5. The Corporate Mind Set as a Precursor for Business Process Change: About Knowledge, Perceptions and Learning (Walter Baets)

This chapter builds on the previous chapters by providing a more detailed analysis on the nature of knowledge and learning. Importance is given to the corporate mind set: a repository of core capabilities. Measurement of the corporate mind set, creation of corporate maps and the development of an approach to support organizational change with these corporate maps are all discussed. This contribution challenges specifically the very foundation of the most recent consultancy solution to business innovation—BPR, a topic to which we return in Chapter 10.

6. The Role of Learning in IS Planning and Implementation (Tapio Reponen)

This chapter draws conclusions from the foregoing issues and examples. Group processes are paid particular attention, as is the process of achieving organizational change. IS planning is treated as an interactive learning process, with attention being paid to using existing systems better. The chapter argues for a less formal/rational approach to strategic thinking, in contrast to much of the existing literature on IS strategy.

3 Innovation, Networks and Corporate Identity

7. Innovations as Precursors of Organizational Performance (Johannes Pennings)

Technical innovation and the bottom line of the company is the subject of this chapter. Pennings questions whether and how technology pays off. Given that IT can be disruptive and has considerable impact on organizations, it could take some time before profits emerge. Based on empirical research, this chapter explores the social lag in implementing IS and questions traditional means of measuring their impact on business performance.

8. EDI, Organizational Change and Flexibility Strategies (Ramon O'Callaghan)

Following a brief introduction as to what EDI and interorganizational systems can imply for organizational structure, this chapter discusses a case concerned with EDI implementation. Conclusions are drawn regarding impacts with respect to logistics, corporate strategy and business re-engineering.

9. An IT Architecture to Support Organizational Transformation (Walter Baets and V. Venugopal)

This chapter draws consequences for considerations of IT architecture of different learning processes and gives an overview of the existing IT tools which can support and enhance a company's development. The chapter proposes a conceptual framework of an integrated intelligent system for supporting organizational transformation. Finally, an example is described briefly of a large financial holding, which is currently experimenting with these concepts and this architecture.

4 IT and Organizational Change

10. Reflections on BPR, IT and Organizational Change (Bob Galliers)

This chapter attempts a synthesis of the major lessons arising from the above treatment of this broad topic. It advocates going "back to the future": learning from past experiences in the related fields of, e.g. strategic management and organizational change, rather than the "obliterate" message of BPR proponents like Hammer (1990). It provides an holistic overview of IS and organizational change. It puts BPR in the context of the IS experience and argues that if we do not include the social dimension in IS-driven change processes, we will have failed to have learned from past experience. The chapter argues for a balanced approach in which we attempt to manage realistic changes rather than always seeking radical change. Variety, involvement, a non-prescriptive attitude and a learning mode are identified as keys to success.

11. The Role of IT in Organizational Transformation (Jon Turner)

This chapter introduces an overview of the opportunities now available through IT, individual examples of which having already been illustrated in previous chapters. This contribution puts into perspective: technology infrastructure; support for (cooperative) work; public networks and information; EDI and interorganizational issues; encoding business knowledge. It argues that IT is an important enabler, but should not be seen as the single, key component in the change processes.

12. LUCIA Accelerates Service Delivery: A Case Study of Business Process Re-engineering (Peter Meester and Jan Post)

This chapter describes an important BPR project: important both in terms of size as well as its impact on the business. Lessons drawn from this experience are twofold. First, BPR is viewed as being successful if it impacts the organization as a whole, and not just a specific business process. Second, successful BPR can be achieved without IT, depending on the company and industry concerned.

5 Afterword

13. Success and Failure in Corporate Transformation Initiatives (Andrew Pettigrew)

Having attempted to paint a picture of what the future might have in stock for us with respect to IT and organizational change, it is as well to reflect on the strengths and weaknesses of management techniques that have been developed since the 1960s, each designed to deliver change in organizations. We decided to end on this aspect of our subject for two reasons. The first is to underscore the point that too much has been written on the subject that is prescriptive and overly confident about future opportunities arising from new developments in IT. The second is to downplay the centrality of IT with respect to organizational transformation, to counter the fadishness of much which surrounds the popular writings on BPR, for example—which built, you will recall, on the fadishness of the IT for competitive advantage movement that preceded it.

THE AIM OF THIS BOOK

It is in many cases easier to say what something is "not", than saying what it aims to be. This is the case with this book. As we have already said, our intention is not to provide cook-book solutions: we think this is futile. We also think that the future opportunities provided by IT will provide exciting challenges in organizations, but that these will prove to be even more difficult to deal with than has been the case up till now. With this book we want to share with our readers insights from recent experiences and new ideas. We want to challenge readers' views on the topic, and in doing so we want to open up the debate about IT and organizational transformation. We can learn so much from each other, but unfortunately we seldom see this taking place, due to our traditional disciplinary straightjackets. We hope this book contributes a little in releasing us from the myopia of single discipline treatments of what we believe to be a complex, multidisiplinary topic.

We also aim to give some additional input into our treatment of the subject of IT and organizational transformation by nurturing the debate between practitioners and researchers. Further, we want to show how new concepts and learning emanating from our multidisiplinary approach are applicable in practice. The view that "there is nothing so practical as a good theory" should be the measure by which this book's contribution is judged. Though this book is mainly targeted for the IS community, we believe it has value for those general managers who, despite past failures, have not entirely turned their backs on IT's potential contribution to organizational change.

In this book we foster breadth, more than depth. We want the different concepts, originating from different disciplines, to cross-fertilize each other in order to give a more integrative approach to IT and organizational transformation. If the reader is unaware of the disciplinary bases of each contribution, the book has succeeded in being truly multidisciplinary.

Last but not least, this book aims to provide new perspectives to IT research and practice. It brings corporate strategy, organizational change and IT closer together, not as distinct disciplines which should meet, but rather as a natural symbiosis. It certainly suggests new research directions for IT scholars but it also challenges IT professionals and business executives to think along new lines regarding the role of IT in their organization. We hope that the book presents a challenge to those in the academic community who have a common interest in IT and organizational change to work together on the new research agenda, and that it provides business and IT executives new insights as to how IT can help to leverage business in the coming years. As we have said, we offer no new solutions; those we believe will be obtained by our readers reflecting on the important messages provided by our contributors.

REFERENCES

Andreu, R. and Ciborra, C., 1996, Organizational Learning and Core Capabilities Development: The Role of IT, *Journal of Strategic Information Systems*, 5(2), June, 111–127.

Argyris C. and Schön D., 1978, *Organizational Learning: A Theory of Action Perspective*, Reading, Massachusetts: Addison-Wesley.

Arthur, B., 1994, Positive Feedbacks in the Economy, *McKinsey Quarterly*, 1, 81–95.

Atkins, M., 1994, Information Technology and IS Perspectives on Business Strategies, *Journal of Strategic Information Systems*, 3(2), June, 123–135.

Baets, W., 1992, Aligning Information Systems with Business Strategy, *Journal of Strategic Information Systems*, 1(4), December, 205–213.

Baets, W., 1995, Artificial Neural Networks: Mapping of Change Processes and Measurement of Learning (Dutch version), Handboek Effektief Opleiden, 4/131.

Baskerville, R. and Smithson, S., 1995, Information Technology and New Organizational Forms: Choosing Chaos over Panaceas, *European Journal of Information Systems*, 4(2), May, 66–73.

Cavaye, A. and Cragg, P., 1995, Factors Contributing to the Success of Customer Oriented Interorganizational Systems, *Journal of Strategic Information Systems*, 4(1), March, 13–30.

Ciborra, C. and Jelassi, T. (eds.), 1994, *Strategic Information Systems: A European Perspective*, Chichester: Wiley.

de Callatay A., 1992, *Natural and Artificial Intelligence: Misconceptions about Brains and Neural Networks*, Amsterdam: North-Holland.

de Geus, A.P., 1988, Planning as Learning, *Harvard Business Review*, 66(2), March-April, 70–74.

Dutta, S. and Doz, Y., 1995, Linking Information Technology to Business Strategy at Banco Commercial Portugues, *Journal of Strategic Information Systems*, 4(1), March, 89–110.

Earl, M.J., 1989, *Management Strategies for Information Technology*, Hemel Hempstead, Hertfordshire: Prentice-Hall.

Earl, M.J. (ed.), 1996, *Information Management: The Organizational Dimension*, Oxford: Clarendon Press.

Firebaugh, M., 1989, *Artificial Intelligence: A Knowledge-Based Approach*, Boston: PWS-Kent.

Galliers, R.D., 1991, Strategic Information Systems Planning: Myths, Reality and Guidelines for Successful Implementation, *European Journal of Information Systems*, 1(1), January, 55–64.

Galliers, R.D., and Swan, J.A., 1997, Against Structured Approaches: Information Requirements Analysis as a Socially Mediated Process. *Proceedings: Thirtieth Hawaii International Conference on Systems Sciences*, Volume III, Los Alamitos, CA: IEEE Computer Society Press, 179–187.

Garvin, D.A., 1993, Building a Learning Organization, *Harvard Business Review*, 71(4), July-August. 78–91.

Hammer, M., 1990, Re-engineering Work: Don't Automate, Obliterate, *Harvard Business Review*, 68(4), 104–112.

Holland, C.P., 1995, Cooperative Supply Chain Management: the Impact of Interorganizational Information Systems, *Journal of Strategic Information Systems*, 4(2), June, 117–133.

Jones M., 1994, Don't Emancipate, Exaggerate: Rhetoric, Reality and Re-engineering, in Baskerville, et al, *Transforming Organizations with Information Technology*, proceedings of the IFIP WG8.2 Conference, Amsterdam: Elsevier Science (North Holland).

Jordan, E. and Tricker, R., 1995, Information Strategy: Alignment with Organization Structure, *Journal of Strategic Information Systems*, 4(4), December, 357–382.

Krcmar, H., Bjørn-Andersen, N. and O'Callaghan R., 1995, *EDI in Europe: How it Works in Practice*, Chichester: Wiley.

Loebbecke, C., Kronen, J.H. and Jelassi, T., 1996, The Role of Information Technology in Retailing: the Case of Supporting Fashion Purchasing at a European Department Store Chain, *Journal of Strategic Information Systems*, 5(1), March, 67–78.

Meier, J., 1995, the Importance of Relationship Management in Establishing Successful Interorganizational Systems, *Journal of Strategic Information Systems*, 4(2), June, 135–148.

Pedler, M., Burgoyne, J. and Boydell, T., 1991, *The Learning Company—A Strategy for Sustainable Development*, London: McGraw Hill.

Porter, M.E., 1980, *Competitive Strategy: Techniques for Analyzing Industries and Competitors*, New York, NY: The Free Press.

Porter, M.E., 1985, *Competitive Advantage: Creating and Sustaining Superior Performance*, New York, NY: The Free Press.

Ramani, K.V. and Pavri, F., 1994, IT Supports Business Strategy Growth at the Development Bank of Singapore, *Journal of Strategic Information Systems*, 3(4), December, 327–337.

Rao, H., Pegels, C., Salam, A. and Hwang, K., 1995, The Impact of EDI Implementation Commitment and Implementation Success on Competitive Advantage and Firm Performance, *Information Systems Journal*, 5(3), July, 185–223.

Roche, E.M., 1996, Multinational Corporations — The Emerging Research Agenda, *Journal of Strategic Information Systems*, 5(2), June, 129–147.

Rumelhart D., and McClelland J., 1986, *Parallel Distributed Processing: Exploration in the Microstructure of Cognition Vols 1 & 2: Foundations*, Cambridge, MA: MIT Press.

Swatman, P.M., Swatman, P.A. and Fowler, D. 1994, A model of EDI Integration and Strategic Business Re-engineering, *Journal of Strategic Information Systems*, 3(1), March, 41–60.

Ward, J., and Peppard, J., 1996, Reconciling the IT/Business Relationship: a Troubled Marriage in Need of Guidance, *Journal of Strategic Information Systems*, 5(1), March, 37–65.

Webster, J., 1995, Networks of Collaboration or Conflict? Electronic Data Interchange and Power in the Supply Chain, *Journal of Strategic Information Systems*, 4(1), March, 31–42.

Whittington, R., 1993, *What is Strategy and Does it Matter?*, London: Routledge.

Yellen, R., Winniford, M. and Sanford, C., 1995, Extraversion and Introversion in Electronically-Supported Meetings, *Information & Management*, 28(1), January.

Part 1
STARTING AFRESH

The purpose of Part 1 is to have you rethink what are perhaps taken-for-granted ideas on the nature of strategic information systems, on IT's role in organizational transformation and on the way we communicate and work together, and on the way strategies are formed and implemented. A more subjective, political and systemic stance is taken here than is perhaps the norm. By deconstructing our thinking on the subject, we may be better prepared for the messages that follow in the subsequent sections. By taking an overtly multidisciplinary perspective, the very ethos of this book comes more clearly into view.

We start with a chapter by Harry Scarbrough which highlights the political nature of what we term strategic applications of IT. Drawing on case study evidence, the subjective quality of the topic is brought sharply into focus, as is the question of how we might go about managing expertise in organizations. This is followed by a chapter written by Liam Bannon, which again challenges our notions of the nature of work and technology, from a somewhat different perspective. In this chapter, Bannon introduces the topic of Computer Supported Cooperative Work (CSCW) and suggests that emerging from this multidisciplinary field will be new ideas about the multiplicity of cooperative work arrangements within organizations. The third chapter in this section, by Niels Bjørn-Andersen and Jon Turner, introduces an alternative approach to change. In it, they describe some of the experiences of Oticon in recent years—a company which changed the very nature of its work practices, and became "95% paperless" in so doing.

While approaching our topic in different ways, the three chapters, each in its own way, help us to rethink our models of IT and Organizational Change, and place the emphasis on individual and team working, rather than on some grandiose plan. IT, while considered an important component in the change process, is not placed centre stage, and the Taylorist engineering paradigm is set aside.

1
Linking Strategy and IT-based Innovation: The Importance of the "Management of Expertise"

HARRY SCARBROUGH
Warwick Business School, UK

INTRODUCTION

The 1980s saw important shifts both in the scope of IT applications and in managerial thinking about their relevance to business needs. One important strand in management thinking and practice which reflected these trends was the attempt to relate IT-based development to the strategic needs of the business. In the late 1980s and beginning of the 1990s, research was carried out in a number of financial sector firms (most of them based in Scotland) to ascertain the extent to which firms were succeeding in linking IT-based innovations to strategic needs of the business.[1] Its focus was on the role of expertise in facilitating or inhibiting such a linkage. As many commentators have noted (e.g. Gunton, 1990 and Grindley, 1991), a crucial element in the strategizing of IT is the existence of a body of knowledge which bridges the technical expertise of IS staff and the organizational and marketing expertise of senior management.

---

[1] This research was funded by the Joint Committee of the ESRC/SERC in the UK. Other members of the research team were Robin Fincham, James Fleck, Robert Procter, Margaret Tierney, and Robin Williams.

This chapter reports on the case study findings of this research. It suggests that expertise is indeed at the heart of the matter: that strategic uses of IT depend very largely upon the interaction between IS expertise and the knowledge controlled by senior management. But it also suggests that such interaction is not driven by the functional needs of the organization, but owes more to politics and processes of learning. Although it is sometimes viewed as a competence to be deployed and developed at senior management's behest, IS expertise is not particularly amenable to functional manipulation. It is generally deeply embedded in the structure and politics of the organization, and often brings with it a distinctive world-view which may not be easily assimilable within the culture and outlook of senior management. It follows that the IS function's role and self-image in the structure and politics of the organization is an important factor here.

This is not to say that the fusion of managerial and IT knowledge is impossible, though the sluggish emergence of "hybrid managers" shows how difficult it is in practice. However, the key theoretical point which comes out of our study is that where such a fusion occurs it is unlikely to reflect the classical model of strategy formulation, i.e. rational adaptation to the contingencies of technology and environment. A focus on expertise makes it clear that the factors which foster strategic IT projects are (a) the IS function's organizational role and knowledge-base; and (b) its ability to make IT a strategic issue against the competing claims of other groups who are equally convinced of the strategic importance of their expertise. The idea of the "social construction of reality" provides a useful theoretical framework here. It allows us to explore this interaction of technology and organization without privileging one over the other.

THEORETICAL FRAMEWORKS

Our research highlights the importance of the management of expertise to the strategic management of IT. This perspective on the relationship between strategy and technology represents a significant departure from more established approaches which have generally fallen into two main camps; the Classical school and the Processual school (Whittington, 1993).

In the still-dominant Classical perspective, organizations are seen as basically market-driven, and having constantly to adapt to the changes and contingencies of the external environment. IT is seen as a resource to be deployed according to the needs and pressures of that environment. Strategy has the job of transmitting such pressures by forging links between internal structure and resources, on the one hand, and external product-market moves, on the other. In brief, this perspective sees the relationship between strategy and IT as essentially to do with recognizing the contingencies of the technology—the stages approach for example—and its potential for application (McFarlan, 1984), and relating these factors to business objectives.

The organization itself hardly figures at all in the Classical approach—in fact, the role of top management is to divorce itself from the operational problems of the organization to gain an Olympian view of its context. The Processual approach, in contrast, rejects formal plans and methodologies as simply the tip of the organizational iceberg. It delights in exposing the hidden world of the organization, where social values, political interests and structural inertia shape the formal instruments of rationality. It rejects the idea that organizations are engaged in a ceaseless struggle to adapt to changing environments. Its focus is more on the ceaseless struggle within the organization, as different groups within the structure of the business compete for power. Again IT represents a resource, but this time it is an instrument for gaining power, not for achieving adaptation. Strategy, claim Processual theorists, is not to be equated with plans which are imposed top-down. Not only are these more like the window-dressing of power than the product of reasoned deliberation, the plans themselves are probably meaningless because implementation is so fraught, problematic, and, of course, political. Processual theorists point out that overcoming the inertia of existing interests and routines is not a frictionless, automatic adjustment. To energize change and make it real involves management commitment, project champions and a supportive context.

In contrast to both these schools of thought, the social constructionist view (Berger & Luckmann, 1967) challenges the fundamental assumption that there is a singular external reality to which organizations have to adapt. It is sceptical about the ability of organizations rationally to identify relevant contingencies in their environment. Equally, it does not subscribe to the view that the internal reality is the dominant one. Rather, its focus is not on the organization as an island in the stream of environmental change but on the way in which social groups within and across organizations actually construct the realities which seem to confront them. In this context, the notion of strategy is neither a concrete reality in its own right nor an outcome, but a resource which groups use to construct reality.

A trite example of such social construction is the way in which accountants and marketing experts construct markets (Morgan, 1990). This is trite because it is obvious that talking about social construction here simply signals a rather complex set of processes, but does not really explain them. On the other hand, this example does indicate one of the key features of the way in which social construction is employed here. If I was only arguing that accountants and marketing people make up the idea of markets—that it is a fiction which they have persuaded others to accept—then I would be guilty of a crude form of idealism, that is, of suggesting that ideas alone shape the world. On the other hand, if we focus on the knowledge and expertise which accountants and marketing people possess we can get a more sophisticated sense of what construction means. Obviously, markets as such do not exist "out there"—they are an aggregate representation of millions of individual interactions and transactions. But when accountants and marketing people construct these aggregate representations they are not simply making them up, or pulling figures out of thin air. They are employing powerful computational techniques, practical experience and formal knowledge which has been legitimated and approved by powerful professional bodies. In other words, their expertise, both collectively and individually, is constructing the market, and is continually testing its interpretations against the raw, unprocessed data that markets produce.

Notice, however, that the market which these experts construct is not the same as a real market—it is a representation which is as much a product of their expertise as it is a reflection of the contingencies and quiddities of the market. Moreover, such expertise, however well it is validated, is clearly not omniscient and infallible. At any point in time, the interpretations of reality developed by expert groups are limited both by the existing state of knowledge, and by the specific cultural context through which their claims are validated. Moreover, the interpretations developed by one expert group are not only subject to revision by changing events and the development of knowledge. Other expert groups are in competition with them to gain acceptance and resources for their own interpretations.

The social construction of reality is a well-established theoretical position. Although the management of expertise is a more novel variant of it, three factors make it especially pertinent here. First, focusing on expertise allows us to deconstruct technology; that is, to view it not simply as concrete artefacts, but as involving different levels of embodied knowledge ranging from specific implementations, through generic designs, to professional and disciplinary knowledge (Scarbrough & Corbett, 1992). Second, the relationship between strategy and IT seems to hinge very largely upon the distribution of particular kinds of knowledge. Where strategy draws upon a detailed complex of market and organizational knowledge, the management of IT requires a specialist understanding of the dynamics of the technology. These knowledges are widely distributed by the management structure of the organization, and are embedded in its politics, practices and routines. This creates a collective gestalt (Miller & Friesen, 1980)—a mind set or culture, if you will—which may be highly resistant to change and which typically provides an almost unbreakable frame for the adoption of new technologies.

In this perspective, strategic IT projects do not emerge spontaneously according to business need or external pressure. Rather, they depend on certain groups—obviously the IS function, in particular—making IT strategic. This involves making space within the existing routines of the organization, cutting across organizational boundaries, and acquiring knowledge from other groups. In doing so, such groups will be exploiting different aspects of their own expertise, including their functional competence in handling problems, their structural relationships with other groups, and their connections with supplier or occupational groupings outside the organization.

SECTORAL CONTEXT

One of the corollaries of the management of expertise view is to highlight the importance of the web of social and occupational networks through which competences and knowledge get developed and disseminated. This web normally develops as part of the evolution of a business sector, though it may also take in other sectors, such as suppliers.

In our study sectoral influences on the management of expertise at firm level were reflected most visibly in the historical emergence of distinctive competences in financial institutions (Abernathy, 1978; Whipp & Clark, 1986). Thus, financial services have typically been delivered through branch networks controlled from a central headquarters. This established the classic infrastructural patterns for computing and IT, where large mainframes served a large number of branch systems. IS expertise inevitably developed around this pattern, with consequences which are still being felt today. The structural factors not only shaped IS expertise, however. They also helped to establish the role of other kinds of expertise through the centrality of financial intermediary functions.

The structural features of financial services have evolved in tandem with the development of competences and knowledges in financial institutions (Scarbrough, 1992). One of the more long-standing connections, for instance, is between the importance of trust in financial markets and the cultivation of a culture of prudence, conservatism and company loyalty amongst financial service workers. Also, the intermediary functions performed by financial firms are dependent on the key banking, accounting and actuarial skills which continue to dominate management in the sector. The latter have inhibited the emergence of general management expertise, including marketing and corporate planning.

Against the dominance of the traditional professions, technological trends in the 1980s and 90s promised to increase the centrality of IS expertise. As financial services are information-based, there seemed to be ample opportunities for new product development and the creation of new electronic delivery systems. Equally, the power of IT to appropriate the expertise of specialist groups seemed to presage greater consumer accessibility to once esoteric intermediary skills. As Child & Loveridge (1990) note:

> "The ability to rationalize service provision through the application of new technology depends upon an ability to codify transactional information which consumers can then use to make their own choices, in principle on a self-service basis." (pp. 36–37)

The extent to which such theoretical possibilities became realities depended, however, not so much on the potential of IT alone as on the management of expertise through which that potential was interpreted and mediated. In part, therefore, the management of expertise was to do with the internal formation of expertise—especially the legacy of skills and values which were embodied in the IS functions of financial firms. But, it was also to do with another feature of the sector, which was the role played by occupational and inter-organizational networks in transmitting general strategic "recipes" (Child & Smith, 1987) and detailed technical knowledge.

A number of studies have highlighted the evolution of sectoral networks which link organizations with customers, suppliers and even with rivals. Management in each firm becomes "part of a social network in which common perceptions, attitudes and behaviours are shaped and moulded" (Shearman & Burrell, 1987: 328). Such networks provide the basis for the exchange of non-price information between organizations, and for the exemplary role of "significant others" such as major competitors. They are particularly important in the development of technological innovations. Von Hippel (1988), for instance, has highlighted the importance of users in shaping innovations.

In the financial sector, an important feature of IS expertise is the development of inter-sectoral networks encompassing hardware and suppliers (the historical influence of IBM is an obvious example here).

There are also important flows of knowledge and information between IS management in different organizations. One IS manager in a building society interviewed for the research described how his staff:

> "are always immensely quick and eager to go to other building societies and ask them about what we should buy and whether a package might be best or whatever. That's one thing about building societies—we're very good at communicating with one another, as compared to, say, insurance companies. They wouldn't tell you if they got a new pencil sharpener."

Such knowledge-trading is affected by competitive pressures, however, as another IT manager acknowledged:

> "We will meet at various times, at various conferences. In DP (*sic*), for example, there is a bi-annual meeting where we all exchange views on what we're doing in relation to technology. At that level, we may not exchange the various products we are working on. The details of those products. But certainly we don't mind saying: 'We've purchased a number of PCs which are going to do this'. Or 'we've purchased a mainframe computer and a network which is going to do this'."

CASE STUDIES

Unlike the Classical or Processual schools, the management of expertise perspective is very much concerned with the counter-factual—the clues offered by the "dog that didn't bark" as Sherlock Holmes would put it. Rather than assuming that organizations respond rationally to their environment, it can explain why IT might be managed in different ways in organizations whose circumstances are actually very similar.

It was axiomatic to this approach that we did not attempt an objective categorization of "strategic" IT projects. We found that it was tremendously difficult to reach a definition which was detailed and unambiguous enough to be useful in research terms. But, apart from these conceptual problems, what mattered to us was the way in which the concept was interpreted and used by different groups in our case study firms. Not only would an objective definition have neglected the specificity of the term's usage, it would also have meant glossing over an important aspect of such usage. This was the tortuous inter-subjective processes through which different groups grappled with and sought to overcome precisely the same problems of objective definition which we had ourselves encountered. It could hardly be otherwise, given the way in which textbook definitions of strategic IT invariably focus on outcomes (competitive advantages, long-term effects etc.), which are by definition unknowable and often highly contestable when a project is at the embryonic stage.

In short, the focus in our research was not on a predefined set of strategic IT projects, but on the organizational processes involved in constructing such concepts and categories. Definitions of strategic IT were the end-point rather than the starting-point of such processes. Moreover, the processes of making IT strategic varied enormously from one company to another. In some firms, the "strategic" tag was simply a symbolic matter, whereas in others it had important consequences for the direction, scale and evaluation of resources. In general though, making IT strategic involved setting the projects (and by implication IS management itself) on a wider stage in which their actions could be justified and evaluated against a different kind of managerial discourse.

To develop this analysis, subsequent sections outline the findings from our various case studies. The findings have been organized so as to provide paired comparisons involving projects where the task, technology and product-market context have some important commonality. The pairs of case studies described here are as follows:

- National Bank Credit Centre and Vogue's Voguepac; customization of card processing packages.
- Caledonian Phonebank and Scotbank Remotebank; remote banking systems.
- National Bank BranchNet and Highland Insurance: a Branch Information Network and a Corporate MIS respectively.

From Contingencies to Symbolism

To begin with the comparison between National Bank Credit Centre and the Vogue case study: in both these cases, the major IT development involved decisions on the acquisition and maintenance of software packages for the processing of credit card accounts. Although there were important issues to do with customization, the technology was well-defined and the IT development process itself was reasonably routine. In short, this IT development conformed to McFarlan's (1984) "Factory IT" model. On the basis of contingencies then, one would expect the operational criteria of cost and efficiency to predominate.

For the most part, this was indeed the case, at least as far as the acquisition of the software package was concerned. However, in the Vogue case, a project which was technologically routine took on an unexpected organizational significance. Vogue was a recently acquired subsidiary of a larger clearing bank group—ScotBank Group. In the previous year, the increasing diversity of the Group had prompted the establishment of a Group Services function, which was dedicated to maximizing the effective use of the Bank's technical resources. As control of IT developments in the Group had previously rested almost exclusively with the in-house IT function of the clearing bank, this aim brought Group Management and IT functional management into direct conflict. When the acquisition of a processing package for Vogue got caught up in this conflict, a routine technology suddenly took on immense organizational significance.

Group Management saw IT developments at Vogue as a unique opportunity to establish their own influence over the allocation of IT resources. Exploiting their new mandate to the full, they were able to insist that both the customization and the maintenance of the new package be turned over to the software supplier. Both of these tasks would normally have been carried out as a matter of course by Scotbank's IT function. Consequently, the effect of excluding the in-house IT function from these tasks was to establish an important precedent for the future organization of IT resources. In other words, the *symbolic* importance of the project was tremendous, with political repercussions extending far beyond immediate questions of efficiency and practicality. The very fact that Voguepac was technologically routine made it a more powerful precedent in defining the role of the in-house IS function. A member of the Group Management team hinted at these repercussions:

> "I think what we're really talking about here is power. We're talking about an historical environment where nothing, but nothing, would happen in a computer development unless it was done either directly or under the control of IS Division. Now the implications of a user getting a system in and running without ever going anywhere near Information Systems . . . if you were in IS Division in a senior position, you would say, 'Wait a minute!'."

The symbolic character of the Vogue case is demonstrated by the comparison with National Bank Credit Centre. As National Bank had not adopted a diversification policy, many of the structural conflicts of ScotBank organization were absent. Decision making was uncontentious, and it was quickly established that the new package would be better customized and maintained by the Bank's in-house IT function.

This comparison establishes that the routineness of an IT development is only one factor in determining its importance to the organization. Equally importance is the symbolic role it may play in structural conflicts within the organization, or, more generally, in issues of power and control between organizations and suppliers.

Symbolism to Strategy

Whatever their political ramifications, neither of these credit card projects prompted management to develop an explicitly "strategic" vocabulary of action for dealing with them. Our second paired comparison, however, shows how the symbolic importance of a project may be parlayed into a full-blown strategic justification if it furthers the expertise of a particular group within the organization. The relevant comparison here is between the development of two remote banking systems. At Caledonian Bank, the in-house IT function both conceived and justified the PhoneBank remote banking system as a strategic project. They argued from the evidence of market and technological trends that remote delivery systems would play an increasingly important part in the Bank's future product range. PhoneBank was conceived as one element in a range of remote banking products, and as an important competitive response in a rapidly changing market-place:

> "So we had made greater sense of home and office banking; we'd taken it a lot further than anyone else had. We'd moved from being second to National Bank, and through the use of this telephone system which was innovative, we've moved ourselves to being market leaders in the UK."

At ScotBank, however, the design of what was actually a more sophisticated remote banking system was conceived and executed without reference to any such strategic concerns. The impetus came from senior management who were aware of similar developments in the US, and were concerned to extend the range of services available to business customers. Far from playing up the long-term or strategic aspects of the new technology, IS management took a decidedly downbeat view:

> "There are business requirements for which we are finding technological solutions ... You can't utilise technology for its own sake."

Again, neither the technological characteristics of the projects, nor the features of what were actually very similar market contexts, can explain the variation in the way the projects were developed. Although both projects clearly derived from a new technological recipe centred on remote delivery systems, the conceptual frameworks within which they were designed and justified were markedly different. That is to say, they were less a reflection of external contingencies than of the internal structuring of expertise in each organization.

In the Caledonian Bank case, we found an IT function which was increasingly unhappy with its role. Caledonian was a relatively small subsidiary of a larger banking group—BritBank—and in recent years the same kind of managerial processes we noted at ScotBank had started to restrict the power and scope of the IT group at Caledonian. In this context, PhoneBank not only represented a way of securing greater autonomy within the group structure, but also of securing a lead role in any future technological developments in that area. This was described by one of the system's major proponents. Phonebank, he said:

> "is not highly important in terms of our own systems; though, remember, it was extremely important at the time. Politically, it was immensely important politically. It was incredibly important that people here could see that we had something outwith the British Bank. Because beyond that point we were able to persuade British Bank that we should project manage the Group developments in home and office banking."

This quote highlights the way in which the political interests of an IS function are not simply given by its structural position but also reflect the collective identity which its managers and employees are seeking to cultivate. Caledonian's IT specialists had been involved in a number of important innovations in the preceding decade, including the development of a unique branch network system, and of a prototype EFTPOS (Electronic Funds Transfer at Point Of Sale) system.

Although the self-image or identity of the IS function is partly a product of its structural position, research on support functions (e.g. Grindley, 1991 on "enthusiasts and pragmatists" and Storey, 1992 on personnel functions) suggests that the way such groups make sense of their role is also a reflection of the aspirations of functional management and of the wider occupational community of which it is a part.

Where the IT function at Caledonian saw themselves as *Innovators,* IS management at ScotBank saw themselves as *Professionals*; that is, they emphasized the need to serve specific needs of the Bank, and prided themselves upon structuring their resources to ensure the closest possible relationships with user groups. Given this image, they were unlikely to pursue "strategic" innovations, but saw developments in remote banking as a logical, incremental response to customer needs.

Organizational Learning and the Pursuit of Strategic IT

The next pairing of cases not only demonstrates that the construction of strategic projects can be a handicap as well as a resource for IS functions, but also highlights the role of organizational learning in determining such outcomes. The cases cited here are, firstly, National Bank's development of BranchNet and, secondly, Highland Insurance's Corporate Management Information System.

The scope of BranchNet certainly lent itself to a strategic conception of its role and implications. As designed by the in-house Management Services Division, this was to be the major infrastructural investment for the Bank's branch network into the 1990s. It would provide on-line customer-based information to branches, replacing a current account-based information flow which involved the daily updating and despatch of thousands of microfiches. It not only involved the development of an information network connecting hundreds of bank branches to central mainframes, but also the integration of existing account records into a central customer database.

By any measure, the BranchNet concept seems to have represented a strategic IT investment. Certainly, it was widely hailed as a major component of the Bank's product strategy for the coming decades. Senior managers within the IS function saw it as almost sacrosanct:

> "Branch Network itself is not a product. Branch Network is a strategy. It's a strategy to attack the market place in the 90s."

The Chief Executive was equally convinced of its importance, even while recognizing the risks:

> "The danger with Branch Network is that you go down a blind alleyway from which you cannot escape. The danger of not doing it is that you go out of business."

With this kind of backing, the massive investment required by Branch-Net managed to escape the normal Return On Investment criteria. In their dealings with colleagues from the Accounting function, IS management were able to argue quite successfully that the singular character of BranchNet freed it from the tiresome necessity of detailed cost-benefit justification:

> "We knew that if we tried to cost justify each application as it came up, we would never be able to do it ... because the infrastructural costs would always be too high. We had to take on a longer-term marketing view and accept that we would have to implement one project that was actually not going to be cost justified ... provided we were sure it was taking us in the right direction."

And even a management accountant was disposed to accept that BranchNet was "a strategic decision, and the cost of not doing it was more important than the cost of doing it."

Yet, without questioning the strategic status attached to BranchNet, it seems permissible to explore the reasons why National Bank had pursued this route at this particular time. Clearly, sectoral recipes to do with quality of service play a part here, as did the sheer business potential associated with new database technology. Moreover, this and other cases suggest that the "strategic" label is sometimes less a reflection of the business impact of a project than of the extent to which it falls within the previous experience and expertise of the specialist function. If a project is highly innovative, at least relative to in-house IS expertise, it seems more likely to get labelled "strategic" because this signifies an area of risk and uncertainty for management.

All of this was certainly true of BranchNet. However, in addition, National Bank's willingness to pursue this expensive and avowedly uncertain option also seems to reflect a wider commitment to IT and beyond that the important role played by the Management Service Division (MSD) in the Bank's affairs. That MSD had come to play such an important role in the Bank's development was a tribute not only to the perceived expertise of its managers and staff, but also to an important process of organizational learning which had led to its current structural form. That process hinged on an important policy error in the late 1970s (Scarbrough & Lannon, 1988). At that time, responsibility for computing services was uneasily divided between two different divisions—Computer Services and Management Services. When ATM technology emerged in the late 1970s, these two divisions produced conflicting assessments of the potential of this new technology. Moreover, the most detailed assessment, which was conducted by Computer Services, confined itself to a cost-benefit analysis based purely on the clerical labour-saving potential of these devices. It concluded that ATMs could not be cost justified, but virtually ignored the marketing benefits offered by this new technology.

When the Bank's greatest rival in the Scottish market embarked on an extensive programme of ATM installations, and began to win large numbers of customers from National Bank, top management acted swiftly. First, the original policy decision on ATMs was rapidly overturned. Second—and here is the critical learning point—top management set about amalgamating the two divisions into one, termed the Management Services Division (MSD). And as its General Manager they appointed an outsider—a highly respected figure who combined a detailed understanding of banking operations with a masterly understanding of the potential use of IT. Equally importantly, the ATM episode effectively sensitized the Bank's top management to the strategic potential of IT. As a result, the newly formed division was not only equipped with a dynamic new General Manager, but also had a powerful mandate to develop strategic applications of IT. It quickly began to deliver the goods—BranchNet being only one of a series of innovative projects—and the function rapidly developed a self-consciously "Strategic" conception of its role in the Bank's affairs.

Contrast this happy (at least for IS afficionados) state of affairs, with developments at Highland Insurance. The development of a Corporate Management Information system may not have had quite the same investment implications as BranchNet, but any system that could tidy up and improve the existing patchy and sporadic information flows to product managers (principally for the setting of premium rates) would certainly have had tremendous importance for the company. At first, things went well. Indeed, in textbook fashion, the director of the IS function began what was termed the "strategy" project by embarking on a rigorous implementation of the Business Systems Planning (BSP) methodology.

The adoption of BSP was partly a reaction to an earlier unsuccessful attempt by another group—the Statistical Services function which had IT development resources of its own—to develop a workable system. Theirs had ultimately foundered on a key oversight; it was belatedly discovered that their up-to-the-minute MIS reports would take many hours or even days of run-time. BSP, however, would avoid such oversights by beginning with a detailed assessment of information needs and then moving logically and carefully onto the possible IT solutions for those needs.

Like other projects described here, one of the principal implications of the strategic status awarded to the Corporate MIS involved freeing it from the standard, highly detailed financial assessment. The only financial justification ever devised for it claimed that it would lead to a "decrease in claims ratio which in turn will be reflected as benefit on the Underwriting profit/loss in a year". It noted the Statistical Services' estimate that a 1% reduction in the ratio would lead to a £5 million benefit across all classes of business. However, while the report claimed that a 1% reduction was a conservative estimate of the impact of a corporate MIS, it did not attempt to substantiate the relationship between the MIS and the quality of rate-setting within the company. One of the report's authors noted of the 1% estimate:

> "There was no grounding for that really. It was just a figure that everyone accepted would be the case."

However, despite (or perhaps because of) the formal and rigorous attempt to link the Corporate MIS to strategic business needs, the project quickly ran into trouble. This was partly because, unlike Branch-Net, the project's design was dependent from its earliest stages on the local knowledge and cooperation of a disparate range of user groups. The complexity of the existing process, and its dependence on tacit knowledge, was one major barrier. It was exacerbated because the IS function—symbolically located on the lowest floor of the headquarters building—lacked the necessary status and credibility to gain the active commitment of top management who were (equally symbolically) located on the top floor. One of the (relatively youthful) team of systems developers noted:

> "The topmost level was banned from us, perhaps because we were pretty scruffy."

As a consequence, the project quickly ran into difficulties as IS developers tried to squeeze a complex reality into a formalized model:

> "We produced organization charts but this was one of the more difficult tasks. In a complex business you may leave areas of responsibility slightly grey. Like the individual Product Managers formally had some responsibilities, but they varied in their approach to product pricing and left different decisions to their product managers ... That was the first big hole we fell down."

Where BranchNet had achieved strategic status by dint of MSD's mandate and its infrastructural implications, the Highland Insurance project fell into the "big hole" of existing organizational practices. The complexity and time demands of the project were further compounded by political pressures from impatient user departments. By 1986, "people were turning against the information strategy idea", and there was a feeling that the IS function had "analyzed it to death". Without support from top management, and in danger of losing face within the organization, a change in IS management facilitated a switch to a more "realistic" and pragmatic approach: "evolution not revolution" as the new IS manager put it. This involved tailoring the MIS, initially, to the specific needs of the largest and most demanding user department.

The contrast between the BranchNet and Highland Insurance cases is revealing. Clearly, simply mapping a strategic methodology onto a development process is not enough to make it strategic. Much depends also on the reputation of the IS function itself, and, relatedly, on its basic competences in making the technology work. In the Highland Insurance case, the low status of the IS function was compounded by its dependence on the local knowledge and cooperation of a variety of user groups. Although BranchNet too was ultimately dependent on its users, the design stage was relatively free of such constraints, allowing MSD management to promote their strategic vision to the full.

Discussion

This study suggests that the strategic nature of a particular IT project is not something which can be determined at the outset. Persuading top management to invest major resources into a project, or to slacken the usual investment criteria, is as much a matter of the internal manage-ment structure and culture of the business as it is the "objective" merits of a particular proposal. In suggesting that such persuasion reflects the social construction of technology, I have sought to show how the expertise of the IS function, combined with the degree of IS knowledge or ignorance amongst top management, can project a compelling world-view in which the strategic possibilities of IT are central. Although it obviously helps if such a world-view is supported by wider sectoral features, the contingencies of the immediate environment are probably secondary to the way in which they are interpreted. In this process, the IS function's history, status and self-image are important factors.

The practical implications of this study are manifold. It suggests that the rational model of strategy is relevant, but only as a resource which is generally available to competing functions and which reflects both the latter groups' aspirations and the problems they experience in handling particular projects. Similarly, the competence of the IS func-tion and of users is also relevant, but again not in a straightforwardly functional way. Perceived competence both influences and reflects credibility and political influence. Moreover, competence is embedded in a specific philosophy or approach which may not be readily inte-grated into the kind of overarching inter-functional framework needed to create the bridging knowledge between business and IT issues.

The social construction perspective cautions against simplistic pre-scriptions; however rational the model or methodology, it will normally come unstuck if it conflicts with what people really "know" in organizations. Instead, it points to the importance of organizational learning in bringing about a more holistic appreciation of IT across the organization. This is not to say that the new ideas and concepts acquired through learning are objectively valid—they will certainly be used to gain power, for instance, and sometimes may have to be unlearned. On the other hand, the more that managers are induced to test their ideas against "reality", the more likely it is that they will be able to construct the kind of reality that they really want.

Conclusions

The experience gleaned from the case studies has a relevance stretching beyond the debates on strategic IT. For one, it questions the common sense assumption that the organizational deployment of IT is driven by the economic forces of competition and globalization. The case studies do not challenge the importance of competitive forces, but suggest that they are vocalized differently within each organization. What uniformity exists in firms' responses to competitive pressures seems to derive from the common currency of "recipes" and cognitive categories (Douglas, 1987) which circulate within firms and sectors.

The account of strategic IT presented in this chapter is an illustration and exploration of this wider point. Outlining the conditions under which IS expertise comes to shape the categories that inform strategic thinking—broadly, the distinction between strategic and non-strategic IT—I have emphasized the importance of blending different knowledge-bases, including sectoral, organizational and technical forms, into a compelling interpretation of the strategic problems, hence solutions (Scarbrough, 1993), confronting top management. This account steers a middle way between competing interpretations of organizational change. It suggests that change is neither a matter of rational adaptation to external competition nor the messy product of internal power-games. The crucial engine of change is found to be the competition between different bodies of expertise and their preferred categories and constructions.

As evidence for the validity of this account, and for its general-izability beyond the domain of strategic IT, I would offer as my final argument the illustration of current trends towards the outsourcing of IT. As many studies (Lacity & Hirschheim, 1995; Willcocks et al., 1995) have indicated, this trend can hardly be taken as an objectively rational response to the economic conditions facing firms, though such forces are often invoked in its support. In fact, despite seeming to be a complete reversal of the trend towards strategic IT, the processes and mechanisms involved are broadly the same. This is essentially another way of classifying IT activities, but is a classification (out- versus in-sourcing) which specifies the sources rather than the applications of IT expertise, and which is driven by an accounting perspective emphasiz-ing cost efficiency rather than an IT perspective emphasizing innovation. Accounting expertise is in the ascendant, and is supported not so much by the competitive forces of the immediate sectoral environment, as by the cross-sectoral links with the major IT consulting firms. In short, the forces which drive outsourcing are ultimately no different to the ones which drove strategic IT but with an important shift in the guiding categories of action and with market relationships securing a more subordinate relationship between IT expertise and the accounting perspective.

Parallels such as this underline the need to explore the dominant interpretations and categories which shape the deployment of IS in organizations. In particular, we need to understand the roots of such interpretations in the formation of specialist expertise and the competi-tion between expert groups. Above and beyond the development of specific technologies in organizations, we find the emergence of different kinds of knowledge *about* technology. Ultimately, it is this level of knowledge which implicitly shapes the management and development of information systems.

REFERENCES

Abernathy, W.J., 1978, *The Productivity Dilemma: Roadblock to Innovation in the Automobile Industry*, Baltimore: Johns Hopkins University Press.

Berger, P. and Luckmann, T., 1967, *The Social Construction of Reality: A Treatise in the Sociology of Knowledge*, New York: Doubleday Anchor Books.

Child, J. and Loveridge R., 1990, *Information Technology in European Services*, Oxford: Basil Blackwell.

Child, J. and Smith, C., 1987, The Context and Process of Organizational Transformations—Cadbury Limited in its Sector, *Journal of Management Studies*, 24, (6), 565–593.

Douglas, M., 1987, *How Institutions Think*, London: Routledge and Kegan Paul.

Grindley, K., 1991, *Managing IT at Board Level*, London: Pitman.

Gunton, T., 1990, *Inside Information Technology*, Hemel Hempstead: Prentice-Hall.

Lacity, M.C. and Hirscheim, R., 1995, *Beyond the Information Systems Outsourcing Bandwagon*, London: Wiley and Sons.

McFarlan, F.W., 1984, Information Technology Changes the Way you Compete, *Harvard Business Review*, May-June, 98–103.

Miller, D. and Friesen, P., 1980, Momentum and Revolution in Organizational Adaptation, *Academy of Management Journal*, 23, 591–614.

Morgan, G., 1990, *Organisations in Society*, London: Macmillan.

Scarbrough, H., 1993, Problem-Solutions in the Management of Information Systems' Expertise, *Journal of Management Studies*, 30, (6), 939–955.

Scarbrough, H., (ed.), *The IT Challenge: Strategy and IT in Financial Services*, Hemel Hempstead: Prentice-Hall.

Scarbrough, H. and Corbett, J.M., 1992, *Technology and Organization: Power, Meaning and Design*, London: Routledge.

Scarbrough, H. and Lannon, R., 1988, The Successful Exploitation of New Technology in Banking, *Journal of General Management*, 13, 38–51.

Shearman, C. and Burrell, G., 1987, The Structures of Industrial Development, *Journal of Management Studies*, 24, 4, 325–345.

Storey, J., 1992, *Developments in the Management of Human Resources*, Oxford: Blackwell.

von Hippel, E., 1988, *The Sources of Innovation*, Oxford: Oxford University Press.

Whipp, R. and Clark, P., 1986, *Innovation and the Auto Industry: Production, Process and Work Organization*, London: Frances Pinter.

Whittington, R., 1993, *What is strategy—and does it matter?*, London: Routledge.

Willcocks, L., Lacity, M. and Fitzgerald, G., 1995, *IT Outsourcing in Europe and the USA: Assessment Issues*, Research and Discussion Paper 95, 2, Oxford Institute of Information Management, Templeton College.

2
Computer Supported Collaborative Working: Challenging Perspectives on Work and Technology

LIAM J. BANNON
CSCW Research Centre, Department of Computer Science
& Information Systems, University of Limerick, Ireland

"Organizations typically display inertia through their established routines, institutionalized practices, and taken-for-granted assumptions that inform and reinforce the status quo . . . Managers not only have vested interests in an existing order, they also tend to be rooted firmly in a given understanding of reality, making acceptance of an alternative structural order and new view of the world problematic"
Wanda Orlikowski, 1991

INTRODUCTION

In recent years, the realization that information technology (IT) and computer-based information systems (CBIS) can be used not simply as a means to improve the efficiency of operations, but also to provide new strategic possibilities for organizational innovation and development, has begun to be recognized. The convergence and integration of computing and telecommunications, the ubiquitous nature of computing in all aspects of daily work life, including the appearance of mobile facilities, means that there are few aspects of business that are not influenced by the use of computer technology. Such a situation opens

Information Technology and Organizational Transformation. Edited by R.D. Galliers and W.R.J. Baets. © 1998 John Wiley & Sons Ltd

up possibilities for both business success and failure. What is evident is that there is little chance of surviving in the game if one simply stands still. The question is not whether one needs to change, but whether one does so reactively or proactively, piecemeal or wholesale. Whatever strategy is selected there are risks associated with it.

The purpose of this chapter is not to discuss information systems (IS) strategy *per se*, or business opportunities arising from IT, but to outline an emerging perspective on the nature of work, learning and the role of technology in the workplace that I believe, if accepted, will have a significant impact on the way we go about both organizational re-design processes and the deployment of IT. This perspective has been most clearly articulated and investigated in the emerging interdisciplinary field entitled Computer Supported Cooperative Work (CSCW) over the past several years. This new field is characterized by a number of at times competing voices, stretching over academic research and development groups, technology companies, organizational change agents, and technologically-oriented businesses. A focus on the multiplicity of cooperative work arrangements to be found in organizations and problems and prospects for their computer augmentation is what makes the area "new".

The differing groups that comprise the field not surprisingly have differing agendas and priorities as to the central issues that need to be confronted in order to produce a technological and information systems infrastructure that will truly support work processes in organizations. The field attracts people from a variety of different disciplinary backgrounds: psychology, sociology, software engineering, design, organizational studies, management, computer science, anthropology, human factors, media studies, etc. Given such a variegated "community", is it any wonder that they do not speak with one voice? It is within this area that I believe there has developed a discussion worth taking note of, that is, a view on the nature of work and organizational learning and its implications for technological and organizational change. It is important to note that while this work has been taken up in the CSCW community, the early studies have come from existing research traditions within the social sciences. This view is different from that prevailing in the field, which I would argue is still dominated, implicitly if not explicitly, by a neo-Tayloristic industrial engineering stance. In CSCW we find alternative perspectives on the relation between work and technology, on the details of work, and on how these details need to be understood as we deploy technologies to "support" it. Key features of these alternative perspectives are a focus on collective work activities rather than individual work tasks, on the way learning occurs within work communities, and on the myriad ways in which people in their work activities innovate with and through technology.

While to some, for example those who subscribe to the Business Process Re-engineering (BPR) school, the centrality of work practices in these approaches may seem too static a view to be useful, and to others the perspective on how learning in organizations occurs may appear too radical, the argument here is that these discussions within the CSCW community are likely to lead to some interesting changes in the years ahead, from both a management and an IS viewpoint. I say this from a pragmatic stance, in terms of business innovation—not simply from an academic standpoint. What I hope to do in the rest of this paper is orient you to some relevant work that has been circulating within the CSCW community concerning the nature of work, recount some stories, and allude to possible implications. In a word, the intent is not to have you embrace CSCW as the answer to all the problems concerning IT and organizational change, but to offer some of the work and technology studies which can be found inhabiting the CSCW arena as interesting signposts towards an alternative path to understanding people, technology and organizational change processes.

THE FIELD OF CSCW

In this section a brief background on the emergence of the CSCW field, and its key claims and features are delineated.

Some Background on CSCW

Workgroup computing, collaborative computing, Groupware, co-ordination technology, augmented business teams, group decision support systems, cooperative work support, are all terms that have become increasingly common in the world of organizational computing in recent years. Despite this interest, there is still considerable confusion about the exact focus of the area commonly labelled "Computer Supported Cooperative Work" (CSCW), and the reasons for its apparent growth. Is it just a fad, a passing fashion, or does it denote a new approach to problems of harnessing information technology to human needs? Whatever the answer, the area of CSCW appears to have become accepted over the past few years as a legitimate sphere of academic research and development activity, with a growing number of interested researchers and the support of many software developers and end user organizations[1]. What exactly is the basis for this interest? We can distinguish at least four distinct perspectives on the nature of the CSCW field (Bannon, 1993):

CSCW as a "Catch-all" Concept

At the most simple level, it can be argued that CSCW is simply an "umbrella term" with little content other than the idea that it is concerned with people, computers and cooperation in some form. The utility of such a seemingly vacuous definition is that it may still allow people from a variety of different disciplines, with partially over-lapping concerns as to the current state of technology development and the understanding of use contexts, to come together and discuss issues of mutual interest. CSCW in this view is an "arena" where different groups vie for the attention of participants, rather than a coherent focused field. Howard (1988) describes two distinct though very varied communities within CSCW. He coined the term "strict construction-ists" to describe those in the field focused on the development of computer systems to support group work, who tend to use themselves as objects of analysis in the provision of support tools. These people, mainly implementers, are interested in building tools and they see the area of CSCW as a possible leverage point for creating novel applica-tions. Most of these people equate the CSCW field with Groupware, as they focus on new software applications. Howard denoted those who make up the remainder of the CSCW field, the larger part, as "loose constructionists," a heterogeneous collection of people, some of whom are drawn to the area by their dissatisfaction with current uses of technology to support work processes, others because they see in this area a chance for communities who traditionally have not had a voice in the design of computer systems to have one. Rob Kling has articulated a somewhat different view of the CSCW community to that of Howard. He sees CSCW as a conjunction of "certain kinds of *technologies*, certain kinds of *users* (usually small self-directed professional teams), and a *worldview* that emphasises convivial work relations" (Kling, 1991). This

---

[1] The first open conference on Computer Supported Cooperative Work was organized in 1986 in Austin, Texas. It brought together people from a variety of backgrounds: artificial intelligence, human-computer interaction, office information systems, computer science, psychology and anthropology. The general focus was on issues concerning technology support for groups. The bi-annual Conference has grown in size and stature over the years, as has the related European Conference. Many journals in the areas of office systems, human-computer interaction, decision support and software engineering now include CSCW in their list of topics, and some new journals with a more specific focus on CSCW have emerged (*CSCW, Organizational Computing*). Monographs and edited collec-tions of papers are also mushrooming (e.g. Baecker, 1992, Greenberg, 1991).

issue, of whether or not CSCW implies anything about shared goals of group members, or convivial work relations, has been the subject of some dispute (Bannon & Schmidt, 1991).

CSCW as a Paradigm Shift

Hughes, Randall & Shapiro (1991) argue that we should conceive of CSCW as a paradigm shift in the way we think of designing computer support systems of all kinds, rather than as a distinct research field concerned with a specific form of work. This position has similarities to the views of Suchman (1989), who describes CSCW as "... the design of computer-based technologies with explicit concern for the socially organised practices of their intended users". Both these views deny any special prerogative to particular user groups, technologies, or forms of work in what constitutes CSCW. Rather the emphasis is on "a return to the social", realizing that much work on people-technology systems has systematically avoided issues of the social organization of work and their implications for the design of appropriate support technology.

CSCW as Software for Groups

A quite different conception of what the field is about can be discerned among those who focus on the computer support of "groups" or teams as the hallmark of the field. This has given rise to the term "Groupware" to distinguish the computer products marketed in this area (Johansen, 1988). While this view is most commonly found among information technology and business consultants, it can also be found among software developers and researchers. For example, Irene Greif, one of the originators of the term CSCW, defines it as "an identifiable research field focused on the role of the computer in group work" (Greif, 1988a). As noted by Kling (1991) and Howard (1988), many adherents of this view tend to focus on small teams or homogeneous groups with convivial work relations, and thus pay little attention to settings in everyday organizational life where issues such as power and politics play a large role. The "group" focus has also been criticized, based on difficulties of enumerating properties of "groups" as found in the workplace.

CSCW as Technological Support of Cooperative Work Forms

Bannon & Schmidt (1991) define CSCW as "an endeavour to understand the nature and characteristics of cooperative work with the objective of designing adequate computer-based technologies". Here the emphasis is on understanding cooperative work as a distinctive form of work (Schmidt, 1990), and on supporting these cooperative work forms with appropriate technology. This broadens the scope of the field considerably beyond that of computer support for groups. In this framework, "cooperative work" does not imply any notion of shared goals or conviviality, but rather people engaged in work processes related as to content. While having some overlap with the paradigm shift perspective described above, this approach focuses on specific work forms and practices, and the nature of the mechanisms that evolve to facilitate the co-ordination of cooperative work. Critics of this approach argue that the distinction between cooperative work and individual work is problematic in everyday work situations, and that this approach has too functionalist a perspective, neglecting subjective factors of participation and cooperation.

CSCW as Participative Design

The CSCW community contains within its ranks a number of people who are proponents or practitioners of participative, or participatory, design (Clement & Van den Besselaar, 1993). Their focus is on developing alternatives to traditional systems design, alternative ways of doing design, of involving users, and so on (Greenbaum & Kyng, 1991). While certainly various forms of user involvement are important to the development of successful CSCW systems, and there is an overlap of interests and concerns, the terms are not by any means completely synonymous. Indeed, many successful participative design practices such as Future Workshops and Wall Charting are noticeable by the complete absence of computers in supporting the ongoing work of the group. Nevertheless, the opinions and experiences of the participative design movement exert an influence on the field.

The purpose of this chapter is to show the relevance of certain work appearing in the CSCW field to the management of organizational change and IT. Thus, I do not wish to dwell on the details of the above distinctions here but simply note that the position taken in this paper is congruent with the paradigm shift and technological support of cooperative work forms perspectives. Put more simply, CSCW involves the exploration of issues concerning cooperative work arrangements and their support via information technology. Such a view of the field opens it up to a wide mix of disciplines—computing and software engineering, cognitive and social psychology, work sociology and anthropology, organizational theory, etc. Our task now is to demonstrate that CSCW is not simply the re-packaging of earlier IS frameworks, but does have some genuinely new insights—insights that are relevant to today's business concerns of organizational change and deployment of new technology. So, the next section describes some of the distinctive features of the CSCW field, before moving on to show how work in this field may impact on organizational understanding and the effective deployment of new technologies.

What's New in CSCW?

For many people working in the information systems field, it is difficult to comprehend the recent surge of interest in CSCW issues as if these were totally new and deserving of particular attention. Surely many of the topics have always been important in information systems. However, a major development that gives impetus to the rise to CSCW *as a distinct field of study* is the current transformation in the organization of work. Changes in the environment in which businesses work require companies to improve their innovative skills, operational flexibility, and product quality. To meet these demands, work organizations must be able to adapt and innovate rapidly and to co-ordinate, in a comprehensive and integrated way, their distributed activities across functions and professional boundaries within the organization or within a network of organizations (Schmidt, 1991). Work organizations thus require support from advanced information systems that can facilitate the co-ordination of distributed decision making. Simultaneously, the proliferation of powerful workstations in cooperative work settings and their interconnection in large-scale networks provide the technological foundation to meet this need. CSCW thus entails both a wider remit than traditional IS as regards the different settings in which it is appropriate to study cooperative work arrangements, as well as a more explicit focus on the support requirements of cooperative work and the way people create, manage, disable, modify, etc. computer-based mechanisms of interaction. Thus studies in areas such as computer-aided design (CAD), computer-integrated manufacturing (CIM), computer-aided software engineering (CASE), etc., are all relevant to the CSCW field to the extent that they study the use of computers to support cooperative work in different domains. A focus on the multiplicity of cooperative work arrangements and problems and prospects for their computer augmentation is what makes the area "new".

For purposes of clarification, and as an aid to understanding the focus of the field, it may be useful to note the relationships between CSCW as currently constituted and other, related fields. We thus note its relationship to the areas of Office Automation (and Office Information Systems), Human Factors, Groupware, Group Decision Support Systems (GDSS) and Business Process Re-engineering (BPR).

Office Automation and CSCW

The early computer systems developed to "automate the office" were built by designers who implicitly assumed much of the traditional procedural conception of office work (Ellis & Nutt, 1980; Hammer & Sirbu, 1980; Zisman, 1977). These types of systems are suitable for office work that is structured around actions where the sequence of activities is similar, but they do not deal well with unanticipated conditions. As Wynn (1979), Suchman (1983), Gerson & Star (1986) and others have shown, much daily office work involves more than the "execution" of office procedures, so the simple procedural model has been discredited (Barber, 1983). The need to develop office systems that play more of a support role for people in their work has been acknowledged. However, as noted by Schmidt & Bannon (1992), building computer systems where the work is seen as simply being concerned with "information flow," and neglecting the articulation work needed to make the "flow" possible, can lead to serious problems. Technological support of work should aim at supporting the self-organization of cooperative ensembles as opposed to disrupting work by computerising formal procedures. The organizational models embedded in CSCW applications should be treated as *resources* for competent and capable workers rather than as executable code. That is, the system should make the underlying model accessible to users and, indeed, support users in interpreting the procedure, to evaluate its rationale and implications. It should support users in applying and adapting the model to the situation at hand. The system should even support users in modifying the underlying model and creating new models where appropriate in accordance with the changing organizational realities and needs. The system should also support the documentation and communication of decisions to adapt, circumvent, execute and modify the underlying model. In discussion of such topics, and the development of supportive systems embodying them, the CSCW community goes well beyond the normal boundaries of IS discussions.

Human Factors and CSCW

While undoubtedly one large topic of discussion within CSCW concerns what could be termed "human factors", it would be a mistake to assume that the usual set of such concerns, expressed, for example, in the concepts and frameworks employed within the human-computer interaction (HCI) community, would adequately cover the conceptual frameworks and research topics encountered in the studies of work and technology found in CSCW. Specifically, traditional human factors approaches focus too much on individual skills and capacities and do not explore the whole issue of the sociality of work. This limitation has in recent years led to the search for extensions to existing conceptual and methodological frameworks in order to take these factors into account (Bannon & Bødker, 1991). For example, within the dominant cognitive science tradition in HCI, we see an extension of the basic conceptual apparatus in a number of directions, for example, examining the role of artifacts in human cognition (Norman, 1991), and the way cognition is distributed among people and artifacts—"distributed cognition" (Hutchins, 1990). Whether or not it is possible that simple extensions to existing frameworks will suffice is still a matter of debate.

CSCW as Groupware

For some, the terms CSCW and Groupware are synonymous. In an earlier paper I discussed why this view was problematic (Bannon & Schmidt, 1991). The problem stems partly from too close a focus on developing software packages for groups, rather than on developing supporting technology for cooperative work forms. Perhaps Greif (1988b) is correct in viewing Groupware as a passing fad in that all software in the future will be Groupware in that it will support cooperative work patterns (e.g., word processors facilitating joint authoring), just as state-of-the-art software is now "user friendly". The term Groupware provides a technological focus which is too narrow for an adequate understanding of the multiplicity of social forms of cooperative work in the world and their technological support requirements.

GDSS and CSCW

Group Decision Support Systems (GDSS) are certainly one aspect of CSCW activities. Nevertheless it is important to note that most of the GDSS work does not share the same set of concerns evident among many of the CSCW community concerning the nature of work and how to study work. The models used tend to be extensions of work in the decision support systems field and tend to eschew detailed study of organizational practices. The approach can be criticized on a number of grounds (Whitaker, 1992). The point here is not that one perspective is necessarily more "correct", but rather to point out that much of the literature that appears under the rubric of GDSS stems from a different tradition and different practices to the work I am focusing on here in CSCW.

The Relation Between BPR and CSCW

While on the surface there may appear to be much in common between the current management fascination with the concept of BPR and some of the issues mentioned in this paper about CSCW, it is important to note that there are some important conceptual differences as well. Central to the BPR view (at least in the writings of Hammer, 1990 and Davenport & Short, 1990) is a conception of work that is deliberately ahistorical, and linked to tasks and workflows. People are not seen as enabling agents but more often simply as elements to keep the flow moving. While the approach does help focus attention on organizational change and on understanding some aspects of business processes, it is in danger of throwing the baby out with the bath water when it advocates "don't automate, obliterate" (Hammer, 1990). This view does not seem to ascribe any importance to what I would refer to as the "archaeology of work". It is true that, in certain cases, the sedimentation of practices that has happened over time has led to an accretion of—from today's perspective—irrelevant practices in the work process. But it is also often the case that aside from the formal written operating procedures there has been built up a wealth of practices shared in the community that help get the work done (see "Uncovering Work in CSCW" below). If this tacit knowledge is obliterated through massive layoffs and restructuring, overall organizational competence may suffer due to the faulty "memory" in the organization, as the requisite information and skill may no longer be available to the new workforce. Also, much of the BPR framework adheres, implicitly or explicitly, to a management model of change and control that is in many respects akin to the original ideas of F.W. Taylor's Scientific Management. Indeed, Davenport is quite explicit about this, arguing that the "new industrial engineering" that he is advocating is the next step in scientific management, using IT and business process redesign to re-engineer the corporation. Within CSCW, however, there is an alternative perspective on the way work is accomplished that puts greater emphasis on work practices. This perspective is based on "the capacity of workers to identify problems, decipher them, interpret them within shifting situations, utilize formal and informal social networks in the organization, and draw upon the fund of knowledge in the community" (Sachs, 1994). This approach places importance on the role of the human actors in accomplishing work, and on their evolving learning in communities as a key to organizational development. Focus is as much on the tacit, informal ways in which people organize and support each other, as on the explicit ways this is done. Technological developments must be fitted into this world rather than simply being imposed, if the changes are to take hold. Of course in our brief discussion here we must also realize that neither BPR nor CSCW are characterized by clear and uniform and univalent approaches, but the characterizations expressed here are prototypical.

UNCOVERING WORK IN CSCW

In this section I argue that, far from CSCW embodying a naive "human relations" orientation, it provides a vitally important perspective from which to understand work processes and practices, with consequent implications for their support with information technology. The perspectives in the field can help in understanding the apparent paradox of change and continuity that is required in organizations. Our conceptions of what work is determine how we believe it can be changed. Attention to the way individuals and communities of people work and learn is vital as a key ingredient in any planned change process, be it technology-related or not. So, rather than focusing on some of the technological factors also being addressed in the field of CSCW, or specific software products, I will concentrate here on research studies in the field that have given us a richer understanding of the way people work and learn, with and through technology. This is not to downplay the other kinds of studies within CSCW, but is a question of focus for this particular chapter, which has as its concern understanding the relation of organizational change and technology[2]. In the next section I briefly relate some key features of different schools of thought evident within CSCW concerning the nature of work and learning and use of technology, followed by a series of short vignettes of specific studies that illuminate aspects of these approaches. The purpose of these accounts is to show the utility of these perspectives as a handle to grasp important issues in developing organizations through information technology. Brown & Duguid (1991) provide a perspective on working, learning and innovation that is very similar in its intent to that described here.

Approaches to Understanding Work

In CSCW, the focus is on cooperative work arrangements that emerge as a result of the nature of the actual work being performed. Thus there

---

[2] In a forthcoming paper, I plan to investigate specific CSCW applications in the context of organizational change.

is an emphasis on field studies in specific work domains. While traditional task and work analysis methods from work psychology and sociology can contribute here, much interest has centred on more qualitative, interpretative, ethnographic studies of work practices in an effort to understand more fully the "artful practices" of ensembles of workers as they accomplish their work activities. While more traditional sociological and anthropological concepts—division of labour, issues of power and control, symbolism, for example, are of importance to CSCW, there has been particular interest in ethnographic studies, chiefly of an ethnomethodological nature (Button, 1993). This perspective is distinct from earlier critiques of neo-Taylorist management approaches, such as that of Braverman and the labour process school, in its emphasis on the detailed observation and understanding of the mundane practicalities of "getting the work done". The emphasis in these studies is on the work that members do in order to make their work accountable to themselves and each other, focusing on the "working division of labour" (Anderson, Sharrock & Hughes, 1987) as distinct from viewing the division of labour as an analytical category. This work seems of particular relevance to designers of CSCW systems, where lack of attention to such matters as how the work is actually accomplished by members of the working community has led at times to the development of systems that fail dramatically (see e.g. Harper, Hughes & Shapiro, 1991).

Ethnography is concerned with describing the activities and practices of people in a setting, though, importantly, it is more than that and "attempts to interpret and give meaning to those activities" (Blomberg, et al, 1993). Hughes et al (1992) characterize their study of air traffic controllers thus:

> "There is no one method of ethnographic analysis ... The field workers immersed themselves in the work by spending several months observing activities on and around the suites, talking to staff, and discussing with them the researchers' developing understanding of what controllers do. While attempting to avoid prejudices and to allow the work situation to 'speak for itself' as much as possible, researchers cannot claim to address it innocent of any theoretical orientation; and their results would be much impoverished if they did. The purpose of an ethnographic approach is not so much to show *that* work is socially organised (which is rather easy) but to show *how* it is socially organised."

Such approaches, inspired by certain groups of sociologists and anthropologists, have been a core component of the new way of viewing work within CSCW. As an example, we can briefly examine the case of office automation. According to the traditional "bureaucratic" conception of organizational work, people perform a number of tasks according to a set of well-specified "procedures" that have been developed by management as efficient and effective means to certain ends. The traditional formal organization chart is presumed to show the actual lines of authority and the "correct" pattern of information flow and communication. However, this understanding has been proved to be highly idealized and grossly inadequate for analyzing and modelling the articulation of real world cooperative work arrangements. Due to the dynamic and contradictory demands posed on a social system of work by the environment, task allocation and articulation are renegotiated more or less continuously. A number of studies of office work, conducted by anthropologists and sociologists, have emphasized the rich nature of many allegedly "routine" activities and the complex pattern of cooperative decision making and negotiation engaged in by co-workers, even at relatively "low" positions within the organization (Wynn, 1979; Suchman, 1983; Gerson & Star, 1986). Suchman gives a concise account of this discrepancy between the office procedures that supposedly govern office work and the practical action carried out by office workers. She notes: "the procedural structure of organizational activities is the *product* of the orderly work of the office, rather than the reflection of some enduring structure that stands behind that work" (Suchman, 1983). It is not that office procedures are irrelevant, it is just that these procedures require problem solving activities and negotiation with co-workers, the result of which can be interpreted as performance according to procedures. The "informal" interactions that take place in the office thus not only serve important psychological functions in terms of acting as a human support network for people, for example, providing companionship and emotional support, but are crucial to the actual conduct of the work process itself. Evidence for this is apparent when workers "work-to-rule", i.e. perform exactly as specified by the office procedures, no more and no less. The result is usually that the office grinds to a halt very quickly.

Yet it is precisely the procedural model of work that has tended to dominate in the early work on office automation and even much more recent office information systems development work as noted earlier. If we are to take on board the observations from ethnographic studies the anthropologist Brigitte Jordan notes how we need to "investigate the ways in which people in the workplace 'co-construct' knowledge and skill, drawing on the social and material resources available to them. Attempts to design CSCW technologies, then, must be grounded in a thorough understanding of ongoing work processes and how they are supported (or not) by the physical layout, artifacts, information systems and databases, as well as the social relationships and arrangements of the workplace" (Jordan, 1996). Jordan points to the distinctions between the concepts embodied in process models and workflow representations currently in vogue versus the tacit, implicit, embodied and unarticulated knowledge inherent in work practices, and points to the importance of the concept of "communities of practice" (Lave & Wenger, 1990)—the basic social unit in which work gets done and in which these skills are shared, learned and evolved.

There are other approaches to understanding work, which while sharing many of the concerns of ethnographers, derive from other traditions, for example, Russian-inspired activity or cultural-historical theory (Wertsch, 1981). This approach is built on the work of Vygotsky, Leont'ev and others in the Soviet Union in the 1920s–1940s and is represented more recently by the work of people such as Cole, Scribner, Engeström, Kuutti and others. Their emphasis is on activity systems, their evolution and development, and on understanding the context in which activities are carried out. "An activity system comprises the individual practitioner, the colleagues and co-workers of the workplace community, the conceptual and practical tools, and the shared objects as a unified dynamic whole" (Engeström, 1991). While the conceptual apparatus of this framework is difficult to apply directly, its focus on the concept of activities, which are inherently collective, not individual, phenomena, and on mediation of activity via instruments, tools, procedures, methods, etc., make it quite appropriate for CSCW. As such, the approach provides an alternative framework for conceptualizing human work activity, mediated by artifacts, and by other people, to the prevalent information processing paradigm in much management and technical work (Bannon, 1990). The Finnish researcher Yrjö Engeström has developed this approach in terms of understanding work activities within a more comprehensive conceptual framework, including a rich fieldwork methodology, entitled Developmental Work Research, which provides mechanisms for understanding both the past history of work practices as well as the development of new work forms (Engeström, 1987; 1991). He claims that this approach challenges many assumptions about work and learning, so that not only do individuals change, but they change their collective practice and its institutional frames as well. This work has begun to be discussed within the CSCW community (Kuutti, 1991) and, even more recently, within a management perspective by Blackler (1993), who recounts how the approach provides an interesting reframing of a number of important issues in management and organizational thinking. Significant features of the approach include: "The social origins of motives, the nature and significance of mediating mechanisms in the enactment of activities, the active nature of participation, the relevance of history, and the significance of inconsistency and conflict in activity systems" (Blackler,

1993). Especially important within the context of this book, Blackler argues, like Harry Scarbrough in Chapter 1, that the approach encourages an orientation "away from a concern with the management of experts to a concern with the management of expertise, from an emphasis on plans and strategy to an analysis of activity and activity systems, and from a preoccupation with objective knowledge to a concern with the management of collective instability". Such an approach would certainly seem to be highly topical in today's business environment.

The anthropologist Pat Sachs draws on both general ethnographic and activity theoretic backgrounds for her perspective on work (Sachs, 1994). Her critique builds on that of figures such as Wynn, Suchman, Blomberg, Orr, Scribner, Hutchins, and herself on the nature and organization of everyday work practices. This body of work, through critical argumentation and extensive field work, has begun to have an impact on a number of fields—including management studies, business administration, information systems development, organizational behaviour, job design, human resource management and training. This increasingly prominent view reconceptualizes the nature of work and organizational life, and the role of information technology support. It emphasizes work practices, and the way learning is accomplished within communities of practice. It argues that learning and action are "situated" (Suchman, 1987), and that work is accomplished via artifacts, in conjunction with others. Much of this work has helped to contribute to the interdisciplinary field of CSCW (Schmidt & Bannon, 1992). Sachs (1994) argues passionately and cogently for the need to reconceptualize the nature of work, away from what she terms an "organizational" view, to one she labels "activity-oriented". To synopsize these perspectives the organizational view is still the predominant one in organizations today, grounded in scientific management ideas, focusing on training, tasks, procedures, workflow and teams, in contrast to the activity-oriented view focusing on learning, know-how, networks, conceptual understanding, work practices, judgement and communities (of practice). In line with Jordan's comments, the contrast is between the "documented, visible and articulatable" versus the tacit, silent and "only-understood-by-the-group". Finally, she notes: "Because the people who design business processes are ordinarily not the individuals who do the hands-on work, and because business process designers tend to think organizationally rather than employing work thinking, the fund of knowledge about details of work process are generally not incorporated into work process designs" (Sachs, 1994).

Work in the area of cooperative systems development by groups in Scandinavia (Ehn, 1988; Greenbaum & Kyng 1991; Kyng, 1994) under the Participative Design label is also relevant to the present discussion, as this approach is concerned directly with building systems that are better fitted to the capabilities of workers, and takes into account both their individual skills and shared practices. A key feature of this work is that computer users are themselves key players in any attempt to improve their work situation. Approaches towards cooperative systems design are well described in Greenbaum & Kyng (1991), which contains several papers by people with an ethnographic background, indicating the linkages existing between the approaches, notwithstanding their separate origins. The Scandinavian work has also focused on the concrete practices of people at work, as the basis for the development of new tools and practices. Kyng (1995) argues for the need to understand present use as the key to future developments as there is a co-evolution of work and artifacts. He is circumspect about the idea of radical change: "innovation is difficult and tied to whatever already is—for better or worse". At the same time, he is aware of the need for us to build flexible, adaptable systems: "our artifacts should be modifiable, or even replaceable". His argument in based on the belief that "many design artifacts such as requirements specifications, are more directed towards managerial needs for control than towards supporting creative design work, no matter who does the work". The problem of how then to design appropriate systems is handled by the notion of "concretization" and simulation of future work through the development of work situation descriptions and use scenarios. He is thus proposing a method by which designers can, in conjunction with end-users, come to explore the possibilities and limitations of specific tools for specific work practices. Rather than imposing change on people, the approach argues for a process of mutual learning. Due to the interest in building appropriate computer systems, this work helps build a bridge between the ethnographic work, with its emphasis on observation and interpretation, and computer systems development work, with its emphasis on actual design and construction. The learning theme runs throughout the book as you will already have seen from Chapter 1. In particular it is taken up in Part 2 (i.e., Chapters 4, 5 and 6).

Some Practical Implications

Let me recap the arguments of the chapter thus far and point to where we are heading. Having set out a landscape for CSCW, as one where interesting debate on the nature of work and its support with IT is being conducted, I have described a set of approaches to understanding work and learning in work that I believe are important for the planning of organizational change, and for supporting innovation in the organization. This view is in conflict with a number of the assumptions built into process analysis perspectives, including the action workflow model of Flores and his colleagues (Medina-Mora, et al, 1992). Inadequate descriptions of work can create serious problems when these are used as the basis for new IS development. We have already noted this when discussing the office automation area. A recent issue of the *Communications of the ACM* contained a number of papers discussing representations of work, including an activity-oriented (Sachs, 1995) and participative design (Kyng, 1995) perspective. These papers are concerned about reshaping the systems development process so that it better reflects the centrality of the work domain for which the computer system is supposed to be designed. The authors wish to support work practices through the (re-)design of work artifacts, and often procedures, processes and settings as well. The work reported differs from much of the literature in business process re-engineering and process modelling in important ways. Specifically, the authors argue that these process approaches tend to leave out far too much of what is involved in the nature of work, specifically the inherent capabilities of the human actors and more particularly the communities of practice around such work.

In the application systems development process, workers are asked to evaluate the descriptions made of their work processes by analysts and designers, yet this is often unproductive, as the representational formalisms adopted are often obscure to the workers. We can question many aspects of this process of representing work. Who makes the representation, who has access to it, what purpose does it have? In many cases, rather than clarifying things, the representations used simply obscure actual work processes in a cloud of abstractions that make little sense to the people whose work is supposedly being modelled. Worse, these abstractions are then utilized as the basis for building the new information system, with the result that the inadequacy of these descriptions becomes clear to all in the failure of the resulting system. So, rather than being able to augment work practices with technology, in these situations the technology actually "gets in the way" of doing the work.

Incorporating the experiences of the workers themselves, or "end-users", through active participation in the design process, is an important aspect of the perspectives adopted and described in the papers by Kyng and by Sachs. Grounding design in a deep understanding of the practical contingencies of work practice is the key insight shared by the authors. My own perspective on these issues has been formed over a number of years through interaction with people in the areas of software engineering, information systems development, human-computer interaction and information technology support in end-user organizations. For a number of years, problems have been surfacing in a variety of areas connected to information technology, including requirements "capture", the usability of the resultant systems, and their lack of organizational impact. There has been much discussion over the validity and utility of developing formalizations of work processes. The argument is not whether some level of abstraction and formalization is possible or desirable, but rather, whether such techniques could in principle "capture" all that is required, how to manage what is left outside the representation, and how to allow scope for technology modification and innovation on the part of the workforce (Robinson & Bannon, 1991; Schmidt, 1991).

There seems, however, to be an emerging consensus within the CSCW community about the necessity for models of aspects of work activities, the limitations of certain kinds of models, and the need to allow for local adaptation and innovation, so the field as a whole has moved forward to richer understandings of work and of how to support the work process through technology. There is recognition of the way both systems and work practices need to co-evolve in use. As Mackay notes: "Software does not remain static when it is introduced into an organization. People in the organization evolve their individual patterns of use, share them with each other, react to external changes, both technical and non-technical, and sometimes pro-actively modify the system to produce significant innovations." (Mackay, 1990). A perspective on either work or technology that neglects such factors is liable to run into problems. Let us now look at some examples of how change has been effected in organizations through IT, and some of the concomitant issues that arose.

INVESTIGATING EXPERIENCES OF IT DEPLOYMENT AND ORGANIZATIONAL CHANGE

In a large survey, Bullen & Bennett (1990) examined a number of different "Groupware" systems and their effects in a variety of organizations. Their conclusions were of interest, from both an IT and organizational change perspective. They point out that much of the functionality of the systems was not being utilized, as the benefits to the people were marginal, or not perceptible. This alludes to an important point, especially relevant when dealing with CSCW systems, that has been pointed out by Grudin (1989), namely that it is often the case with these systems that certain people stand to benefit from their use, while others are required to do more work. At another point, Bullen & Bennett (1990) take some of the IT people to task, noting: "rather than looking at 'fancy' innovative functions for Groupware systems, designers should be focusing on how to better solve the basic need of office workers, i.e. managing large volumes of information". Their major claim was that organizations were not seriously considering the nature of work and how it could be redesigned, and how technology could help to enhance work processes. Their finding showed that most people were just using new technology to perform the old routines. Once again, the study also pointed to the need for champions within the organization to promote change, for matching people's expectations of the technology to reality, for the need to improve the quality and focus of training, and for the need to allow time for use of systems to evolve in the organization.

As a specific example of the kinds of issues that Bullen and Bennett describe, the field study by Wanda Orlikowski (1992) on the implementation and uptake of Lotus Notes in one branch of a large consulting firm is instructive. Notes has generated an enormous amount of interest since it was first announced (Marshak, 1990). While difficult to describe succinctly, it can be seen as providing a client-server architecture for developing a number of applications to support communication and information sharing in an organization. Orlikowski's research has pointed out a number of problems in the implementation strategy adopted by this particular firm, which was a "brute force approach", with minimal education of users about the utility of the system for their daily work. She notes the discrepancy between the organizational culture evident in the firm—a competitive, individualistic environment—and the purported intent of Notes to foster "sharing" of information among people in the organization. "In situations where the premises underlying Groupware are incongruent with those of the organization's culture, policies, and reward systems, it is unlikely that effective cooperative computing will result without a change in structural properties. Such changes are difficult to accomplish, and usually meet with resistance." (Orlikowski, 1992).

Rather than revolutionising the work environment Orlikowski describes how the system was being used to build applications supporting individual, not group productivity, and mechanizing existing workflows, rather than developing new work arrangements. This field study took place during the initial six months of implementation of the Notes system in the organization, so it is possible that over time changes will take place, and new work practices will evolve. What the account does tell us, however, is that we need to be careful in assuming that simply installing the technology will produce far-reaching changes in the organization. We also need to be aware that, because Notes is such a general purpose environment, it will be difficult to discuss general aspects concerning the success or failure of Notes, as much will depend on the quality of the local programming applications built on top of the Notes substrate. Other studies that I have had access to tell a similar story—that organizational change is only observed when there is a sustained high-level commitment to change, of which the technology is but a part. Simple "technology-push" strategies will not reshape the organization—a point taken up in Chapter 3.

In the paper referred to earlier, Sachs (1995) describes an interesting case of an operational support system in an organization, called the Trouble Ticketing System (TTS). This system was a large database that also functioned as a scheduling, work-routing and record-keeping technology. This computerized dispatching system, while deemed "organizationally" more effective on certain criteria, was systematically making the work of the people on the ground more difficult. She notes: "The translation of each turn of talk into a single ticket reduced an effective network of co-workers who could troubleshoot together into something like a relay race, handing off pieces of work to the next runner, creating an aggregate of dissociated workers" (Sachs, 1995). Sachs shows several instances of how this system systematically reduced the competencies of the people using the system, and thus effectively reduced the overall competence of the organization. Some of the measures of effectiveness used to evaluate the system totally ignored aspects such as training on the job, an important part of the work. So, for example, the system was configured so that "efficient work" for an individual was interpreted as doing several jobs a day and simply accumulating tickets, irrespective of whether such a work pattern actually created further problems down the line and actually increased workload in the overall system.

What makes this case doubly interesting is that Sachs and her colleagues not only point to the deficits of this system, but, having analyzed the assumptions built into the original TTS, they had the opportunity to redesign the system, in order to put back into the system some possibility for workers to communicate with other workers about the problems they were encountering. They were able to re-establish some sense of a community of workers, who could support each other on the job. The new system is in use and by all accounts is effective. One consequence noted by Sachs is that managers are now thinking more about the concept of work activities than simply work tasks.

The final study I wish to refer to here is related to the previous one, in that it also deals with the attempt to support work activities through technology. The focus of Orr's (1992) work is on organizational learning, and how this can be made manifest. Unfortunately the study tells as much about the difficulties of embedding a changed view of the workplace and workers in the organization as it does about change with or through technology. While the technology employed in this case (portable radios) is a little unusual, Orr documents how this tool was introduced and used among a community of repair technicians over several months. Orr notes how the goals of the project were threefold: to enhance the view of the worth of the repairmen's role in the company (related to that much abused term "empowerment"); to look for unnecessary hindrances to practice; and to see ways in which technology might hinder practice. One rule was that from the outset managers were not allowed to have radios, a clear negation of one of the tenets of scientific management concerning the locus of control in the organization. From the perspective of the technicians, Orr notes several important benefits. The feeling of not being alone was one important factor; another was a strengthening of the feeling of belonging to a workgroup. Technical consultation and moral support was also possible. So the introduction of the radios did seem to support the development of the work community, which was one of the major goals of the study.

At another level, change was not so evident, however. For example, Orr notes that the relationship of the workers to the corporation did not change. Partly, he sees this as due to organizational obduracy. Since this initiative did not emerge from the corporate centre tasked with developing IT to support the service people, support from this centre was lacking. Secondly, during the trial study, emphasis switched to demonstrating "improved productivity" rather than enhanced work practice, and so the bottom line was to be in terms of "reduced headcount" as a result of the new technology. Finally, focus moved to the technology per se, the radios, rather than to how the technicians developed their practice with radios. So, the study gives an honest appraisal of the difficulties that can still be encountered, even within a progressive organization, when one tries to move away from the "organizational thinking" described by Sachs to an activity-oriented one.

CONCLUDING REMARKS

Due to the variety of issues and concepts discussed in this paper, and the somewhat different orientations evident in the material, the reader at this stage may be a little confused as to this chapter's central theme. Let me try to restate the position. Organizations are undergoing change irrespective of technological developments, although the technology can be a key contributing factor. Likewise, technological developments may also create organizational restructuring, even if such organizational changes were not planned as a part of the technological change. There are thus a large variety of ways in which technology and organization can interact. But, ultimately, changes in technology and/ or organization depend on and affect people in work. Our perspective on the nature of work thus has an important bearing on how we implement changes in technology or the organization, or, most likely nowadays, both.

A key message has been my critique of management orthodoxy, based on industrial engineering perspectives, as to the "location" of knowledge about work. This knowledge exists most firmly in communities of practice, and not directly in the management. Thus, any attempt to support work through information technology must be sensitive to these communities, and build on, rather than destroy successful practices. It is here that the Participative Design work described earlier can help us. Yet often we find that in the design of applications, the representations of work that are used as the basis for the design are seriously flawed. Designers are "automating a fiction" as Beau Sheil (1983) so aptly put it. Similar criticisms of process engineering models of work are made. Once again there is a gap between representation and practice. Even after specific technologies have been developed, their deployment in organizations and their impact are not deterministic. Recently, much attention has been paid to how technologies evolve in use, and thus use can be seen as the basis for innovation. The upshot of all this is that both computer-based information systems designers and organizational change agents need to understand:

- the inherent complexity and vitality of existing work communities
- the fact that learning at work often occurs at such sites
- the need to introduce change in a way that supports key aspects of these practices
- that adaptation and innovation occurs in these communities.

If we take these points on board, then our views on organizational and technological matters must undergo a radical transformation from the existing norm. The approach adopted here goes beyond enlightened HRM positions, expressed for example by Peter Keen (1991), when he says: "Business needs to treat people like machines. It accords the machinery of IT—the hardware, software, and other components— care, long-term planning, and commitment . . . much rarer is the firm that acknowledges the importance of education, which is the equivalent of maintenance for people, and has a formal organizational plan that looks ahead in detail at job, career, and skill changes and needs." While

Keen's sentiments are an improvement over traditional management nostrums, they still tend to partition aspects of work into individual tasks and competencies, and do not focus on either the details of work, nor more importantly, of work *communities* for learning and innovation. Of course, such communities may on occasion also act as constraints, but I wish to emphasize their positive contribution—which has often been insufficiently appreciated.

With respect to technology, this new approach has an impact on the way system requirements are gathered and how we represent work activities in systems. Regarding organizational learning and development, this approach breaks down the artificial doors that have existed at times between the concepts of working and learning, and throws light on the activities of working communities as the site for learning and innovation in the organization. It is my belief that within the CSCW field these messages are currently being learned. The intent is not to tout CSCW as some solution to the problems facing organizations today in their development and use of IT, but as an arena in which important perspectives are available on the nature of work, learning and the use of technology, which if taken seriously, could lead to innovations in how organizational change is planned and initiated. One aspect of this approach would be the realization that work communities should not be viewed as seedbeds of recalcitrance but as containing rich tapestries of stories and anecdotes on how work is done. As such, it can be the basis for evolving new practices and even innovations—if given the chance. Management practices today are still dominated by a limited view of how people work, which affects both the change process and the utilization of IT in organizations. Paying attention to the details of work can provide useful insight into what aspects of work could benefit from redesign, in a way quite different to the usual depictions of process analysis. I have attempted to show how over the past few years a richer perspective on work has been evolving within the design community, one that is informed by ethnographic and other forms of field studies of work. It is the incorporation and discussion of the implications of such views for the design of IT that makes the area of CSCW so pertinent to the concerns of people regarding IT and organizational change.

ACKNOWLEDGEMENTS

My views on CSCW have been developed over the years in interaction with a number of colleagues engaged in the EC COST CO-Tech Work Programme and the EU ESPRIT COMIC Basic Research Action, especially with Kjeld Schmidt, concerning the nature of cooperative work, Mike Robinson, on the role of models, John Hughes on ethnography, Kari Kuutti on activity, and Susanne Bødker, Pelle Ehn and Morten Kyng on participative design. Thanks also to the Work, Practice and Technology group at Xerox PARC. Finally, thanks to Heleen Riper for comments on the manuscript. Support for this work was provided by the EU ESPRIT Project No. 6225.

REFERENCES

Anderson, R., Sharrock, W. and Hughes, J., 1987, The Division of Labour, *Action Analysis and Conversation Analysis*, Maison des Sciences de l'Homme, Sept. 1987.

Baecker, R., (ed.), 1992, *Readings in Groupware and Computer-Supported Cooperative Work*, San Mateo: Morgan Kaufmann.

Bannon, L., 1990, A Pilgrim's Progress: From Cognitive Science to Cooperative Design, *AI & Society*, 4, 4, 259–275.

Bannon, L. (1996) Use, Design, and Evaluation: Steps towards an Integration, in D. Shapiro, M. Tauber & R. Traunmueller (eds.) *The Design of Computer-Supported Cooperative Work and Groupware Systems* (series 'Human Factors in Information Systems' volume 12) Amsterdam, The Netherlands: North-Holland.

Bannon, L. and Bødker, S., 1991, Beyond the Interface: Encountering Artifacts in Use, in J. Carroll (ed.) *Designing Interaction: Psychology at the Human-Computer Interface*, Cambridge: Cambridge University Press, 227–253.

Bannon, L. and Schmidt, K., 1991, CSCW: Four Characters in Search of a Context, in J. Bowers and S. Benford, (eds), (1991) *Studies in Computer Supported Cooperative Work: Theory, Practice and Design*, Amsterdam: North-Holland. 3–16.

Barber, G.R., 1983, Supporting Organizational Problem Solving with a Work Station, *ACM Transactions on Office Information Systems*, 1, 1, 45–67.

Blackler, F., 1993, Knowledge and the Theory of Organizations: Organizations as Activity Systems and the Reframing of Management, *Journal of Management Studies*, 30, 6, 863–884.

Blomberg, J., Giacomi, J., Mosher, A. and Swenton-Wall, P., 1993, Ethnographic Field Methods and their Relation to Design, in D. Schuler, and A. Namioka (eds.) *Participatory Design: Principles and Practices*, New Jersey: Erlbaum.

Bødker, S. et al, 1988, Computer Support for Cooperative Design, in *Proceedings of CSCW '88 Conference*, Portland, September, 377–394.

Brown, J.S. and Duguid, P., 1991, Organizational Learning and Communities-of-Practice: Toward a Unified View of Working, Learning, and Innovation, *Organization Science*, 2, 1, 40–57.

Bullen, C. and Bennett, J., 1990, Learning from User Experience with Groupware, in *Proceedings of CSCW '90 Conference*, October, Los Angeles, California, 291–302.

Button, G. (ed.), 1993, *Technology in Working Order*, London: Routledge.

Clement, A. and Van den Besselaar, P., 1993, Participatory Design Projects: A Retrospective Look, *Communications of the ACM*, 36, 6, June.

Davenport, T. and Short, J., 1990, The New Industrial Engineering: Information Technology and Business Process Redesign, *Sloan Management Review*, Summer, 11–27.

Ehn, P., 1988, *Work Oriented Design of Computer Artifacts*, Stockholm: Arbetslivscentrum and Erlbaum.

Ehrlich, S., 1987, Strategies for Encouraging Successful Adoption of Office Communication Systems, *ACM Transactions on Office Information Systems*, 5, 340–357.

Ellis, C.A. and Nutt, G.J., 1980, Office Information Systems and Computer Science, *Computing Surveys*, 12, 1, 27–60.

Engeström, Y., 1987, *Learning by Expanding: An Activity-Theoretical Approach to Developmental Research*, Helsinki: Orienta-Konsultit.

Engeström, Y., 1991, Developmental Work Research: Reconstructing Expertise Through Expansive Learning, in M. Nurminen and G. Weir (eds.) *Human Jobs and Computer Interfaces*, Amsterdam: North-Holland.

Gerson, E.M., and Star, S.L., 1986, Analyzing Due Process in the Workplace, *ACM Transactions on Office Information Systems*, 4, 3, July, 257–270.

Greenbaum, J. and Kyng, M., (eds.), 1991. *Design at Work: Cooperative Design of Computer Systems*, Hillsdale, NJ: Lawrence Erlbaum Associates.

Greenberg, S. (ed.), 1991, *Computer-Supported Cooperative Work and Groupware*, London: Academic Press.

Greif, I., (ed.), 1988a, *Computer-Supported Cooperative Work: A Book of Readings*, San Mateo, CA: Morgan Kaufmann.

Greif, I., 1988b, Panel Remarks : CSCW: What Does it Mean? (L. Bannon, Moderator). Proceedings of CSCW '88 Conference, Portland, September.

Grudin, J., 1989, Why Groupware Applications Fail: Problems in Design and Evaluation. *Office: Technology and People*, 4, 3, 245–264.

Hammer, M., 1990, Re-engineering Work: Don't Automate, Obliterate, *Harvard Business Review*, July-August.

Hammer, M. and Sirbu, M., 1980, What is Office Automation? in *Proceedings. First Office Automation Conference*, Atlanta, Georgia, March.

Harper, R., Hughes, J. and Shapiro, D., 1991, Harmonious Working and CSCW: Computer Technology and Air Traffic Control, in J. Bowers and S. Benford (eds.) *Studies in Computer Supported Cooperative Work: Theory, Practice and Design*, Amsterdam: North-Holland.

Howard, R., 1988, Panel Remarks: CSCW: What Does it Mean? (L. Bannon, Moderator). Proceedings of CSCW '88 Conference, Portland, September.

Hughes, J., Randall, D. and Shapiro, D., 1991, CSCW: Discipline or Paradigm? in L. Bannon, M. Robinson, and K. Schmidt, (eds.) *Proceedings of the Second European Conference on CSCW—ECSCW '91*. Dordrecht: Kluwer, 309–323.

Hughes, J. A., Randall, D. and Shapiro, D., 1992, Faltering from Ethnography to Design, in Proceedings of CSCW '92, the Fourth International Conference on Computer Supported Cooperative Work, Toronto, 2–4 November 1992, 115–122.

Hutchins, E., 1990, The Technology of Team Navigation, in J. Galegher, R. Kraut, and C. Egido (eds.) *Intellectual Teamwork*, New Jersey: Erlbaum.

Johansen, R., 1988, *Groupware. Computer Support for Business Teams*, The Free Press: New York and London.

Jordan, B. (1996) Ethnographic Workplace Studies and CSCW, in D. Shapiro, M. Tauber & R. Traunmueller (eds.) *The Design of Computer-Supported Cooperative*

Work and Groupware Systems (series 'Human Factors in Information Systems' volume 12) Amsterdam, The Netherlands: North-Holland.

Keen, P., 1991, Shaping the Future: Business Design through Information Technology, Boston: Harvard Business School Press.

Kling, R., 1991, Cooperation, Coordination and control in Computer-Supported Work, Communications of the ACM, 34, 12, 83–88.

Kuutti, K., 1991, The Concept of Activity as a Basic Unit of Analysis for CSCW Research, in L. Bannon, M. Robinson, and K. Schmidt, (eds.) Proceedings of the Second European Conference on CSCW—ECSCW '91, Dordrecht: Kluwer, 249–264.

Kyng, M. (1995) Making Representations Work. Communications of the ACM, vol. 38, no. 9, pp. 46–55, Sept. 1995.

Lave, J. and Wenger, E., 1991, Situated Learning: Legitimate Peripheral Participation, New York: Cambridge University Press.

Mackay, W., 1990, Users and Customizable Software: A Co-Adaptive Phenomenon, Doctoral dissertation, Sloan School of Management, MIT.

Marshak, D., 1990, Lotus Notes: A Platform for Developing Workgroup Applications, Patricia Seybold's Office Computing Report, 13, 7, July, 1–14.

Medina-Mora, R., Winograd, T., Flores, R., and Flores, F., 1992, The Action Workflow Approach to Workflow Management Technology, in Proceedings of CSCW '92 Conference, Toronto, November.

Norman, D., 1991, Cognitive Artifacts, in J.M. Carroll (ed.), 1991, Designing Interaction: Psychology at the Human-Computer Interface, New York: Cambridge University Press, 17–38.

Orlikowski, W., 1991, Integrated Information Environment or Matrix of Control? The Contradictory Implications of Information Technology, Accounting, Management and Information Technologies, 1, 1, 9–42.

Orlikowski, W., 1992, Learning from Notes: Organizational Issues in Groupware Implementation, in Proceedings of CSCW '92 Conference, November.

Orr, J., 1992, Ethnography and Organizational Learning: In Pursuit of Learning at Work, in Proceedings NATO Advanced Research Workshop, Organizational Learning and Technological Change, Siena, Italy, Sept. 22–26.

Robinson, M. and Bannon, L., 1991, Questioning Representations, in L. Bannon, M. Robinson, and K. Schmidt, (eds.) Proceedings of the Second European Conference on CSCW Dordrecht: Kluwer, 219–233.

Sachs, P. (1995) Tranforming Work: Collaboration, Learning and Design. Communications of the ACM, vol. 38, no. 9, pp. 36–44, Sept. 1995.

Schmidt, K., 1990, Analysis of Cooperative Work. A Conceptual Framework, Risø National Laboratory, Roskilde, Denmark, June 1990.

Schmidt, K., 1991, Riding a Tiger, or Computer Supported Cooperative Work, in L., Bannon, M. Robinson, and K. Schmidt, (eds), Proceedings of the Second European Conference on CSCW, Dordrecht: Kluwer, 1–16.

Schmidt, K. and Bannon, L., 1992, Taking CSCW Seriously: Supporting Articulation Work, Computer Supported Cooperative Work, 1, 1–2, 7–40.

Sheil, B., 1983, Coping with Complexity, Office: Technology and People, 1.

Suchman, L A., 1983, Office Procedures as Practical Action: Models of Work and System Design, ACM Transactions on Office Information Systems, 1, 4, October, 320–328.

Suchman, L., 1987, Plans and Situated Actions: The Problem of Human-Computer Communication, Cambridge: Cambridge University Press.

Suchman, L., 1989, Notes on Computer Support for Cooperative Work, Working

Paper WP-12, Dept. of Computer Science, University of Jyvaskyla, SF-40100, Jyvaskyla, Finland.

Wertsch, J. V. (ed.), 1981, *The Concept of Activity in Soviet Psychology*, Armonk, NY: Sharpe.

Whitaker, R., 1992, *Venues for Contexture: A Critical Analysis and Enactive Reformulation of Group Decision Support Systems*, Dept. of Information Processing, Umeå University, UMADP-RRIPCS 15.92, Sweden.

Wynn, E., 1979, *Office Conversation as an Information Medium*, PhD. dissertation, University of California, Berkeley, California.

Zisman, M.D., 1977, *Representation, Specification and Automation of Office Procedures*, PhD. dissertation, Dept. of Decision Sciences, The Wharton School, University of Pennsylvania, PA.

3
The Metamorphosis of Oticon

NIELS BJØRN-ANDERSEN[1] AND JON TURNER[2]
[1]Copenhagen Business School, Denmark and
[2]Stern School of Business, New York University, USA

ABSTRACT

The chapter is an analysis of the organizational transformation which took place in the Danish hearing aid company Oticon, which transformed its headquarters from a traditional bureaucratic organization into an information age "spaghetti-type" flexible, innovative and learning organization.

The case focuses especially on the role of IT in the transformation process. Although IT by no means was the driving force, and although a large part of the new organizational structure could have been implemented without any major change in the IT support, the change to become 95% paperless was a key enabler in the organizational transformation.

The analysis focuses especially on how the strategy pursued in Oticon was radically different from current Business Process Re-engineering and Computer Support for Cooperative Work approaches.

INTRODUCTION

We take the view that the hierarchical, bureaucratic organization with its underlying assumptions of authority and control is basically a relic

Information Technology and Organizational Transformation. Edited by R.D. Galliers and W.R.J. Baets. © 1998 John Wiley & Sons Ltd

of the past. It is a way of organizing which is deeply rooted in the "Industrial Age". It is not suited for the "Information Age". In other words, it is not given by nature, it has not provided a high level of job satisfaction for its members, and it is certainly not the most effective way of satisfying customer demands. It is a bad habit inherited from the church and the army! In the former it was necessary to have unity of command in order to establish what was ethical/morally right, and in the latter to establish where and how a total strike on the enemy was to be launched. In both cases only one solution was valid.

Not so in the "Information Age". In order to be competitive, it is important that authority, tools and information are delegated to the lowest level in the organization where the threats and opportunities are first detected. However, at the same time, the employee meeting these threats and opportunities should ideally be able to call upon the consolidated resources of the company if need be. And if need be, the organization should be flexible enough totally to reconfigure its organization and business processes to meet new challenges or benefit from new opportunities.

In Chapter 10, it is argued that potentially IT has a significant role to play in the transformation of the organization from an industrial-type organization to an information age-type organization due to its very nature of facilitation, co-ordination and communication.

This chapter provides an analysis of a case where this issue is explored. It is an analysis of the fascinating organizational transformation in the headquarters of the Danish hearing aid producer Oticon which has totally transformed itself from a traditional bureaucracy to a post-industrial, so-called "spaghetti-type" organization. In the story that unfolds it can be seen that Oticon has taken a very different route to the present dominating paradigm of Business Process Re-engineering (BPR). Oticon has not focused on business processes as a starting point, but has aimed at creating a team-based, flexible, learning organization, where business processes emerge as a result of individuals and project groups perceiving a need.

In order to enable this change, Oticon decided that it was necessary to install a totally new IT system which would mean that the company was able to eliminate 95% of all paper as its information storage medium. The IT solution will be described, and the role of IT as a key enabler in the organizational transformation will be analyzed. It will be shown how the company has taken a giant step towards establishing a "corporate knowledge base" where almost all information stored by individuals is made publicly available for everyone to draw upon.

It will also be shown how the solution achieved is radically different from the dominating CSCW rationale discussed in the preceding chapter. In almost all CSCW applications, IT is used to ameliorate the problems of having people separated in time and space by providing a means of communication/co-ordination. In Oticon, IT is used to allow employees almost total flexibility to move around the headquarters since virtually all information is stored in the IT system and not on paper. IT should not be seen as the driving force in this change, however; this came about as a result of leadership and collective will.

OTICON

Oticon is one of the five largest producers of hearing aids in the world, with about 1200 employees and annual sales of approximately DKK 750 million (at current exchange rate about 100 million ECU) in 1994. Oticon is truly an international firm exporting more than 90% of its production to more than 100 countries through subsidiaries and agents. Oticon has its own basic research department, its own production facilities and attempts to position itself as the preferred partner for leading hearing aid clinics around the world.

Consistent with this philosophy, Oticon has always stressed the quality of its hearing aids, relying strongly on its engineering and product design capability. Towards the end of the 1970s, however, customer demand changed from a relatively large, high quality device behind the ear to a more discrete but somewhat poorer hearing quality device inside the ear. This trend was strongly exploited by a US and German competitor, and Oticon, who was number one in the industry in 1979 and a market leader until the mid 1980s, was faced with decreasing market share (especially on the US market). Oticon suffered its first ever financial loss in 1986.

A new CEO, Lars Kolind, was recruited in 1988, and managed to get the company into the black by 1989 by being extremely cost conscious. Every single expenditure had to be approved by him personally. Kolind realised after a couple of years, however, that they had reached the end of the trail of cost cutting. Only very marginal savings could be achieved from further conventional automation and cost reductions in production, and he turned his attention to the head office functions.

The real issue was to transform Oticon from an industrial organiza-tion producing high quality standardized hearing aids to ''a high quality service organization with a physical product in the form of a hearing aid''. In the old organization there were four independent company functions: sales, production, administration and R&D. These were hierarchically structured as machine bureaucracies (Mintzberg, 1983). This structure was fairly efficient in turning out standard products, but not very efficient, for example, in handling claims or responding to changing demands. If a sales representative in Atlanta had a problem, he would contact his superior who would then contact the regional manager who in turn would contact the sales director in Copenhagen. From him the problem would be passed to the R&D director, and perhaps a couple of levels down, until the problem was finally presented to someone who could solve it.

In the new organization Kolind envisioned, the various functional units would have to work together in a truly integrated manner to craft innovative customer driven services and products and be more responsive to customer demands. This could not be achieved by normal structural or procedural change. It was necessary to create a completely new, innovative, flexible, and learning organization. In the process of wrestling with these problems, Kolind explained:

> "I sat down on New Year's Day in 1990 and tried to think the unthinkable: a vision for the company of tomorrow. It would be a company where jobs were shaped to fit the person instead of the other way around. Each person would be given more functions and a job would emerge by the individual accumulating a portfolio of functions" (Morsing, 1993)

Kolind called his new vision a "spaghetti organization" because the multiple roles people were to play were so intertwined. But he would also compare the organization with a bowl of spaghetti, because "you cannot describe how spaghetti hangs together, but somehow it does".

On September 9, 1991 all employees in headquarters and other administrative staff, who had previously been located in two different buildings, were moved into a new building. This building had been designed especially for Oticon as part of the organizational metamorphosis[1]. This was also when the new IT system was to be used for the first time.

What did Oticon do?[2]

Four types of organizational changes[3] were initiated in order to reduce the overhead costs and to create a more flexible and innovative organization.

---

[1] The concept of metamorphosis is used here in order to characterize a very radical change for an organization where changes take place on almost all dimensions.

[2] The Oticon story has been told among others by Peters (1992), Holtham (1992), Morsing (1993), Thygesen-Poulsen (1993), CNN, and the BBC, and has been the topic of an almost countless number of newspaper/journal articles in Denmark.

[3] The following discussion pertains only to a totally restructured head office with roughly 130 employees concerned with marketing, accounting, R&D, production management and servicing of the sales force and their customers. The production facilities were not changed as part of the transformation.

Elimination of the Traditional Departments

Instead of organizing the company into different departments, headquarters was turned into one large department, and all work was organized as projects in order to highlight its temporary nature. This discouraged the departments from attending to their own interests instead of those of the company as a whole. It also discouraged managers of the various departments from fighting for power for their own functional areas rather than working in the interest of the total organization. The absence of departments also provided for much more flexibility in responding to unexpected work demands.

Marketing, for example, was an area where workload fluctuated throughout the year. August through November were particularly busy with preparations for exhibitions and trade shows. During the autumn, marketing could easily use 30 people. Under the new structure, however, instead of having a fixed number of employees working in marketing throughout the year, a much smaller number of people (around five) permanently worked there including the (project) head. As the workload increased over summer and early autumn in preparation for exhibitions, more people were recruited internally from the other project groups (e.g. from R&D) to staff an expanded and concentrated marketing effort.

Organization of Work in the Form of Projects

A project team comprised a project manager and a number of workers. The project manager was appointed by top management. It was then the job of the project manager to recruit and form the team to carry out the task.

The original idea was that project managers would advertise projects on an electronic (company) bulletin board accessible to all employees and that employees would then voluntarily sign up for a particular project. The idea was employees could sign up for whatever project they cared to, and in that way take on board more tasks if they could handle them. They were only allowed to give up tasks (i.e. leave projects) if their present project managers were happy for them to do so, or if they could sell their present task to somebody else (i.e. find a replacement). If, for instance, someone identified a new business opportunity and could obtain top management support for it (including the necessary resources), he or she could become the project manager for this opportunity and could start recruiting staff immediately. Within a couple of hours a new project could be formed and work on it could be started. This would have had a significant effect in improving Oticon's response to unanticipated demands from clients, and its ability to be proactive.

As it turned out, however, employees would not voluntarily sign up for new tasks. People were shy to come forward and claim that they felt confident working with new tasks, and most of the time employees felt that they already had enough on their plate. Accordingly, after a few months a more personal procedure was established under which project managers for newly appointed project groups would solicit group members by personally talking to those with whom they wanted to cooperate.

Employees Occupy Several Positions

After the change, employees could work on several tasks at the same time and in this way on several projects. This meant that they had an opportunity to use their skills in ways which were much more satisfying to them than would have been the case with just one job. It was also a much more versatile manner for organizing work since it allowed the company to make more use of the diverse skills that most employees possess.

The organization of project work permitted employees who wanted to develop their skills further and who were willing to get involved in different projects to do so. As Kolind explained, "there is no room for employees that stick to the old concept of one job, one person". For instance, it was found that employees in accounting and in production could contribute in an innovative way to the production of marketing material. Hearing aids are a product for the end-consumer, and employees in accounting might have views on Oticon products that marketing employees had not thought about. Having workers with diverse backgrounds and perspectives on a project brings diversity into play in a natural manner.

A New Control Philosophy

Top management at Oticon believed that employees who had chosen to sign up for a particular project would prove to be much more interested in their work tasks than if they had been assigned to tasks by their manager. Thus, they would be more responsible for their own work and more motivated to do it as effectively as they possibly could. This meant that managerial resources were freed up as there was no longer a need for project leaders to act as monitors; workers themselves had proved effective in this role. Instead, the demand now was for leaders to act as innovators and motivators.

These four sets of organizational changes could not have been achieved if it had not been for two distinct changes: a new open plan office layout, and a new IT system which, as indicated, led to almost total elimination of paper. While we shall deal with the IT solution in the section that follows, the background for the open plan solution will be discussed first.

No Private Offices

Oticon decided to do away with private offices for everyone in the firm, including Kolind. They took down all the walls, and created one large open space (or rather two open spaces since the new head office was now located on two floors). All employees had identical desks and chairs with only a workstation and a mobile phone/charger on the desk. The principle was that if employees needed to work on different projects with different people, it was not practical to have them placed in fixed locations. Accordingly, employees and projects were relocated and set up where there was space available.

Private flasks for coffee were also banned in order to encourage employees to get up and walk to the stand-up coffee bars for fresh supplies. "When employees meet each other it facilitates informal communication that we would like to encourage" explained Torben Petersen, head of IT. Furthermore, at each coffee bar a white board was installed for recording informal discussions and assisting in the exchange of ideas.

Since employees no longer had a private office or even a private desk that they could count on having "permanently", they were confined to storing all their personal belongings in a small lockable caddie with one drawer for personal things and a couple of shelves for storing up to 10 files. Whenever an employee needed to move he or she would simply wheel the caddie to an empty desk where he or she could continue working after initialising the workstation. All physical artefacts were in the caddie, and access to employee-specific information was through the workstation. As an example, it was decided in December 1993 to undertake a major reshuffle of desks. Eighty employees changed desks, and two hours later everyone was fully operational.

In the late summer of 1994 Oticon took yet another decisive step in its transformation from an industrial to an information age company through outsourcing half its production facilities. The background was that Oticon until that time had two factories: one in Thisted and one in Copenhagen. The former was the newer, mainly oriented towards inside-the-ear digital technology, while the latter was producing hearing aids based on analogue technology. The latter facility had spare capacity, and Oticon found that it was difficult for them to operate this factory satisfactorily. Different solutions were contemplated including new organizational forms with no middle managers and advanced multi-media learning systems for the operators of the pick-and-place machines, but even given such changes it would be pretty difficult to make the production profitable with the rather limited sales at the time. However, if the factory was independent of Oticon, it could conceivably also produce components for other hearing aid producers. Accordingly it was established as an independent company, and Oticon has since entered into a long term agreement for its supply of components for the analogue based hearing aids.

The IT Solution Chosen in Oticon

One of Kolind's initial visions was for a "paperless office", where everyone would have an identical workstation. This would solve two major problems. If everybody had large paper files and bookshelves it would be difficult to move physically, and the organization would not be flexible in its creation of workgroups sitting near to each other. Secondly, if all information was stored electronically, a much larger part of the information would become available to others, and a large step towards an integrated corporate database would be achieved. Information could be shared and re-used for purposes not foreseen at the time of initial filing—another prerequisite of a flexible, innovative organization.

Kolind did not personally know a lot about IT, and an IT manager was recruited from outside the company. Even with this addition, however, the IT knowledge in Oticon was not at a level permitting them to design and develop such an innovative and technically challenging solution by themselves. This would also be far too risky, since a total failure would almost certainly jeopardise the survival of the company. Such a risky technical IT solution could only be achieved through what Oticon saw as a strategic alliance with the IT suppliers.

The three main technical challenges were: scanning all incoming messages in order to store them electronically; building the database in such a way that information could also be retrieved by somebody else than the originator; and the question of moving from DOS to a more user friendly interface. Many different solutions were investigated, but it was clear that there was no integrated solution on the market solving the three problems. Hewlett Packard (HP) had an acceptable solution for the interface as well as the database. HP had further developed the Windows interface into New Wave, a user-friendly GUI office platform with e-mail. HP also had a database system in the form of AIMS

(Advanced Information Management System) based on an Informix database, running on several installations in North America, and even though it was running under UNIX, HP was interested in moving it to the PC platform and New Wave.

Regarding the third problem of scanning documents and storing these for easy access there were a number of applications, but most of these were fairly simple high volume standardized documents. There were almost no commercial applications available where "all" documents were scanned and where there was a need for very easy retrieval of different sorts which could not be specified in advance. The task of developing this software was put in the hands of Andersen Consulting. Since Oticon did not want to be left hanging between two independent suppliers, HP became the main contractor and Andersen became the subcontractor to HP.

In the requirements stage of the process all employees were asked about their information requirements, and almost everybody requested some sort of database more or less specifically structured to their needs (e.g. some people asked for a database of patents). This was mind-blowing to the IT manager, because the capacity to develop and maintain that many databases vastly exceeded the capacity he had foreseen. Later on in the development process it became a relief that the actual information needs could be satisfied by having a consolidated database. It was decided that it was easier to teach employees to use some sort of common database than to maintain 20 different data-bases!

Since the installation of the PCs took place in September 1991, the state of the art workstation for everyone's use at this time was the HP Vectra 386 PC with 8 Mb memory running Windows and New Wave. Everyone was provided with the same workstation, except for a few technicians, who required more specialist equipment. The local area network installed was LanManager. New Wave included tools for creating, transmitting, duplicating and storing documents that may contain text, drawings, and graphics.

This technical solution permitted all employees to access the common set of office applications and all their own files on the servers, independently of which workstation they used. More importantly, once the personal ID code was entered, access was provided to central files and a personal calendar. In this way, employees were not tied to a physical location within the building, but could move around according to the cooperative tasks they were involved with at the time.

As indicated, the system eliminated 95% of the paper in the office, since all incoming documents were scanned as they were received and all documents originating in Oticon were stored electronically. Employees were not allowed to keep paper-based files. Contrary to the original idea of just walking to the new desk and letting the PC reconfigure itself automatically with the old interface etc., Oticon discovered later on that it was easier simply to move the PC along on the caddie and just plug it into the network and the monitor.

The advanced office system with all information in electronic form, and the identical workspace for everybody meant that one could easily change desks in order to join a new workgroup and everyone was treated in exactly the same way. Once when Kolind was out of the office, a group of employees decided that they needed his desk and moved him somewhere else!

The physical layout could easily be retro-fitted to match any new task structure. For example, if there was a customer complaint from a hearing aid clinic in Atlanta, it was possible to create a new project group to cope with the issue within a matter of hours. The project manager appointed for the workgroup would distribute the task description to all members of the group via the network, together with instructions on where the group might physically convene in order to cope with the new challenge. A few hours after the complaint had been received, the full project group could be established with desks next to each other working to solve the customer's problem. In this manner, Oticon was able to bring the full range of its resources to bear on a problem much more quickly than it had been able to do in the past and—more importantly—more quickly than its competitors.

In order further to enhance the IT support for the collaborative mode of work, Oticon acquired Group Systems V in late 1993, a group decision support system primarily supporting groups meeting at the same time and place. This system was placed in a separate meeting room which was used frequently for both meetings of employees in headquarters, and for meetings with employees from other parts of the organization.

Analysis of the Oticon Transformation

We have described the main characteristics of the organizational transformation in Oticon, and the IT solution supporting this organizational transformation. In this section we shall analyze the organizational transformation and argue that it is radically different from the presently very popular strategies promoted under the label of Business Process Re-engineering (BPR) or similar concepts like Business Process Redesign (Davenport & Short, 1990), Core Process Redesign (a concept used by McKinsey & Co.) or Process Innovation (used by Ernst & Young).

We shall argue that bringing about massive organizational transformation as in the Oticon case requires more than rethinking basic business functions. Even if key processes involved in delivering a service or product were recognized and streamlined it would not result in sufficient performance improvement. The types of changes in Oticon required a complete reconceptualization of the business—not just its mission or the tasks workers performed (their content and sequence), but also the fundamental way people related to each other, the work they did, how they were managed and supervised, the way they were compensated and otherwise rewarded, as well as a complete change in their physical environment. We have previously called this complete rebirth of a firm a "Metamorphosis" (Bjørn-Andersen & Turner, 1994). In order to illustrate the extent to which a metamorphosis moves beyond BPR and similar strategies as they are typically conceived by, for example, Davenport (1993), Hammer & Champy (1993) and Andrews & Stalick (1994), let us consider some dimensions of the change that took place in Oticon.

Holistic Vision

Almost all proponents of BPR (e.g. Jones, 1994) argue that in some way or other the BPR has to be driven by a vision. Hammer & Champy (1993) provide a number of good examples of company visions of the type "50% more effective", "save $45 million", "shorten our develop-ment process by 30%", or "be the number one". Lars Kolind also expressed his vision in those terms when he proclaimed that Oticon should "be the number one hearing aid company by 1997". However, many of these visions are either very abstract or are relatively straight-forward business objectives which may be achieved with something less than metamorphosis. It is also characteristic that in the work by Davenport (1993) in particular, the visions are identified *after* the identification of business processes—the visions are reduced to be "process visions". Not so in Oticon. Kolind went much further than formulating this business objective. He presented a much richer and much more comprehensive vision with his "spaghetti" organization, where "Think the Unthinkable" became the slogan used internally[4].

The transformations in Oticon involved changes regarding the prod-uct it was selling (not just a mass manufactured product but a service with a product); redefining its customers (not the hearing aid clinics but also the end consumer (i.e. the person wearing the hearing aid); a totally new organizational structure (no hierarchy but flexible project groups); a new reward and incentive structure (less structured and more based

---

[4] This is also the title of a popular book by Thygesen-Poulsen (1993) about Oticon.

on individual informal performance appraisals from all project managers one is working for); new control structures (no middle managers); new office layout (from individual offices to open space); new technology (a new and never before implemented integrated IT system with the latest in collaborative technologies); and focus on individual skills (rather than on business processes).

Focus on Employees Rather than Business Processes

If there is any common denominator in BPR methodologies and implementations, it is the focus on business processes, which must cross existing functional boundaries. Business processes are obviously extremely important in any business, but focusing on these might, paradoxically, preserve the old ways and might prove too inflexible to cope with the demands of the future. Focusing strongly on redesigning new business processes might in fact risk freezing these new processes, preventing innovation in the future.

The metamorphosis approach, like the one in Oticon, is, despite the radical pretentions of the BPR protagonists, a much more radical approach. Oticon did not want to establish permanent new structures in the form of new business processes. In fact it did not look at business processes at all. Instead, the focus was on enhancing the skills of each individual employee. The expectation was that if it removed all constraints on the employees and provided them with the most advanced productivity enhancement tools, the employees could be given a much broader job (cf., empowerment), and would more or less automatically perform much more in the interests of the company and its customers. It would not need to look at business processes, these would simply emerge from the work of the individuals and the sharing of the work with other colleagues in face to face project groups.

Commitment

However, if a metamorphosis along the lines suggested here is to succeed, employee commitment over and above that created by fear of losing one's job, has to be preserved. In Oticon several measures were taken to achieve this. One decision was to increase Oticon's share capital by issuing employee shares every year. The intention was to reach 25% ownership. Another major contributing factor was the creation of a "fish-bowl" effect. Lars Kolind very skilfully utilized public relations to reinforce organizational metamorphosis. The fairy tale called "Oticon" had been told over and over again in the Danish media and elsewhere. This meant that every employee, in quite different spheres, received a lot of positive comments, and everyone outside the company was keen to know what it was like to work for such a wonderful company. It would have required a very hard-nosed and stubborn character to argue against the metamorphosis since everybody outside expected it to be so wonderful. If an employee did not agree, then why was he or she still there?!

Participative rather than Expert Driven Approach

Contrary to most organizational transformations, as for instance those described in the BPR literature (e.g. Venkatraman, 1991), the process followed at Oticon was very participative. Although it was driven by the above mentioned top management vision, and although there is no doubt that the charismatic leadership style of Lars Kolind drove the process, it was very open. It involved the majority of employees in head office discussing and deciding upon the vision's elaboration and implementation.

It is often argued that participation is good for handling evolution and gradual change, but that it is not effective for a radical change since nobody will be willing to "cut one's own throat". At Oticon, there was a guarantee that nobody would lose their job due to the metamorphosis. This guarantee was a necessary prerequisite. But there was also such an emphasis on enhancing the skills and capabilities of the employees that it would be almost impossible to have the process driven exclusively by some external consultant. While Oticon's project manager was recruited from outside, his role was not that of an external consultant. He was recruited as just another employee, and he is still employed in the company.

Accordingly, the work on thrashing out all elements of the metamorphosis was not restricted to the managers. It was carried out in a number of project groups, where everyone had the opportunity of participating, and where more than half of the employees took a very active role. Everyone was kept informed and everyone was involved in one way or other. This high level of involvement seems to be key to the process.

User Training

A large number of the employees did not have experience of using PCs or terminals prior to the change over. Since everybody was to work on PCs, a major training effort had to take place. In order to make this work, employees were given the opportunity of getting a PC to use at home. This was not given free of charge as this would have had tax implications, but a clever arrangement was set up in such a way that the employees leased the PC for the cost of 100 DKK (approximately 13.5 ECU) per month. This incurred no costs to the company. Employees were then given the necessary software and applications for different tasks in order that they could familiarize themselves with the new tool and a graphical interface.

Culture

A metamorphosis of the type argued here requires the kind of employee-oriented culture which was to be found at Oticon. It is quite clear that Kolind was keen to make sure that there was little distance between the top and the bottom in the hierarchy. He would even argue that there was no top or bottom after the change. As an example, when he joined the company, he was offered the royal-blue Jaguar XJ Sovereign 6.2 with leather seats and mahogany panels which had been driven by the former CEO (Oticon had five classes of company car depending on managerial level). Kolind responded by announcing that his old Saab was good enough for him. It did not take that long before the standard of company cars had adjusted itself to the kind of ascetic set by Kolind (Morsing, 1993). Furthermore, Kolind did not request an office of his own, but took a desk in the middle of the open office just like everyone else. The hierarchical distance was indeed made as invisible as possible.

The Role of IT in the Metamorphosis

IT was never the starting point of the organizational metamorphosis. Kolind had a vague idea of what technology could do but he formulated his vision without any detailed analysis of IT. There was never an articulated IT strategy aligned to the business strategy as suggested in the literature (e.g. Venkatraman, 1991). However, Kolind did believe that IT was at a level where in principle it would be possible to have information in whatever form and shape available anywhere in the company.

An outside project manager was recruited who could help realize what at that time was a vague dream of creating the paperless office in a manufacturing firm. That had not been done elsewhere before and, as indicated above, Oticon could not have developed this system by itself. Accordingly a strategic alliance was established with HP as the hardware vendor and Andersen Consulting as the software vendor. It was only by having these three organizations pool their resources that it was possible to come up with a practical and economical feasible IT solution that would support the vision of the "spaghetti" organization.

Accordingly, IT was not the cause of the radical organizational transformation that we have termed metamorphosis. The spaghetti organization was feasible in principle even without advanced IT systems. There was, however, a very high probability that the spaghetti organization concept would not be have been effective in this type of organization without advanced IT. Several reasons have been mentioned. The IT solution enabled the physical mobility of employees, it enabled to a very large extent the sharing of information, and it enabled a significant enhancement of personal productivity. Before the metamorphosis, a development engineer used up to two thirds of his or her time on writing, documenting and searching for information according to analyses carried out in Oticon. A significant reduction in this time occurred as a result of the change. There is no doubt therefore that IT was a key enabler in the organizational metamorphosis in Oticon.

Furthermore, the IT solution chosen in Oticon is a good example of a CSCW application. It is interesting to note, though, that the role of the CSCW application in Oticon is significantly different from "typical" CSCW applications. Typically, CSCW applications are used to connect people working in different places and sometimes at different times. The purpose of the CSCW application is to provide a communication link which is almost as good as being together in solving the task. In Oticon, the result of the application of IT was that it enabled employee mobility. In other words, rather than using the CSCW for moving information around, it was used for enabling people to move around with all their belongings—just like a snail carrying its house.

Results Obtained so Far in Oticon

No independent formal assessment of costs and benefits has been carried out so far of the organizational metamorphosis in Oticon. Accordingly, it is only possible to provide an impression of some of the implications and the overall effect, and this we shall do with respect to the individual, the organizational structure and the financial impact.

In the transitional period from 1 January 1991 to 1 June 1992 no one lost their job and nobody actually resigned due to the changes taking place. However, after the transition period approximately 10% of head office staff were laid off; mostly former secretaries and administrative support staff. This was due to the fact that almost all staff were able to handle most of the systems themselves. Since then there has been a gradual recruitment (especially academics), and the total number of head office staff is now actually greater than before the metamorphosis.

Furthermore, job satisfaction "is up" if one asks the employees. Oticon has become a much more "interesting place" to work, and the tasks "are more challenging". No one wants to return to the old system. One of the unexpected results from the metamorphosis, though, has been the lack of willingness of employees to sign up for new tasks over and above the ones they already had. This could be because almost everybody would testify that they now worked harder and longer hours than they did before. There seems to be more pressure due to social control than with a traditional managerial control system. Project organization seems to have worked extremely well in addition. Even though the role of head office, seen from the point of view of other departments, was evidently hard to comprehend at times, it seems to function extremely well internally.

As regards the IT system, one of the more or less unexpected consequences has been that it has turned out to be difficult to classify and categorize the incoming documents in such a way that they are easily accessible for everyone's use. The storing and retrieval of documents is a constant challenge, and the system has been modified over time. On a more technical issue, the number of key words seems to have grown too fast, and worse yet, it is difficult to see how this can be avoided.

On the financial side, the results obtained so far have been extremely positive. Even though many of the changes are not likely in the short run to show up on the bottom line (e.g., market share obtained through new innovative products or better service to clinics) there are clear indications that Oticon has improved its competitive position. The profits declared for 1992 were nine times better than those of 1989 and 1990 (1991 had a deficit). Sales were up 20% from 1992 to 1993, and again 13% from 1993 to 1994. Profits were 84 million DKK in 1993, and a staggering and almost embarrassing 134 million DKK in 1994. Profits are now no less than 18%![5]

More importantly, however, the company believes that it has been possible to reduce the time-to-market for new products significantly. It is a company estimate that the recently introduced Multifocus System, where the hearing aid adjusts itself to the level of environmental background noise, was brought to the market six months earlier than would have been possible under the old system, a reduction of the development cycle from 24 to 18 months.

---

[5] Oticon, where 65% of the shares are owned by a foundation, decided to go public on May 8, 1995. Twenty per cent of the shares were sold, and the tender was oversubscribed seven times. While the initial cost per share was 20 DKK, it rose to 1200 by the end of 1996.

Oticon used part of this advantageous situation to buy one of its Swiss competitors early in 1995. This means that Oticon now has approximately 20% of the world market, like its two largest competitors, Siemens and Starkey.

In the words of Fortune (November 1992), the management and employees in Oticon have created a "Terminator II type organization", or in the confident words of Kolind, "I would not like to be one of our competitors in 1996!".

CONCLUSION

Oticon was reborn through a major organizational change that we have termed an "organizational metamorphosis". In line with the ethos of this book, we do not believe that its strategy is necessarily valid for others. There are obvious scalability problems for large organizations, and the management strategy presupposes a high level of education and commitment, which might not be available everywhere. But Oticon does represent a very interesting candidate for what might constitute a 21st century organization.

Oticon very clearly applied an integrated approach with a number of characteristics making the change difficult to copy directly. In summary, some of the more important changes were:

Strategy and Market

- From analogue to digital technology for its products
- From delivering a product (hearing aid) to delivering a service (better hearing) with a customized Product
- From selling to clinics to focusing on the end customer (i.e. the user of the hearing aid)

Structure

- From a hierarchically organized company to a spaghetti type organization
- From relatively narrowly defined tasks to a situation where potentially everybody could draw upon the consolidated set of human and other resources
- From having functional managers to having project managers who could very easily and frequently be changed
- From a traditional reward structure to reward on merit as perceived by the project managers in the different groups in which the employees work
- From a control-oriented management style to a motivational style, where the skills of the project manager are measured by his or her ability to motivate project members

People

- From employees having just one job to employees having several jobs
- From a situation with clearly defined job specifications to one where the individual frequently has to (re)define his or her job
- From a stable situation where experience was a valuable resource to a situation where there is a much higher level of learning

It is evident that most of the above could have been achieved without the advanced IT system that was installed. However, for the record, this had the following characteristics.

IT Solution

- Scanning of all incoming documents
- Establishing a corporate database with all incoming and internally produced documents available
- Removal of barriers in the way of physical movement by having all information available on the servers
- The provision of state of the art personal productivity tools for the creation, filing and retrieval of documents
- Making all files publicly available
- Facilitation of group work

To sum up, IT was not the root cause of the organizational metamorphosis in Oticon but was a key enabler in this organizational transformation. Oticon could not have implemented the vision of the spaghetti organization effectively if it had not been possible to put in place a completely new IT solution aligning IT to the organizational strategy. Theoretically, we have demonstrated how the metamorphosis followed by Oticon had very different characteristics from that of BPR, and how the IT solution represents an interesting alternative argument to the reasoning behind most CSCW applications. We hope we have provided some food for thought in so doing.

REFERENCES

Andrews, D.C. and Stalick, S.K., 1994, *Business Re-engineering—The Survival Guide*, Yourdon Press, Prentice Hall, Englewood Cliffs, New Jersey.

Beer, M., Eisenstat, R.A. and Spector, B., 1990, Why Change Programs Don't Produce Change, *Harvard Business Review*, November–December, 158–166.

Bjørn-Andersen, N., Eason, K. and Robey, D, 1966, *Managing Computer Impact*, New Jersey, Ablex.

Bjørn-Andersen, N. and Turner, J, 1994, Creating the Twenty-First Century Organization: The Metamorphosis of Oticon in R. Baskerville, et al, (eds.), *Transforming Organizations with Information Technology*, Elsevier Science B.V., 379–394.

Davenport, T., 1993, *Process Innovation: Re-engineering Work through Information Technology*, Harvard Business School Press, Boston.

Davenport, T.H. and Short, J.E., 1990, The New Industrial Engineering: Information Technology and Business Process Redesign. *Sloan Management Review*, 31, Winter, 11–27.

Drucker, P.F., 1988, The Coming of the New Organization Re-engineering Work: Don't Automate. *Harvard Business Review*, January–February, 45–53.

Hammer, M. Re-engineering Work: Don't Automate, Obliterate, 1990. *Harvard Business Review*, July–August, 104–111.

Hammer, M. and Champy, J., 1993, *Re-engineering the Corporation: A Manifesto for Business Revolutions*, Harper Business, New York.

Holtham, C., 1992, Improving the Performance of Work Groups through Information Technology. *A Business Review*, City University Business School, London.

Jones, M., 1994, Don't Emancipate, Exaggerate: Rhetoric, Reality and Re-engineering, in R. Baskerville, et al, (eds.), *Transforming Organizations with Information Technology*, Elsevier Science, 357–378.

Malone, T.W. and Rockart, J.F., 1983, Computers, Networks, and the Corporation. *Scientific American*, 235(3), September, 128–136.

Mintzberg, H., 1983, *Structure in Fives. Designing Effective Organizations*, Prentice Hall, Englewood Cliffs, New Jersey.

Morsing, M., 1993, *Organisatorisk Læring i Praksis—analyse af En Transformation (Creating a Learning Organization*, in Danish), Unpublished PhD. thesis, Copenhagen Business School.

Peters, T., 1992, *Liberation Management*, New York, Alfred A. Knopf.

Thygesen-Poulsen, P., 1993, *Tænk det Utænkelige, (Think the Unthinkable)*, Copenhagen, Schultz.

Turner, J.A., 1984, Computer Mediated Work: The Interplay between Technology and Structured Jobs. *Communications of the ACM*, 27(12), 1210–1217.

Venkatraman, N., 1991, IT-Induced Business Reconfiguration. In M.S. Scott Morton (ed.) *The Corporation of the 1990s*, New York, Oxford University Press.

Williamsson, O., 1975, *Markets and Hierarchies*, Free Press, New York.

Part 2
IT AND THE LEARNING ORGANIZATION

The emphasis in Part 1 was on team working and on a more subjective, political and humanistic stance to our topic of IT and organizational transformation. In this second part, we change the focus somewhat by concentrating more on the means by which individuals in organizations and organizations as a whole may develop their core competencies and utilize learning to make best use of their IT investments.

Much attention has been paid to the organizational learning concept in the management literature since the early writings of Argyris and Schön on this topic. The primary focus has been—for the most part at least—on organizational learning at the corporate level and on core competencies; it is only in the more recent past that linkages have been made between individual and organizational learning (for example, Kim's *Sloan Management Review* article in 1993) and on the role that information systems might play in retaining the corporate memory, notwithstanding the rapidly changing commercial environment and the high levels of staff turnover that many organizations have experienced and are experiencing of late. This part aims to redress the balance by refocusing on these issues in some detail.

We start with a chapter by Claudio Ciborra and Rafael Andreu which identifies the role that information systems can play in capability development and organizational learning. This is followed by a chapter from Walter Baets which provides a means by which the corporate mind set might be measured and mapped. The chapter goes on to discuss the role that a particular information technology—neural networks—might play in this process. The part is brought to a close by a chapter contributed by Tapio Reponen that provides yet another perspective on IT and the learning organization. In it he reflects on the IS planning process as one which is more to do with group learning than with the kind of objective, rational, formalized strategic analysis that characterized the field in the 1980s and early 1990s. By so doing, the philosophy underpinning, and the learning arising out of Part 1 is reinforced.

4
Organizational Learning and Core Capabilities Development: The Role of IT

CLAUDIO CIBORRA[1] AND RAFAEL ANDREU[2]
[1]Institut Theseus, Sophia Antipolis, France and
Università di Bologna, Italy
[2]IESE, International Graduate School of Business,
Barcelona, Spain

INTRODUCTION

The resource-based view of the firm (RBVF) focuses on the firm's resources and capabilities to understand business strategy and to provide direction to strategy formulation. This chapter emphasizes the learning aspects of capability development and explores how information technology (IT) can contribute to it.

As a standardized resource widely available, IT can participate in the fundamental process that transforms resources into capabilities and eventually into core capabilities. In this way, IT can become— embedded in core capabilities—an active component of the firm's competitive advantages.

The process by which resources end up being components of core capabilities in firms is a learning process that can be described and

Information Technology and Organizational Transformation. Edited by R. Galliers and W.R.J. Baets. Published 1998 John Wiley & Sons Ltd.

© Elsevier Science 1996. Reprinted with permission from *The Journal of Strategic Information Systems.*

understood using RBVF concepts. Furthermore, the development of IT strategic applications (also called "strategic information systems", or SIS) follows patterns that closely parallel the structure of that learning process. For this reason we propose an organizational learning model based on the RBVF, and use it to derive guidelines for management action aimed at improving IT effectiveness in organizations.

The chapter is organized as follows: the RBVF framework is summarized, including the concepts of capabilities and core capabilities and the organizational processes that lead to them. Next, an organizational learning model is presented: an interpretation of capability development that emphasizes situated learning and knowledge accumulation. The model is then used to show how IT can contribute to core capability formation in a firm: management action can mould the process to some extent, although it often unfolds "naturally" embedded in an organizational context that is both determined by and determinant of learning. Finally, guidelines are discussed to come up and build strategic IT applications, based on the previous analysis. Short conclusions follow.

1. THE RESOURCE-BASED VIEW OF THE FIRM FRAMEWORK

The resource-based view of the firm (RBVF) conceives a firm as seeking to acquire hard to imitate, valuable resources and capabilities:

> For managers the challenge is to identify, develop, protect and deploy resources and capabilities in a way that provides the firm with a sustainable competitive advantage and, thereby, a superior return on capital. (Amit and Schoemaker, 1993)

The firm's quest for differentiation is a process that develops distinctive capabilities, also called *core capabilities*. Core capabilities are "capabilities that differentiate a company strategically, fostering beneficial behaviors not observed in competitive firms" (Leonard-Barton, 1992). A capability has *strategic potential*, and thus becomes core, with potential for competitive advantage, when it is (Barney, 1991): (1) *valuable* (i.e. exploits opportunities and/or neutralizes threats in a firm's environment), (2) *rare* (i.e. the number of firms that possess a particular capability is less than the number needed to generate perfect competition in an industry (Hirshleifer, 1980), (3) *imperfectly imitable* (for instance because of unique conditions in its acquisition process, because the link between the capability and sustainable advantage is causally ambiguous (Lippman and Rumelt, 1982), or because it is socially complex), and (4) *with no strategically equivalent substitutes* (i.e. with no alternative ways of achieving the same results).

Core capabilities develop in organizations through a transformation process by which undifferentiated resources, available in open markets (where all firms can acquire them), are used and combined, within the *organizational context* of each firm, with *organizational routines* to produce *capabilities*, which in turn can become core and the source of competitive advantages if the above conditions are met. Since this transformation process takes place within an organizational context and uses specific organizational routines, the resulting (core) capabilities are highly dependent on them. As the process unfolds, the *path- or acquisition-dependency degree* increases, making the results more and more idiosyncratic to the firm in which they develop. Hence, the transformation is a path-dependent learning process. We consider now, in more detail, its major phases.

Although iterative and evolving, the process starts with a set of existing *resources*. A *resource* is "any available factor owned [. . .] by a firm" (Amit and Schoemaker, 1993). We may add that resources are assets available in the firm without specific organizational effort. IT is understood as a resource in this sense.

Capabilities are developed by combining and using resources (and/or other capabilities) with the aid of *organizational routines*. An *organizational routine* is a particular way of doing what an organization has developed and *learned*, and in the utilization of which that organization is very efficient and effective, to the point of becoming almost automatic, a "natural" reflection of its "way of being". These routines embed organizational knowledge acquired through learning (Nelson and Winter, 1982; Dosi et al., 1990; Grant, 1992); consequently they have a strong tacit dimension which makes them difficult to imitate and change.[1]

Capabilities are seen in the RBVF literature from many different perspectives. Teece et al. (1990) define them as "a set of differentiated skills, complementary assets, and routines that provide the basis for a firm's capacities in a particular business". Amit and Schoemaker (1993) define capabilities *vis-à-vis* resources:

> *Capabilities* refer to a firm's capacity to deploy *Resources*, usually in combina-

---

[1] Other definitions of the organizational routine concept have been proposed in the literature. Grant (1992), for example, defines them as "regular and predictable patterns of activity which are made up of a sequence of coordinated actions by individuals". Furthermore, they are conceived as dynamic entities that continuously evolve: Collis (1991), for example, refers to "dynamic routines" as "the managerial capability to improve and upgrade firm efficiency and effectiveness". See also Kogut and Zander (1992), and Lado et al. (1992).

tion, using organizational processes, to effect a desired end. [...] Unlike
Resources, Capabilities are based on developing, carrying, and exchanging
information through the firm's human capital.

Consequently, developing capabilities involves organizational learning: learning how to combine and use resources, and also the learning
already embedded in the organizational routines employed. The interplay among resources, organizational routines and capabilities is very
rich: existing capabilities can be made more sophisticated by combining
some of them into new ones with the aid of organizational routines;
new organizational routines may also develop by combining old ones
with available capabilities. At a given point in time an organization is
characterized by specific and interrelated sets of "stocks" of resources,
capabilities and organizational routines.

Since learning takes place within a firm's organizational context, core
capabilities are *path-dependent*—their *specificity degree* is high. This is
crucial for making them difficult to imitate and hence resulting in
advantages sustainable and durable. *Path-dependency* means that the
way a firm owns an asset (a capability) depends on the process through
which it acquired it (Dierickx and Cool, 1989; Dosi et al., 1990; Collis,
1991). The concept of *specificity degree* relates to the idea of "specific
purpose": as capabilities develop through a process that uses idiosyncratic routines and takes place in a specific organizational context, the
results become less and less "general purpose" (i.e. less and less
efficient/effective if they are taken away from where they originated)
(Montgomery and Wernerfelt, 1988).

Fig. 4.1 summarizes the process. It is complex and not necessarily
planned for; many times it "just happens". Planning and making it
happen, however, are genuine management activities, as discussed
below. In general, the degree of specificity and path dependency
increases from bottom to top in Fig. 4.1, as more learning and selection
are involved.

2. LEARNING IN THE CAPABILITY DEVELOPMENT PROCESS

The transformation process that produces core capabilities from resources involves learning. Learning is important because (1) it implies
path-dependency and specificity in the resulting core capabilities, and
(2) consequently, it is one of the causes of their inimitability, which is
crucial for competitive advantage. By analyzing in detail the learning
processes involved we will derive practical suggestions on how to
harness IT as a key component of a firm's core capabilities.

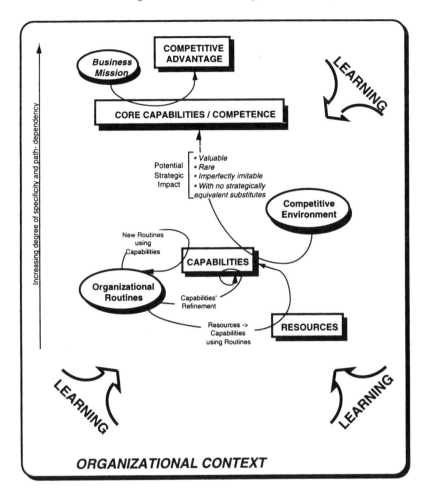

Figure 4.1   *The capability development process: from resources to competitive advantage*

The first transformation step develops capabilities from standard resources. Two different types of learning take place at this step: The first aims at *mastering the use of standard resources*, and produces what we call *efficient work practices*. Individuals and groups in the firm learn how to use resources in the context of a given organizational situation. The quest for better work practices may even trigger a search for new resources, more appropriate for the practices under development. Or, the appearance of new resources (say new technologies) may motivate individuals and groups to "take advantage of them" through new work practices. Thus, there is in fact a *learning loop* between resources and work practices. We call it the *routinization learning loop*. The environment in which learning occurs is an organizational context, which influences the learning process and is in turn influenced by its result (i.e. new working practices become part of the context, thus increasing the knowledge base of the organization (Giddens, 1984; Orlikowski, 1992). Such an organizational context has the characteristics of a *formative context* (Ciborra and Lanzara, 1990; Muñoz-Seca and Riverola, 1994).[2] Work practices are "formed" within it, and receive their meaning and scope from it. Work practices resulting from this learning loop are concrete, detailed, specific and operative, close to the concept of *skills*; they are instances of what has been called *modus operandi* (Bourdieu, 1977)—in fact, they tend to lose their value when taken away from the specific situation in which they were developed and are afterwards used. From a different perspective, work practices are the first step in the firm's "internalization" of resources. Mastering the usage of a spreadsheet by an individual or a team in a specific department is an example of this type of learning.

The second type of learning creates capabilities from existing work practices. Several characteristics of this learning are important: (1) it involves combining work practices and organizational routines; (2) the result has a strong *potential* connotation, as capabilities convey what an organization is *capable* of doing if properly triggered—i.e. capabilities involve *generalizing* work practices and putting them in a wider context that defines *how* they work, so that they are instances of opus operatum (Bourdieu, 1977); (3) the result—capabilities—is easily described in terms of *what* they do and *how* they do it, but *for what* they do it is taken for granted, not necessarily well defined and rarely challenged; and (4) since needs for new routines for work practices can be detected during the process, it also becomes a learning loop, that we call the *capability learning loop*. The objectives of the learning involved in both these loops are close to the concept of *static efficiency* (Ashby, 1954; Ghemawat and Ricart, 1993).

To summarize, learning at this basic level results in a continuously improving set of capabilities—specialized and idiosyncratic ways of using resources for given purposes. These purposes are functionally

---

[2] A formative context is defined as "the set of preexisting institutional arrangements, cognitive frames and imageries that actors bring and routinely enact in a situation of action" (Ciborra and Lanzara, 1990). That groups are influenced by their organizational entourage is widely recognized—the parts of an organization's memory that are relevant for organizational learning are "those that constitute active memory—those that define what an organization pays attention to, how it chooses to act, what it chooses to remember from its experience" (Kim, 1993).

well defined and stable over time, although how they are attained may change even drastically, for example with the emergence of a radically new technology (resource) or a revolutionary new use of an old resource (Penrose, 1959). The driving force for continuous capability improvement is static efficiency, and the change agents are individuals and groups in the organization who become the repositories of the resulting capabilities. The learning processes often occur spontaneously, although the organizational climate and context, and the incentives, power and motivational systems are ultimately responsible for differences in the quality of the process from one organization to another. Although efficient, capabilities lack a sense of *why* they exist, or at least the reasons for their existence are seldom challenged at this level. This sense develops as they evolve into core capabilities through yet another learning loop. See Fig. 4.2.

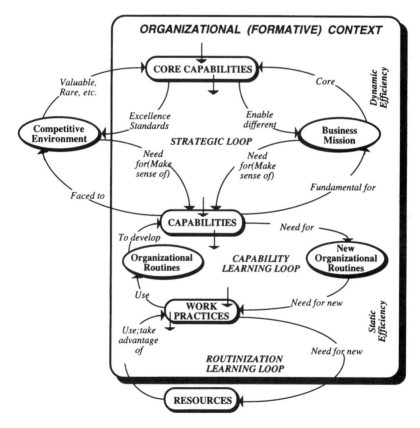

Figure 4.2 *Learning in the capabilities and core capabilities development processes*

In the next learning process capabilities evolve into core capabilities. Core capabilities are "capabilities that differentiate a company strategically, [...] fostering beneficial behaviors not observed in competitors". There are two main reference points against which capabilities can be calibrated to check their potential to become core: *the competitive environment* and *the business mission of the firm*.

When faced to its competitive environment, a firm learns why some capabilities have strategic potential (they are rare, valuable, etc.) A converse influence, from core capabilities to capabilities also exists through the competitive environment, as (1) core capabilities of different firms competing in a given environment (industry) define the "standards of excellence" in that environment, and so they point out what capabilities each firm should develop in order to compete effectively; and (2) it is when confronted with the competitive environment that capabilities acquire a sense of *why* they are important, thus clarifying their role and scope. In addition, capabilities are difficult to imitate in part because of the learning involved in the routinization and capabilities loops: to develop similar capabilities, competitors must go through those learning loops.

A firm's business mission is also relevant for identifying core capabilities. It is in it context that capabilities acquire meaning, as some of them emerge as fundamental for carrying it out. Capabilities fundamental in this sense are candidates to become core. Again, there is a converse influence. Core capabilities can enable new missions which if accepted as such, trigger new capabilities → core capabilities transformations. All these interrelationships give rise to another learning loop linking capabilities and core capabilities; we call it the *strategic learning loop* (Fig. 4.2).

The strategic learning loop also takes place within the firm's organizational (formative) context, and so it is influenced by the context. Furthermore, its outcome— core capabilities—in turn reshape the context itself. At this level capabilities can be described and understood not only in terms of *what* they do and *how* they do it, but also in terms of *why*, beyond the static efficiency criterion that dominates the other two learning loops. In a context where it is clear which capabilities are core and why, these loops are given added motivation and direction (e.g. in the search for new organizational routines or resources); we are in the realm of dynamic efficiency. For example, competitive environment changes can render a highly efficient (in the static sense) capability worthless because it becomes irrelevant to compete under the new conditions. Continuously checking the interrelationships among capabilities, core capabilities, competitive environment, business mission and organizational context, and responding to the challenges that arise as the firm and its environment evolve over time, is the essence of the strategic learning loop.

Finally, it must be noted that inertia belongs to the very nature of organizational contexts, as a consequence of the learning involved in their continuous development and updating (Kim, 1993). Consequently, *drastically changing* the context is difficult, although sometimes necessary—for example to respond to radical environment or business mission shifts. However, drastic changes in the mission of the firm are not likely to happen, as its evolution also occurs within the organizational context. Hence, revolutionary changes in organizational context or business mission require *radical learning*—becoming aware of what the context is and explicitly stepping out in order to innovate in a radical manner. As core capabilities are components of the organizational context, radical learning means learning how to *do* radically new things (in the bottom learning loop of Fig. 4.2), that are *important in radically new ways* (which implies activity in the top learning loops) (Argyris and Schön, 1978).

Fig. 4.3 is a summary of Fig. 4.2. We conceptualize the RBVF framework as involving three learning loops, which develop firm's capabilities and core capabilities starting with resources, using organizational routines and taking into account the firm's competitive environment and its business mission. One basic loop routinizes work practices using resources; a second one combines work practices and organizational routines to form capabilities; and the third gives meaning to capabilities in the context of the firm's competitive environment and business mission, thus identifying core capabilities. The knowledge of "which capabilities are distinctive and fundamental to compete" is strategic in nature and becomes part of the organizational (formative) context in which all firm's activities, including learning, occur. Those learning loops tend to unfold spontaneously, and they depend strongly on the individuals' and groups' perceptions of the environment, the business mission, and even their own learning abilities. Management actions aim at giving to the learning processes the appropriate direction at a given point in time (Argyris, 1993).

3. THE CASE OF IT: FROM A RESOURCE TO A KEY COMPONENT OF CORE CAPABILITIES

We now turn to information technology (IT). By IT we mean all computer and telecommunications technologies available in open markets, where firms can acquire them. IT is an enabling technology, although it may also play the role of a constraint, in the sense of "not

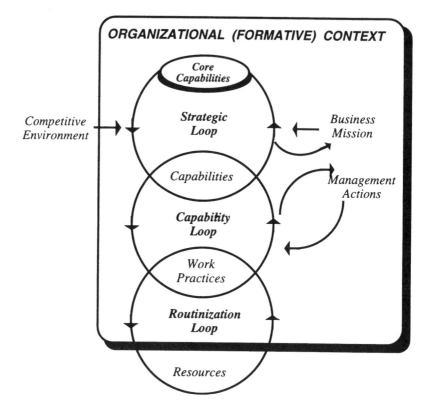

Figure 4.3   *Basic learning processes in the core capabilities formation process*

being enabling enough'' (Scott-Morton, 1991).

In this section we use the learning model just introduced to explain how IT applications can help develop core capabilities in companies. The topic relates to IT applications known as strategic information systems (SIS), since these help to shape core capabilities in the companies that develop them. The goal is twofold: (1) revising a few cases that have led to well known SIS shows that they followed the pattern suggested by the model, and (2) applying the model to the case where IT is one of the resources employed throws light into how the corresponding transformation process could be managed.

One well known SIS is ASAP, launched by AHS Corporation (now Baxter Healthcare). ASAP started as an operational, localized response to a customer need (Short and Venkatraman, 1992). Because of difficulties in serving a hospital effectively, a manager of a local AHS office started to give prepunched cards to the hospital's purchasing department, so that ordering clerks could transfer orders expeditiously through a phone terminal. This local, ad hoc solution gradually led to linking more customer hospitals in the same way, eventually through PCs. AHS management realized the positive impacts on profits of such an electronic link with customers, and allocated resources for its further development (Ciborra, 1992, 1994). The parallel of this process with the basic structure of Fig. 4.2 is clear. Initially, IT was a resource used in a new work practice to solve a localized client's problem. It was an unsophisticated response to a specific operative problem. Generalizing the solution and making it available to more clients is a clear example of what in the learning model is the development of capabilities. The *potential* characteristic is present, and organizational routines used in the relationships with clients are not only brought into play, but also refined as the second learning loop of the model would predict. Furthermore, the capability had strategic potential, as it was valuable and difficult to imitate, in particular by some of the AHS's competitors. It was *valuable* because ASAP *effectively contributed to the positioning of AHS as the "prime vendor"* (Short and Venkatraman, 1992) *for hospitals*; it was *difficult to imitate* because *the important competitors (for example Johnson & Johnson) just couldn't play the same game, at least in the short run, as they were organized in too many decentralized divisions in order to respond quickly enough*. Thus, ASAP actively contributed to the competitive positioning of the firm by exploiting an environmental opportunity: the so called "incumbent's inertia" (Lieberman and Montgomery, 1988) of the major competitor. A valuable organizational and competitive positioning fit was built in the system, which became a major ingredient in the core capabilities' arsenal of AHS. Furthermore, the system evolution led to a shift in "distinctive business competence" (Short and Venkatraman, 1992) that helped to *sustain* competitive advantage.

A different illustration of IT impact on core capabilities is Mrs Fields' Cookies (INC., 1987)[3] Mrs Fields' business started to commercialize the cookies that Mrs Fields had prepared at home for years. The first store was under tight personal control of Mrs Fields herself, who designed not only the cookies' recipes, but also a definite approach to sales, promotion, store style and even personnel recruitment and management. As the number of stores grew, a computerized information system was developed using commodity technology. The system was a bread-and-butter application, that recorded operations data from the stores and reported them to headquarters for centralized control.

---

[3] The fact that this company has had trouble after its first very successful years is irrelevant for the argument that follows.

Although it permitted the operation to run with a remarkably low number of staff workers, it evolved into a system whose main impact was a very different one: it turned into *a way to convey to all stores the "Mrs Fields' way of doing things", independently of the (usually not too well trained and highly mobile) personnel, and also a means by which all personnel could communicate, as often as they liked and in a person to person basis, with Mrs Fields herself.* The case again illustrates how work practices developed with the aid of commodity IT, followed by a period of generalization, as the organizational routines used by Mrs Fields in the first stores were "encapsulated" and effectively transmitted to other stores, finally spreading the "Mrs Fields' way" throughout more than a thousand of them. It also illustrates an interesting and fundamental characteristic of IT. To the extent that the communications infrastructure and systems put in place were a central ingredient of the company's core capabilities (because of their impact in replicating the Mrs Fields' way throughout the organization), they *were an important part of the organizational context, that furthermore they contributed to effectively transmit to the whole organization.* Thus, IT-based applications can not only be instrumental in shaping up the firm's core capabilities, but also in *effectively incorporating them to the firm's organizational context, thereby making them apparent to all organizational levels and giving meaning to all learning processes, which otherwise would operate more "in a limbo"* (Ciborra and Lanzara, 1990).

Another interesting case deals with changing the organizational context. IT applications, consistently with the structure of the above learning model, can effectively contribute to make the shift actually happen in organizations. Consider what a Spanish savings bank did recently. In order to make branch managers responsible for all their activities, as dictated by a decentralization move that top management wanted quickly implemented, they used an existing IT application that permitted each branch manager to check, as often as s/he wanted, her/his performance against objectives. Under the application's new use, *any* branch manager can now check, in real time, how *any other branch* is doing against its objectives. Strong competition among branches developed, thereby contributing to the emergence of a new "way of doing things" at the branches, consistent with what management wanted to implement. The existing application was a basic one developed for control purposes. Once a fundamental shift in the firm's organizational structure was decided upon, the application became central for a completely different purpose, similar to that in Mrs Fields', but different in a fundamental aspect: the organizational context to be communicated was radically new. Thus, IT applications can also play an active role in the difficult task of making the slow evolving organizational contexts change faster.

All the examples show that the proposed organizational learning model is useful to describe how IT applications can contribute to core capabilities development and thereby become part (even a fundamental one) of the resulting core capabilities. Although more detailed field research is needed to explore this claim in depth, the model helps us understand how IT can contribute effectively to firms' competitiveness. Furthermore, it allows us to consistently think about what kind of management actions are needed to improve the IT transformation process, from a commodity to a strategic asset—i.e. management actions to improve the effectiveness of all learning processes involved. In what follows we suggest how to do so in the context of the learning loops of Fig. 4.3.

The *routinization loop* seeks the static efficiency of work practices. Individuals and groups involved should be motivated to experiment and seek alternatives to continuously improve efficiency. Within a concrete organizational context, the work practices formation process should be nurtured and properly organized, and learning reinforced. Such objectives directly suggest basic characteristics for management actions:

- *Nurture the process.* Make sure that individuals and groups are aware of the current organizational context in which learning occurs.
- *Organize the learning process* for effectiveness. Foster a climate in which sharing of existing work practices and experimentation about new ones can occur, so that individuals and groups can effectively "listen to" the accumulated experience of which they themselves are depositories (Brown and Duguid, 1991; Kim, 1993).

An intelligent use of IT can also contribute to attaining such actions' objectives, thus reinforcing IT's potential for support to the overall process—not only to the actual learning, but to its management. For example, IT/IS can contribute to the routinization and capability learning loops in several ways, facilitating the learning that takes place and spreading it to all the individuals and groups involved. For example:

- *Support the firm's work practice development process.* One way is through IT applications that facilitate experimentation with new resources, in particular with new sources of information and with IT itself (e.g. encouraging the use of new technologies in pilot projects, etc. (see Tyre and Orlikowski, 1993)).

- *Share work practices and facilitate communication within groups and among groups.* An "individual" work practice effectively shared among the individuals of a group is often a new work practice in itself. At the same time, a good communication base facilitates the creation of more efficient work practices, in a way directly relevant to the goal of the routinization learning loop. Groupware is a technology directly relevant for all these purposes, in all its forms. Even straightforward applications based on simple electronic mail infrastructures may be very effective in facilitating work practice sharing, and in putting different work practices, "owned" by different individuals or groups even geographically dispersed, to work effectively together.

The *capability learning loop* generalizes work practices so that their essence is learned and combined with organizational routines to produce capabilities. One basic characteristic of the management actions needed is:

- Put emphasis on *detaching capabilities from the specific and local connotations* that they have as a result of how the routinization learning loop works. *Generalize;* describe capabilities in terms of their essential characteristics, free from unnecessary details. Explicitly try to apply locally generated practices to more general contexts.

IT-based support is also feasible here:

- *Support the firm's capability creation process.* Although few IT applications specifically designed for this purpose seem to exist today, the idea is feasible: data gathered during the ongoing process of capability development can conceivably be stored and made available to further such processes, thus making future learning more effective. Tools such as knowledge-based (e.g. the so-called *case based reasoning,* or CBR) can be used for this purpose, as can other less sophisticated approaches. Yet another way may come about through the so-called "electronic brainstorming" processes (Gallupe and Cooper, 1993).
- *Sharing capabilities.* Capability sharing not only contributes to the creation of new ones, but also to the goal of spreading them in the organization, thus effectively helping to communicate and share the organizational context to the extent that those capabilities are part of it.
- *Facilitate reflection, experimentation and training on routines and capabilities.* Routines and basic capabilities must not only be shared and

spread in order to become effectively available to the whole organization, but they must also be understood—i.e. be effectively learned: why they work and the fundamentals behind them, thus effectively going beyond the so-called operational learning, towards conceptual learning (Kim, 1993). There are many ways in which IT applications can contribute to this goal, for example by facilitating experimentation through simulations or expert systems, or through all kinds of decision support systems (DSS).

- *Support and enable capability diffusion.* This is achieved through what have been called "systems of scope", i.e. systems that help in the "sharing of global knowledge" in the firm. For example, J.C. Penney, the large department store in the USA, has put in place a video link infrastructure that permits store managers (more than 1500 across the USA) to be actively involved in the purchasing decisions *without losing the know-how of experienced central purchasers.* The result is better purchasing decisions because the system allows the store managers' local market knowledge to be brought effectively into play without renouncing to economies of scale inherent to a centralized purchasing department and to the experience and knowledge of the central purchasing function. Eventually, as store managers learn about purchasing, they actually develop new capabilities that enable dencentralization. Other examples include using expert systems to make expertise, knowledge and know-how available throughout the organization, etc.

The *strategic loop*, dealing with core capabilities identification and with the definition of new ones needed to cope with environment changes, involves different management challenges:

- *Make sure that know-how embedded in capabilities is checked against environment conditions and the firm's business mission.* This implies establishing the communication and information channels needed to reach all individuals and groups involved.
- *Make explicit how capabilities contribute to the formation and functioning of core competence.* Make individuals and groups well aware of what the core capabilities are, why, and how they contribute to them.

There is also room for IT-based support in this loop management and actual learning. For example:

- *IT applications that provide information about the competitive environment.* This information is relevant because it conditions core capabilities' identification, organizational context updating and, eventually, business mission reconsideration. Thus, IT applications facilitating access to such information contribute to make management actions more effective—e.g. applications explicitly designed to record information about competitors' actions in the market place.

- *IT applications that disseminate the business mission.* The idea is to help to "spread the word" about the business mission. Examples include all kinds of quality level information displaying systems used in production plants, or even transactional or procedural applications that effectively "force" individuals and groups in the organization to behave in a way consistent with the current business mission of the firm.

4. EMBEDDING IT INTO CORE CAPABILITIES: SOME GUIDELINES

The RBVF, coupled with our learning model, allow us to derive practical guidelines for the process that competent managers should foster to come up with and build strategic IT applications (Feeny and Ives, 1989).

Apart from IT support in the routinization and capability loops, it is interesting to consider how IT can contribute positively to the strategic learning loop. IT can be instrumental in making capabilities become core (i.e. making them rare, valuable, difficult to imitate, and with no strategically equivalent substitutes). Guidelines to achieve this purpose are:

- *Look out for IT applications that help to make capabilities rare.* At the beginning of the computerized reservation systems in the airline industry, such systems were rare as only a few of the competitors, who took the lead in deciding to develop them, had them. In the savings banks industry in Spain, for quite some time only one could offer a 24 hours debit card service because its telecommunications and IT base were rare, the result of a bold investment decision made well ahead of its competitors.
- *Concentrate on IT applications that make capabilities valuable.* The ASAP-AHS example is a case in point: the IT application contributed to the competitive positioning of the firm while exploiting an environmental opportunity (the incumbent's inertia of a major competitor). Similar comments can be made of the Federal Express COSMOS system (Smith, 1991). Several procedures have been proposed for precisely the identification of this type of IT applications (Gongla et al., 1989; Andreu et al., 1992).

- *Identify IT contributions that make capabilities difficult to imitate.* Core capabilities can be difficult to imitate for several reasons (in AHS, for instance, organizational impediments on the competitors' side made their responses slow). The IT-based part of core capabilities can also contribute to their inimitability. Reservation system pioneers in the airline industry couldn't be easily copied simply because at the time those systems were complex—they required advanced software techniques not available to every player in the industry (and even if they had been, they still would have had to be learned, through the two bottom loops in Fig. 4.2). More recently, a savings bank in Spain developed a system that allows its debit cards and ATM network to be used to make ticket reservations for theater or opera shows, sporting events, concerts, etc. For this purpose it developed, in a joint venture with a computer manufacturer, a special purpose ATM that displays complete theater layouts to choose seats and so on. Owning part of the special purpose ATM design, this bank was able to impose delays in the machine becoming available to competitors, thus making its approach to the entertainment business distribution channel more difficult to imitate than it would had been otherwise. Introducing IT aspects in the classical competitors' analysis during strategy design is a way of identifying IT applications in this area.
- *Concentrate on IT applications with no clear strategically equivalent substitutes.* To the extent that the functionality of applications cannot be achieved by other means, IT contributes to the lack of substitution. One of the competitors of the bank just mentioned tried to achieve the same functionality and also sell tickets at its branches, using its telecommunications network for seat reservation purposes. However, instead of being based on automatic teller machines (ATMs), the system requires customers to go to the counter, ask the clerk and wait for a layout of the theater to be printed out before being able to make their choices; they then have to tell it to the clerk, who makes the reservations and the corresponding payment—while other customers wait in line probably to make more mundane banking transactions (and maybe another customer at a different branch just took the tickets in the meantime!). It is unclear whether this bank is competing effectively; some say that its approach is jeopardizing its banking business. Identifying IT applications in this area is, again, a matter of enriching strategic analysis and design with IT points of view.

All of these guidelines have strong implications for management practices in the IT field. An important one has to do with the background and training of the people involved. They should be aware of and fully understand not only the learning processes, but also the firm's organizational context, its business mission and competitive environ-ment, and how individuals and groups behave when confronted with the different types of learning necessary to develop core capabilities. This is, we think, a direct consequence of IT permeating and affecting all activities in organizations (Zuboff, 1988; Scott-Morton, 1991). Appropriate management responses to this challenge can be con-sistently thought of and designed with the aid of the model presented in this chapter.

5. CONCLUDING REMARKS

We have drawn upon a stream of different research programs to address in a new way the by-now classic problem of how to make better use of IT in business organizations. First, the resource-based view of the firm has been invoked to indicate that whatever we do, using a com-modity resource such as IT, to increase a firm's competitiveness, must aim at transforming a standard resource into a firm's core capability. Second, a due consideration of the literature on organizational learning has helped us to build a structured model of this strategic transforma-tion process. We have identified three different learning loops, that range from the concreteness of learning-by-doing to the strategic, and at times radical, reflection on the firm's capabilities, mission and environ-mental opportunities. Third, the recent theories of structuration have helped us in showing the continuous interplay between transforma-tion, learning and context where these processes take place, and exploit their strategic relevance. Finally, the studies and cases of strategic information systems have shown how our learning-based model can actually be used to recount the spontaneous emergence of strategic IT applications and discuss the limits of their sustainability. Furthermore, the model suggests management actions and practical guidelines that can enhance the learning processes taking place in the organization, and hence make the transformation process more effective, by better embedding IT into the core capabilities of the organization.

We are firmly convinced that further research can lead to a new approach to design and develop IT applications geared to the dynamics and varied nature of organizational learning processes that take place within and across the firm's boundaries.

REFERENCES

Amit, R. and Schoemaker, P.J.H. 1993. Strategic assets and organizational rent. *Strategic Management Journal*, 14: 33–46.

Andreu, R., Ricart, J.R. and Valor, J. 1992. *Information Systems Strategic Planning: A Source of Competitive Advantage*. NCC Blackwell, Oxford.

Argyris, C. 1993. *Knowledge for Action*. San Francisco.

Argyris, C. and Schön, D. 1978. *Organizational Learning: A Theory of Action Perspective*. Addison-Wesley, Reading, MA, USA.

Ashby, W.R. 1954. *Design for a Brain: The Origin of Adaptive Behaviour*. Chapman and Hall, London.

Barney, J. 1991. Firm resources and sustained competitive advantage. *Journal of Management*, 17: 1.

Bourdieu, P. 1977. *Outline of a Theory of Practice*. Cambridge University Press, Cambridge.

Brown, J.S. and Duguid, P. 1991. Organizational learning and communities of practice: toward a unified view of working, learning and innovation. *Organization Science*. 2: 40–57.

Ciborra, C. 1992. From thinking to tinkering: the grassroots of strategic information systems. *The Information Society*, 8: 297–309.

Ciborra, C. 1994. The grassroots of IT and strategy. In: C. Ciborra and T. Jelassi (eds) *Strategic Information Systems: A European Perspective*. John Wiley, Chichester.

Ciborra, C. and Lanzara, G.F. 1990. Designing dynamic artifacts: computer systems as formative contexts. In: P. Galiardi (ed.) *Symbols and Artifacts*. De Gruiter, Berlin.

Collis, D. 1991. A resource-based analysis of global competition: the case of the bearings industry. *Strategic Management Journal*, 12: 49–68.

Dierickx, I. and Cool, K. 1989. Asset stock accumulation and sustainability of competitive advantage. *Management Science*, 35(12).

Dosi, G., Teece, D.J. and Winter, S. 1990. Towards a theory of corporate coherence: preliminary remarks. Mimeo, March.

Feeny, D. and Ives, B. 1989. In search of sustainability—reaping long term advantage from investments in information technology. *Journal of Management Information Systems*, 7(1): 27–46.

Callupe, R.B. and Cooper, W.H. 1993. Brainstorming electronically. *Sloan Management Review*, Fall: 27–36.

Ghemawat, P. and Ricart, J.E. 1993. The organizational tension between static and dynamic efficiency. Research paper no. 255, IESE.

Giddens, A. 1984. *The Constitution of Society*. California University Press, Berkeley, CA.

Gongla, P., Sakamoto, G., Black-Hock, A., Goldweic, P., Ramos, L., Sprowls, R.C. and Kim, C.-K. 1989. SPARK: a knowledge-based system for identifying competitive uses of information technology. *IBM Systems Journal*, 28: 628–645.

Grant, R.M. 1992. *Contemporary Strategic Analysis: Concepts, Techniques, Applications*, Basil Blackwell, Cambridge, MA, USA.

Hirschleifer, J. 1980. *Price Theory and Applications*, 2nd edition. Prentice-Hall, Englewood Cliffs, NJ.

INC. 1987. Mrs Fields' Secret Ingredient. *INC. Magazine*, October.

Kim, D.H. 1993. The link between individual and organizational learning. *Sloan Management Review*, Fall.

Kogut, B. and Zander, U. 1992. Knowledge in the firm, combinative capabilities, and the replication of technology. *Organization Science*, 13: August.

Lado, A., Boyd, N.G. and Wright, P. 1992. A competency-based model of sustainable competitive advantage: towards a conceptual integration. *Journal of Management*, 18(1).

Leonard-Barton, D. 1992. Core capabilities and core rigidities: a paradox in managing new product development. *Strategic Management Journal*, 13: 111–125.

Lieberman, M. and Montgomery, D. 1988. First mover advantages. *Strategic Management Journal*, 9: 41–58.

Lippman, S. and Rumelt, R. 1982. Uncertain imitability: an analysis of interfirm difference in efficiency under competition. *Bell Journal of Economics*, 418–438.

Montgomery, C.A. and Wernerfelt, B. 1988. Diversification, Ricardian rents, and Tobin's *q*. *RAND Journal of Economics*, 19(4): Winter.

Muñoz-Seca, B. and Riverola, J. 1994. The improvement dynamics: knowledge and knowledge generation. Technical note 0–694–044, IESE, February.

Nelson, R.R. and Winter, S.G. 1982. *An Evolutionary Theory of Economic Change*. Belknap, Cambridge, MA, USA.

Orlikowski, W.I. 1992. The duality of technology: rethinking the concept of technology in organizations. *Organization Science*, 3(2): 398–427.

Penrose, E. 1959. *The Theory of the Growth of the Firm*. Basil Blackwell, London.

Scott-Morton, M.S. (ed.) 1991. *The Corporation of the 1990s: Information Technology and Organizational Transformation*. Oxford University Press, Oxford.

Short, J.E. and Venkatraman, N. 1992. Beyond business process redesign: redefining Baxter's business network. *Sloan Management Review*, Fall.

Smith, F. 1991. The distribution revolution: time flies at Federal Express. In: J. Blackburn (ed.) *Time-Based Competition*. Business One Irwin.

Teece, D., Pisano, G. and Shuen, A. 1990. Firm capabilities, resources and the concept of corporate strategy. Consortium on Competitiveness and Cooperation W.P. 90–9, University of California at Berkeley, Center for Research in Management, Berkeley, CA.

Tyre and Orlikowski, W. 1993. Exploiting opportunities for technological improvement in organization. *Sloan Management Review*, Fall.

Zuboff, S. 1989. *In the Age of the Smart Machine*. Basic Books, New York.

5
The Corporate Mind Set as a Precursor for Business Process Change: About Knowledge, Perceptions and Learning

WALTER BAETS
Euro-Arab Management School, Granada, Spain

ABSTRACT

This chapter investigates issues of importance with respect to the broader understanding of business processes. It concentrates on knowledge and perceptions and the way processes can form the basis of organizational change—Business Process Re-engineering (BPR) being a notable, recent example. In a broader perspective, organizational learning as a corporate attitude is also introduced.

This chapter describes and explores:

> individual experiences—individual tacit knowledge—individual mental model—shared mental model—repository of corporate knowledge—repository of core competencies—proactive management—positive feed-back loops

as the basic logic of the knowledge-creating company. Learning is viewed as being a process based on the manager's ability to take part in

Information Technology and Organizational Transformation. Edited by R.D. Galliers and W.R.J. Baets. © 1998 John Wiley & Sons Ltd

such a knowledge-creating company. Artificial neural networks are proposed and explored with the aim of creating a moving picture of the shared mental model.

It is argued that the most difficult step in the above cycle is to grasp the shared mental model, but a methodology is proposed that helps in this context.

INTRODUCTION

Based on experience and research both in industry and banking (Johansson et al, 1993; Baets, 1992, 1993a), it appears that business processes are poorly understood amongst managers. Most managers focus on their day-to-day job to the degree that they often miss the overall picture. In line with a new management paradigm which makes the distinction between management of the "whole" versus management of "operations" ("immediate management" is the term used by Borucki & Byosiere, 1992), it appears that in both sectors, managers tend not to have an holistic and/or multidisciplinary view of their business. Notwithstanding, integration of social, managerial and technical issues with respect to the business process appears to be key for better understanding of the overall business. These findings challenge many of the assumptions on which much current BPR practice is based.

It is perhaps an obvious point to make that within the broad area of Information Technology and Organizational Change (Scott Morton, 1991), BPR as a means of obtaining radical organizational change has received most attention amongst managers in recent years (e.g. Ramaswami et al, 1992; Benjamin & Blunt, 1992; Rockart & Hofman, 1992; Niederman et al, 1991). It is claimed that BPR is a key for gaining competitive advantage within a sector (Knorr, 1991; Johansson et al, 1993; Peppard & Rowland, 1995). The company which is able to reorganise its business processes (with minimum slack), integrating customers and suppliers in a chain also has the ability to create important barriers for its competitors. In this respect, BPR is often seen as key to organizational success, despite the failures and more recent concerns regarding its limitations (Davenport, 1996; see also Chapters 10 and 13).

The claim is that BPR enables the identification of the core processes and thence competencies that a company should have. Core competencies have received increasing attention with respect to (re)focusing a business (Kaplan & Murdock, 1990; Hamel & Prahalad, 1989; Prahalad & Hamel, 1990). One could consider BPR as a dynamic way of reshaping the company around its core competencies. The synergy and/or balance between BPR and core competencies creates the potential for an organizational change process. This process of organizational change is facilitated if it incorporates a learning process (de Geus, 1988; Senge, 1990; Leonard-Barton, 1992). Organizational learning—seen as a corporate mind set regarding change—can be an enabling attitude in this context (see also, Chapter 4).

A number of reasons can be identified for the difficulties which organizations seem to have with organizational change. An important one, relevant to BPR, is that managers have difficulties in formulating the desired direction of change. It could be questioned whether they are able to define this direction at all if the above experiences are anything to go by. This may arise because of a fragmented view as to their own situation as a manager, or a rapidly changing business environment (e.g., increased competition, chaotic behaviour of markets) (Stacey, 1993). Hence, the process of BPR should be a dynamic one, demonstrating flexibility with respect to the continuously changing environment, but also the different perceptions which top executives and line managers have, and the limited time available to them to contemplate radical change.

This chapter investigates the issues of importance with respect to gaining a better understanding of business processes. It will concentrate on knowledge and perceptions and the way they can be used to improve the understanding of processes as a means of achieving organizational change. In so doing, organizational learning as a corporate attitude is considered and a methodology to deal with these issues is proposed. The chapter begins by considering the related topics of knowledge and learning.

KNOWLEDGE AND EXPERIENCE

Much work has been undertaken, for example in the cognitive sciences, in order to identify and define knowledge. Unfortunately, however, in management sciences we know very little about what managerial knowledge really is, and though we may have a vague feeling for what this kind of knowledge is, there are few definitions or descriptions available. Kim (1993) suggests that knowledge is a combination of "know-how" and "know-why", while others (such as Firebaugh, 1989, and Nonaka et al, 1994) identify two types of knowledge. *Explicit* knowledge is transmittable in formal, systematic language. This is the kind of knowledge that has been codified in knowledge based systems. *Implicit* or *tacit* knowledge deserves most of our attention, however.

Originally, implicit knowledge was defined as that knowledge which is logically embedded in the system, for example the process of deduction (Firebaugh, 1989). Tacit knowledge is more personalised; it is deeply rooted in action, commitment and involvement in a specific context (Nonaka et al, 1994). Tacit knowledge involves cognitive and technical elements.

It is clear that tacit knowledge is used in managerial tasks. Key to acquiring tacit knowledge is experience. A good example of tacit knowledge in management is the decision-making behaviour of dealers in financial markets. Based on their experience, the things they read and hear and sensing the market "climate", they make decisions on buying and selling in an instant. We like to call this "instinct" or "finger-spitzengefuhl" but the behaviour of individual dealers differs. Each individual dealer seems to have his or her own way of dealing, based on his or her experience and reference framework. It is extremely difficult to extract this kind of "knowledge". However, since some dealers are persistently better than others, it would be of interest to understand why they score better, in the hope that we might be able to reproduce this behaviour. Were a dealer to acquire this experience and knowledge within a particular bank, that bank would be keen to hold on to this acquired knowledge (asset), especially in the event of the dealer leaving for pastures new.

The cognitive elements involved seem to centre on "mental models" (Johnson-Laird, 1983) in which human beings form working models of the world by creating and manipulating analogies in their minds. Senge (1990) describes mental models as deeply held internal images of how the world works, which have a powerful influence on what we do because they also affect what we see. Mental models represent a person's view of the world, including explicit and implicit under-standing. Mental models provide the context in which to view and interpret new material and they determine how stored information is relevant to a given situation (Kim, 1993). Based on these definitions and analogues to individual learning, organizational learning is defined as increasing an organization's capacity to take effective action (*ibid.*). What seems to matter is not "reality" but perceptions of reality.

This capacity of an organization to take effective action is based on tacit corporate knowledge (Baets, 1993b). The more this corporate knowledge is explicit and shared the easier it becomes to take advan-tage of it. Since perceptions of reality are more important for management than "reality", the role of corporate mental models becomes extremely important. In that case, fundamental to corporate learning, and hence proactive management, is a shared mental model (Kim, 1993). One might consider it to be a key management role to identify the shared elements within the diversity (complexity) (Van der Linden, 1993): management of corporate (tacit) knowledge could therefore be seen as a strategic mission.

Furthermore, we do have an idea of how the human brain works. The PDP Research Group (Rumelhart & McClelland, 1986) has demonstrated, based on extensive research, that the human brain is characterized by a high degree of parallelism and a micro structure of cognition (distributed knowledge) of which it is built. The human brain has no clear equation for what happens in a given situation, but is able to reconstruct solutions and actions quickly and easily, based on this micro structure of knowledge. Consequently, we can assume that knowledge is not sequential but parallel and capable of dealing with variety and not just the norm.

Despite the many problems with definitions, the organizational capability for knowledge creation is gaining momentum in managerial sciences and some consider it as a potential source of competitive advantage for companies (Toffler, 1990; Badaracca, 1991; Quinn, 1992). Whereas companies have long been dominated by a paradigm that conceptualizes the organization as a system that "processes" information and/or "solves" problems, we now consider an organisation as a knowledge-creating system (Nonaka et al, 1994; Borucki & Byosiere, 1992).

This body of knowledge, this repository of core competencies, this capacity to manage knowledge and to learn from it, has recently attracted attention in management research. A number of concepts point to the body of differentiating ideas, skills, capacities, etc. of a company. Eden (1988) has introduced the idea of a "cognitive map" as a sort of pool of knowledge in the company; Haeckel & Nolan (1993) introduced the "corporate IQ" for the same "repository", while Keen (1993) argues for a more quantitative representation of this "repository" and calls this a "fusion map". All aim to identify and make explicit the differentiating core competencies of a company. If we could agree that eventually business processes should be re-engineered around these core competencies, it might be well worth paying considerable attention to such concepts.

LEARNING AND MENTAL MODELS

Learning in itself is a complex issue and can only briefly be considered here. Kolb (1984) defines learning as the process whereby knowledge is created through the transformation of experience. This definition of learning mirrors the "know-how" and "know-why" distinction of Kim

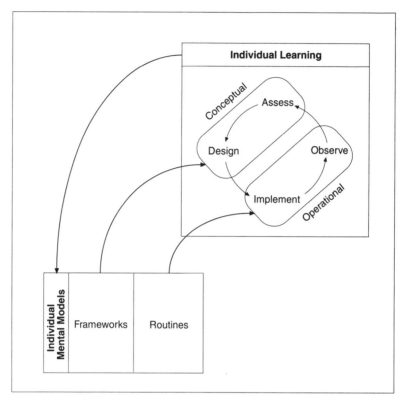

Figure 5.1 *Simple model of individual learning: the OADI-cycle*
Reprinted from *The Link between Individual and Organisational Learning* by
D. Kim. Sloan Management Review, 3513 Fall, by permission of publisher.
Copyright 1993 by Sloan Management Review Association. All rights reserved.

(1993). According to this definition, learning takes place in a cycle: from
experience; making observations and reflections on that experience;
forming abstract concepts and generalizations based on these reflections; testing these ideas in a new situation which gives new
experiences. Kim (1993) calls this cyclical learning loop the OADI-cycle
(Observe; Assess; Design; Implement).

Based on this OADI-cycle, Kim proposes a simple model of Individual Learning, where he links individual learning with individual
Mental Models as illustrated in Figure 5.1. This demonstrates in a way
a double loop learning process in the sense that it includes both learning
based on external impulses (OADI-cycle) and the connection of this
learning with the individual mental models. The reason to put so much
emphasis on mental models is that mental models in individuals' heads
are where the vast majority of an organisation's knowledge (both
know-how and know-why) lies.

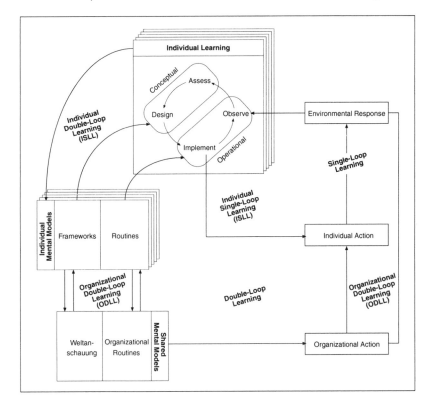

Figure 5.2 *An Integrated Model of Organisational Learning: OADI-shared mental models cycle* Reprinted from *The Link between Individual and Organisational Learning* by D. Kim. Sloan Management Review, 3513 Fall, by permission of publisher. Copyright 1993 by Sloan Management Review Association. All rights reserved.

A comparable double loop learning model can be designed at the level of the organization (Figure 5.2). The upper left corner of Figure 5.2 is the model of individual learning of Figure 5.1. In addition to Figure 5.1, the cycle of individual single-loop learning is added, which was omitted from Figure 5.1. This individual single-loop learning links the implementation phase of the OADI-cycle with an individual action, which in turn creates an environmental response. This response is a new input to the OADI cycle.

The organizational level is introduced in Figure 5.2 in two different ways. Comparable to the single-loop learning of the individual model, each individual action can be part of an organizational action (the lower right hand corner of Figure 5.2) which in turn causes an additional environmental response. Organizational double-loop learning takes place when the individual mental models are in line with the shared

LEARNING AND MANAGEMENT OF KNOWLEDGE

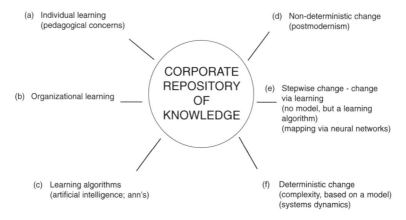

Figure 5.3   *Learning, Knowledge and Change (Baets, 1995, figure 1)*

mental models (shared on a corporate or group level), which in turn have an influence on the individual mental models. In Figure 5.2 shared mental models are pictured with two facets: the "weltanschauung" (taken-for-granted worldview) and the organizational routines. Improved learning via knowledge creation and management takes place, for the most part, in the organizational double-loop learning in the lower left hand corner of Figure 5.2. Explicit shared models (explicit "weltanschauung" and organizational routines) will improve the learning ability of an organization.

When we concentrate on the "shared mental model" of Figure 5.2, we could represent this "map" as in Figure 5.3. We can also rearrange the inputs and outputs in order to be able to construct the repository itself.

Figure 5.3 pictures three different levels of learning: individual learning, organizational learning and learning of algorithms (systems). Each of them has an input in the corporate knowledge repository. This repository is used in order to feed three different types of change processes: deterministic change, stepwise-learning change, and non-deterministic processes.

Probably best known is individual learning {a}. School systems are based on pedagogical theories about individual learning and many in-company courses are also based on these. Some years old, but recently revamped, are the ideas of organizational learning {b} (Argyris & Schön, 1978). Senge's (1990) writings have given these ideas something of a new lease of life. Here, groups and organizations show characteristics which allow individuals to learn more within the group than they would be able to on their own. The question remains unanswered though, whether learning is an individual or a group process (Nonaka, 1994).

More recently, some successes have been obtained in applying the theory of learning algorithms {c}. Within the broader area of artificial intelligence there is considerable interest in systems which appear to demonstrate learning behaviour. Artificial neural networks are only one example of these systems (Dayhoff, 1990). Experiments with such learning algorithms or self-regulating systems (Morin, 1990a, b) give insight into how systems behave when they learn, despite the absence of guidelines.

These three forms of learning contribute to the creation of the corporate knowledge repository on which a number of corporate actions are based. This repository is sometimes called "corporate intelligence": the real distinctive quality between one organization and another. For that reason some have argued that probably the only durable competitive advantage for a company is the capacity to learn continuously (e.g. de Geus, 1988). Taking the argument further, Nonaka (1994) suggests that the capacity to create and manage knowledge is in fact the only durable competitive advantage. This "corporate intelligence" is the basis for successful activities in a company, of which change processes are only a subset and this "intelligence" can be used in a number of different ways. Figure 5.3 illustrates the point.

Our classical, rational, economic thinking about managerial problems has known success in what is "scientific management". Deterministic, quantitative thinking became the common way of considering business processes. Economic phenomena are analyzed via reductive thinking to fit linear, deterministic and non-dynamic models. The "real" world of today, however, appears to be different. Chaos theory (Cohen & Stewart, 1994), complexity theory (Nicolis & Prigogine, 1989) and research into artificial life (Langton, 1989) have changed our understanding of our world. The Santa Fe Institute has produced remarkable work on these topics. We now have a better understanding of the underlying constructs of managerial problems. But we have yet to agree how we can improve management practice. There are (at least) three types of change processes that warrant attention.

Foremost, complex but deterministic processes {d} are often cited. These differ from more classical approaches in the form of the equations of the models used. These equations can be non-linear and dynamic, in which the latter appears via feed-forward phenomena. Complexity theory is one example; others include systems dynamics (originated in the 1970s but once again popular nowadays) and knowledge based systems. The basic idea of this approach towards change processes is that a deterministic (change) model can be represented by a set of complex equations or rules.

A second approach relates to stepwise or "learning" processes {e}. This approach also accepts the existence of a (deterministic) model but, in addition, it assumes that it is impossible to describe this with equations or rules. In this approach a "workable" change process is more important than a single "best" solution. Stepwise change is considered normal and, during the change process, adaptation and learning take place. The debate is between the need for a simplified but detailed model and a less detailed but richer picture of "reality". In addition, this second type of model is prepared to change during the process, which makes it even less accessible for detailed representation. Artificial neural networks, used to map change processes, are an application of this approach and will be dealt with later in this chapter.

One further approach is that associated with non-deterministic change {f}. This approach does not assume any model behind change processes, and its adherents claim that one should not lose time trying to find such a model. Some theories on the learning organization are based on this theorem (e.g. Swieringa & Wierdsma, 1993). Though it could seem contradictory, a manager could try and guide such change processes in combination with approaches focusing on managerial leadership and empowerment. This might be seen as postmodernist (Hassard & Parkers, 1993; Hassard, 1993) and therefore of current interest, but it is not a topic we shall dwell on in this chapter.

In summary: learning is not the accumulation of useful knowledge. Rather, it is the operationalization of perceptions and experiences. We do not really know what knowledge looks like, only that there exist different types (e.g. explicit and tacit) and that most probably knowledge exists in a distributed form. Corporate intelligence is a "repository" of knowledge which probably drives corporate change processes. It would be useful to have an idea of the processes, as they are perceived by the stakeholders, before attempting to change them. Based on what we have described, however, this appears to be difficult to achieve were we not to change our belief in the capacity of reductionist deterministic models to describe or represent knowledge.

If we wanted to model or map this "repository", we would need to investigate new analytical techniques and/or new ways of thinking which would require a vast improvement compared to the Operations Research and/or Decision Support Systems efforts of the 1970s and 1980s. Most of these techniques were prescriptive and failed to deal with variety. Arguing along similar lines to Soft Systems Methodology (Checkland, 1981; Checkland & Scholes, 1990), it is debatable whether it is possible even to try to be prescriptive in managerial processes. These analytical techniques assume that the business process would be something existing "objectively" "outside" the manager. It can be argued that the manager perceives the business process through her or his own filters or mind set. For that reason there is no one single way to manage, but a choice needs to be made between different possible approaches to a particular situation and different aspects of each situation to be dealt with (Van der Linden, 1993). The best combination of "approach" and "aspects dealt with" will constitute the managerial act. The "repository" will be the input for the manager who is trying to handle a particular situation.

In order to improve this process of knowledge creation, management and learning, an approach is proposed in this chapter which is new in a number of respects. The approach attacks business process via the mind sets (and not the claimed knowledge of the processes) of the stakeholders concerned (and not only the managers concerned). This approach keeps the diversity of mind sets accessible for all the people involved. They are translated into an IT-based tool, which facilitates individual learning. Furthermore, this tool can guide the process of creation of shared beliefs, which could be a useful first step of BPR.

For the transfer of issues to relationships, of individual to corporate mind sets and of perceptions to knowledge, we propose that neural networks demonstrate considerable promise (de Callatay, 1992; Firebaugh, 1989) and, since they are computer-based, they are also able to deal with larger numbers of the people concerned.

MEASUREMENT AND MAPPING OF MIND SETS

We argue, then, that process engineering has to do with mapping business processes via mind sets; first, individual mind sets and second, corporate mind sets. A number of techniques exist, most of them tools for organizational learning which attempt to generate a common shared perception (Senge, 1990). The best known are probably scenario analysis, brainstorming, systems dynamics models and simulations. A disadvantage of most methods dealing with group processes (and attempting to create corporate mind sets) is that they are based on a specific consensus, reached in a specific (limited) group at a specific time. There is, therefore, limited guarantee that this consensus is general given that the concerned group as a whole (people involved in the business process re-engineering) is likely to be much larger.

We need to reorientate our thinking if we are to improve these techniques. First, more people should be involved in the process of creating shared beliefs and values. Second, we should find a way (a tool) to communicate these shared beliefs throughout the organization. Third, diversity should prevail over consensus. Postmodernism (Hassard & Parkers, 1993) even advocates that unity or a consensus (or central tendency) cannot be reached. For postmodernists, management is dealing with limited order in chaos. Finally, individuals should be the focus of our attention given that it is generally accepted that most learning takes place at the level of the individual (Kim, 1993).

Explicitation of relationships and measurement of maps or models can be achieved, for the most part, by quantitative (statistical) methods. Research in the banking industry (Ramaswami, et al, 1992; Baets, 1993a) dealing with the indirect and direct impact of organizational context factors (such as strategy and environment) on the emphasis placed by firms on strategic information support, has enabled the identification of limitations of classic measurement. However, if we want to measure and map mind sets with the aim specified above, the choice of neural networks is an alternative which allows the creation of relationships, as close as possible to equations (Norden, 1993), avoiding most of the problems associated with this kind of perception-like data.

The "quality" of the data (observations) and the relationships are characterized by the fact that:

- equations are non-linear, dynamic and most certainly very complex;
- the data deal with perceptions and have by definition qualitative characteristics;
- the observations are highly contingent and interconnected.

Neural network techniques, through their parallel distributed processing, imitate our brain-like thinking, filtering data and establishing perceptions. The classic sequential equation approach needs a valid theory to underpin estimation and needs the definition of these complex equations. Sufficient knowledge does not as yet exist to write this kind of complex (dynamic and non-linear) equation in enough detail (Venugopal & Baets, 1994).

Solving knowledge maps needs a research approach which is able to simulate this kind of "assimilated thinking". Earlier experiments with neural networks for this purpose show promise (Lodewijk & Deng, 1993; Fletcher & Goss, 1993; Baets, 1993b), and this is confirmed by conceptual comparison of neural networks with statistical techniques (*ibid.*). We will now take a look, in somewhat greater detail, at neural networks not only as a tool and technique for knowledge generation but also as a way of thinking about managerial mind sets.

Neural Networks: a Tool and Method for Knowledge Generation

Qualities of Artificial Neural Networks

Neural networks are a highly interdisciplinary way of looking at problems and bring together mathematics, computer science, psychology, biology, etc. Inspired by physiology and biology, they mimic the neurones and synaptic connections of a human brain. These techniques are "by-products" of the search for understanding (and imitation) of the operation of the human brain (Wasserman, 1989).

Neural networks are used successfully in quite a wide range of applications: weather forecasting; speech recognition; adaptive control; adaptive noise filtering (Widrow & Stearns, 1985); financial evaluations and stock value forecasting (Collins, et al, 1988); image analysis (Duda & Hart, 1973); medical diagnosis (Yoon, et al, 1989); jet engine failure detection and related automotive problems (Dietz, et al, 1989); classification problems (Hart, 1992); market response modelling (Van Wezel & Baets, 1995). For an overview of the success stories, we would refer you to Dayhoff (1990). Most of these applications have the shared characteristic that they are based on a form of pattern recognition. It is in applications where pattern recognition is key that neural networks have proved to be most successful.

It has proved difficult in the past to produce equations that describe managerial processes—even the most common ones. Where the human brain has shown its mettle is its ability to filter data quickly, and condense these data into maps or patterns, based on enormous volumes. The way managers deal with complexity is impressive and flexible, but it has one major disadvantage for corporate use: it is extremely difficult to communicate, let alone to share amongst colleagues.

It is generally the case that managers are faced with ill-structured and turbulent environments in which the operations for which they are responsible take place today. But, as we have argued, most of the classical techniques are not able to deal with the non-linear and highly dynamic behaviour of these processes. Neural networks are a promising means of analysing ill-structured and turbulent environments, bringing some system into the "chaos" (Stacey, 1992). However, it would be worth analyzing in more depth how physicists deal with bringing some stability into chaos since management scientists could potentially learn much from physicists' experience (Gleick, 1988; Holden, 1986; Peters, 1991).

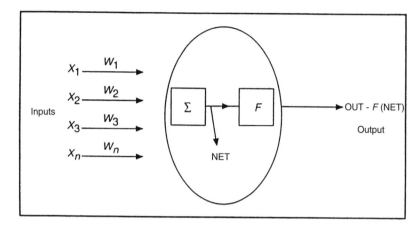

Figure 5.4   *Artificial neurone (Venugopal & Baets, 1994)*

Overall, then, the successful applications of artificial neural networks suggest an important resemblance between neural networks and characteristics of the human brain (Wasserman, 1989). They learn from experiment. Neural networks generalize from previous examples. They seem to be able to abstract essential characteristics from "irrelevant" data.

What Artificial Neural Networks Do

Artificial Neural Networks (ANN) attempt to model the architecture of biological neural systems. Biological neural networks are made of simple, tightly interconnected processing elements called neurones. The interconnections are made by the outgoing branches, the "axons", which themselves form several connections ("synapses") with the other neurones. When a neurone receives a number of stimuli and when the sum of the received stimuli exceeds a certain threshold value, it will fire and transmit the stimulus to adjacent neurones. The aim of ANNs is to extract concepts from biological networks, with which new powerful computational methodologies can be developed.

ANNs consist of many non-linear computational elements called nodes. The nodes are densely interconnected through directed links. Nodes take one or more input values and combine them into a single value to transform them into an output value. Figure 5.4 illustrates a node that implements the macroscopic idea of a biological neurone.

Here, a set of inputs labelled $X_1, X_2, \ldots, X_n$ is sent to a node. Each input is multiplied by the weights of the interconnections $W_1, W_2, \ldots, W_n$

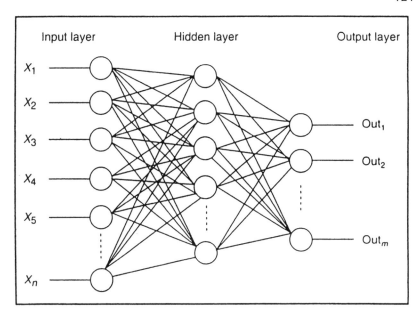

Figure 5.5 *Schematic representation of a three layer Neural Network (Venugopal & Baets, 1994)*

before it is applied to the summation block. Each weight corresponds to the strength of a synaptic connection. The summation block adds all the weighted inputs algebraically, producing an output denoted as NET. The block labelled F accepts the NET output. If the NET output exceeds the threshold level, the OUT node is said to be activated.

The power of neural computing comes from connecting artificial neurones into artificial neural networks. The simplest network is a group of neurones arranged in a layer. Multilayer networks may be formed by simply cascading a group of single layers. Figure 5.5 shows a three-layer neural network: an input layer, an output layer and, between the two, a so-called hidden layer. The nodes of different layers are densely interconnected through directed links. The nodes at the input layer receive the signals (values of the input variables) and propagate concurrently through the network, layer by layer.

The numbers of layers and neurones and the weights to be attached to the connections from neurone to neurone can be decided in such a way that they give the best possible fit to a set of data. Different types of neural network models have been developed in the literature.

ANN models are characterized by their properties, viz., the structure of the network (topology), how and what the network computes (i.e. its computational property) and how and what the network learns to compute (i.e. its learning or training property). Learning means here the process by which a set of input values is presented sequentially to the input of the networks and the network weights are adjusted such that similar inputs give the same output. Learning strategies are categorized as supervized and unsupervized.

Supervized learning requires the pairing of each input value with a target value representing the desired output and a teacher who provides error information. In unsupervized learning, the training set consists of input vectors only. The output is determined by the network during the course of training. The unsupervized learning procedures construct internal models that capture regularities in their input values without receiving any additional information.

The massive number of processing elements makes neural computing faster than conventional computing. It is robust and fault tolerant due to its parallelity. It is fault tolerant in the sense that its performance does not degrade significantly even if one of the nodes fails. Also, based on current results, neural networks adapt themselves (i.e. adapt their structure and/or connection weights) to achieve a better performance.

Relevance of Neural Networks for Mental Model Mapping

When we choose neural networks as an alternative to measure business processes via human perceptions, we are interested in obtaining a map of those individual and shared mental models, which are indicated in Figure 5.2 and explained earlier. If we can construct such a map, we can get a little closer to the "tacit knowledge" existing in a company. But neural networks not only allow the mapping of mental models. If they did they would probably be less promising for BPR purposes because BPR is dealing with complex processes of change, and durable change can only take place if it fits the appropriate mental models or if these mental models are themselves part of the change process. That is probably where learning and change meet. Hence, we need to consider where learning in interaction with change can take place when we use a neural network approach (as described in detail later in this chapter) in relation to the figures described earlier.

We can consider at least two moments in the creation and development of a neural network where learning can take place: the design of the neural network and the training stage. During the creation and development of the neural network, we are working with concepts and operational issues at the level of the individual. We try to identify and list all relevant issues, without linking them with individual mental models. The learning and change moments take place during the elicitation of these issues. During the training phase, neural networks try to develop the mental models, based on the issues and concepts encountered. In as far as the first phase included elements of organizational frameworks (weltanschauung at the corporate level) and organizational routines, we will be able to obtain insight in some shared mental models: shared not in the sense that all people involved tend to share a specific vision but in the sense that the variety in the shared mental model remains operational. This variety in the shared mental model is where the know-how and know-why of company is "stored".

What we have not discussed as yet is in what way a trained neural network could be an explication of tacit knowledge. An ANN is in a way comparable to a moving picture of a corporate mental model. As such, an ANN makes (mostly tacit) knowledge explicit, manages it but also assists in creating knowledge. If managers are interested in managing pro-actively they need to learn from experience. They need to be able to adapt their mental models as well as to fit new experiences into their individual mental models and the corporate mental model. The reflection of experience into a mental model (whether individual or corporate) will be much easier if an explicit form of such a mental model were to exist. Learning could take place more easily and, hence, change could take place more easily.

The paradigm of:

individual experiences—individual tacit knowledge—individual mental model—shared mental model—repository of corporate knowledge—repository of core competencies—proactive management—positive feed-back loops

is the basic logic of the knowledge-creating organisation. Learning is then a process based on the manager's ability to take part in such knowledge creation. A trained neural network can be used to make a moving picture of the shared mental model. A learning organization is an organization able to manage this cycle of knowledge creation and apply it in its daily operational and tactical management.

An Example of an Application

In this section, an example is given of an application of the above in the chemical industry in order to clarify the proposed approach. The desired change process centres on quality management, about which a number of different stakeholders have different perceptions. The chemical company concerned wants to renew a production plant and process. The company is responsible for delivering good quality product and, of course, there is pressure to produce at the lowest possible cost. There are at least two more factors to take into account. First, there are the environmental rules and regulations which the company should follow. It is likely that these rules are at variance with the aim of low production cost and possibly also with the desired quality level. Furthermore, these rules are not always clear and strict and they leave some possibility for interpretation. This implies that the application of these rules is based on the perceptions of both parties involved (company and government). A third stakeholder group are the people living in the neighbourhood of the plant. The way they perceive the plant is almost exclusively based on perceptions and very rarely on facts.

This is a typical example of a situation where neural networks can be used in order to picture the business process under consideration, as well as the change process related to it. In summary, there are imprecise, multiple and often opposing aims expressed by a number of different stakeholders. Elements cannot necessarily be measured objectively. In many cases there may be mistrust between the different stakeholders. The stakeholders often do not agree on definitions of, for example, quality and quality of life.

In such cases, it adds value to be able to draw a "picture" of the stakes involved in a way which does not confront different stakeholder views at the very outset. Direct meetings between stakeholder groups in this stage of the process often lead to debates with little prospect of solution. Concensus is elusive. Furthermore, in such processes it is rather difficult to define relationships between "fuzzy" variables. Stakeholders know which elements play a role, but it is extremely difficult to define the relationships between the different elements. If we can construct a "picture" of the process and show this to the different stakeholders with the aim of them learning from it without immediately having to debate basic principles, then progress can be made.

Via different sources (existing studies, interviews, internal memos, for example) information is gathered as to the possible issues of importance for the process under consideration. At no stage are relationships or influences between issues questioned, since they are based on the individual mental maps of the different people involved (Kim, 1993). Since the ultimate aim is to influence the individual mental maps we want to avoid at this stage existing mental maps interfering with the ultimate goal.

In order to validate the issues raised, testing takes place with a number of representatives from each of the different stakeholder groups. After validation, a questionnaire is constructed in which the importance of the different issues can be scored on a Likert-type 1 to 10 scale. The questionnaires are distributed amongst all stakeholder groups.

Via unsupervised learning algorithms a possible structure is identified in the data. This procedure may show not only a different set of issues than those considered beforehand, but it could also show a different structure and/or sequence of issues. It could well be that issues always considered by the marketing department as crucial hitherto do not turn out to be important for other stakeholders. It may also be that, although people do not agree on definitions of quality, in actuality they turn out to have a common understanding of the issue. Eventually a representation will allow the identification of possible structures which emerge out of perceptions and not out of predetermined mental models.

In order to communicate this structure and allow the emergence of common mental maps about the process, a map is constructed. For this we can construct interactive software tools which facilitate use by stakeholders. Via networks (e.g. Groupware) these pictures can be distributed, but also discussed amongst stakeholders. The impact of this approach can be much greater than with other classical communication tools (paper, workshops) (Chen, et al, 1994) potentially in situations where many individuals and/or groups are involved.

The map which is created in this way does not present a common average perception, but contains the different views, the diversity and variety of opinion that exist. Compared to other cognitive mapping techniques (Eden, 1988) this is clearly a strength of neural networks. Cognitive mapping, according to Eden, strives for a concensus that may not exist. Concensus is not precluded in this approach to change but what underpins it is the need to be able to work with different stakeholder groups, to retain as far as is possible the diversity of opinion and not to strive from the beginning for consensus.

The result of a trained neural network is a matrix of values where virtual groups, comprising members of different stakeholder groups, set out to consider the issues. Both on the issues and the number of groups a range of options is possible. The more virtual groups one allows, the more detailed information one keeps but the overall picture is less accessible. If one chooses fewer groups, detail is lost but "behaviour" is easier to understand. There is no best choice in this respect and experience in a particular situation will show what is workable.

The matrix can be represented in a number of different ways. An easy example is a graph representation where the result resembles a wheel of a bicycle. On each of the spokes an issue is represented. The user clicks on a spoke, obtains the issue and a scale to score it. If a user does this for a number of issues, the system calculates which virtual group the user is most probably part of and shows all the other issues of that virtual group on the graph. This produces an immediate overall picture of the mind set of the virtual group in respect to this particular business process. This picture can be commented on and discussed with a view to improving understanding. If the problem size is large, one may want to limit the number of spokes purely as a matter of practicality. The more that is invested in the user-friendliness of the interface, the higher the communicative power.

A possible additional use of such a system can be to allow the system to "auto-adapt". Each request for information is then translated into a new observation and the neural network is recalculated. In this way a pseudo-living system of evolving perceptions is created. In this chapter this enhancement is not considered in more detail, so the reader is referred to Kim (1993) for an explanation of the basics of these concepts and Baets et al (1995) for some more detail on their application.

CONSEQUENCES FOR IS ARCHITECTURE AND DESIGN

These views not only have consequences for the way we consider business processes, but also for how IT architectures could look in the future. Chapter 13 looks at this in some depth, but it may be useful to summarize some elements here (see also Venugopal & Baets, 1995).

The success of an organization in the global competitive race depends not only on the knowledge of its members and their ability to make appropriate business moves but also on having the requisite skills dynamically to update and put knowledge into practice. Hence, a learning organization enables each of its members to learn continually thereby helping to generate new ideas and thinking. By this process, organizations continuously learn from their own experience and that of others and adapt themselves so as to improve their ability to make progress towards their strategic vision. In a way, learning organizations aim at converting themselves into "knowledge-based" organizations by creating, acquiring and transferring knowledge so as to improve their planning and actions.

In order to become a learning organization, they should be skilled at systematic problem solving, learning from their own experience, learning from the experiences of others, transferring knowledge quickly and efficiently amongst employees and other stakeholders and experimenting with new approaches (Garvin, 1993). Developments in information systems and information technology (IS/IT) can be harnessed to help in this regard: intelligent IT tools which are capable of supporting certain aspects of learning processes are already commercially available.

"Creating a learning/knowledge-based organization is simple but not easy" (Honey, 1991). Possible (IT) techniques which can support the creation of a knowledge-based/learning organizations are: Case-Based Reasoning Systems (CBRS), Expert Systems (ES), Group Decision Support Systems (GDSS), Cognitive Mapping and Artificial Neural Networks.

Lessem (1991) has defined organizational learning-constructs, viz., knowledge origination, knowledge development, knowledge refinement, knowledge promotion, knowledge adaptation, knowledge implementation (dissemination), and knowledge application. He suggested that organizations build on these constructs to enhance their learning capability.

To be specific, learning in the context of organizations occurs when:

- individual members of the organization *form* their views/ knowledge ("mental models") on actions in response to a changing environment;
- individual members *share* (or pose) their knowledge and form a pooled knowledge;
- individual members *update* their knowledge as the environment changes.

CONCLUSIONS

Business processes are complex processes in which perceptions of stakeholders play an important role. If we want to re-engineer our processes or if we want to re-orient our organization to become more knowledge creating in order better to manage the overall complexity, we have argued in this chapter that we should put greater emphasis on mind sets, learning and knowledge. This has consequences, both for approaches and for structures (architectures). However, we still have a long way to go.

Some approaches appear to have potential in this respect and have already demonstrated their value. Based on our own research we know that artificial neural networks can be used to picture complex managerial processes and monitor/facilitate change processes. They can be used as a basis for process re-engineering, and for systems design.

It would appear then that knowledge management in business situations could benefit from joint efforts and developments between artificial intelligence, cognitive sciences and modern human resource management (Nonaka, 1994). Ideas on organizational learning could be boosted by such cooperation.

While at this stage major conclusions are difficult to draw, we can at least indicate possible directions to explore. Further research in real life cases will be required in order to provide further learning, and in this context the application and integration of such IS/IT tools as Case-Based Reasoning Systems, Knowledge-Based Systems, Cognitive Mapping Systems, and Neural Networks appear to offer considerable promise.

REFERENCES

Argyris, C. and Schön, D., 1978, *Organizational Learning: A Theory of Action Perspective*, Reading, MA: Addison-Wesley.

Baets, W., 1992, Aligning Information Systems with Business Strategy, *Journal of Strategic Information Systems*, 1 (4), 205–213.

Baets, W., 1993a, *Information Systems Strategic Alignment: A Case in Banking*, Working Paper, Nijenrode University, The Netherlands.

Baets, W., 1993b, IT for Organisational Change: Beyond Business Process Engineering, *Business Change & Re-engineering*, 1 (2), Autumn.

Baets, W., 1995, Artificial Neural Networks: Mapping of Change Processes and Measurement of Learning (Dutch version), *Handboek Effektief Opleiden*, 4/131.

Baets, W., Brunenberg, L., van Wezel, M. and Venugopal, V., 1995, Corporate Cognitive Mapping: Mapping of Corporate Change Processes, *Fourth International Conference on Artificial Neural Networks*, Cambridge, UK.

Badaracco, J., 1991, *The Knowledge Link: Competitive Advantage through Strategic Alliances*, Boston: Harvard Business School Press.

Benjamin, R. and Blunt, J., 1992, Critical IT Issues: The Next Ten Years, *Sloan Management Review*, Summer, 33 (4).

Borucki, C. and Byosiere, P., 1992, Toward a Theory of Enlightenment of Middle Management in Globally Competitive Firms, *Annual Meeting of the Academy of Management*, Las Vegas, Nevada, August.

Checkland, P., 1981, *Systems Thinking, Systems Practice*, Chichester: Wiley.

Checkland, P. and Scholes, J., 1990, *Soft Systems Methodology in Action*, Chichester: Wiley.

Chen, H., et al, 1994, Automatic Concept Classification of Text from Electronic Meetings, *Communications of the ACM*, October, 37 (10).

Cohen, J. and Stewart, I., 1994, *The Collapse of Chaos*, Viking.

Collins, E., Ghosh, S. and Scofield C., 1988, An Application of a Multiple Neural Network Learning System to Evaluation of Mortgage Underwriting Judgement, *IEEE International Conference on Neural Networks*, II: 459–466.

Davenport, T.H., 1996 Why Re-engineering Failed: the Fad that Forgot People, *Fast Company*, Premier Issue, 70–74.

Dayhoff, J., 1990, *Neural Network Architectures*, New York: Von Nostrand Reinhold.

de Callatay, A., 1992, *Natural and Artificial Intelligence: Misconceptions about Brains and Neural Networks*, Amsterdam, North-Holland.

de Geus, A., 1988, Planning as Learning, *Harvard Business Review*, March/April.

Dietz, W., Kiech, E., Ali, M., 1989, Jet and Rocket Engine Fault Diagnosis in Real Time, *Journal on Neural Network Computing*, 1(1), 5–18.

Duda, R. and Hart, P., 1973, *Pattern Classification and Scene Analysis*, New York: Wiley Interscience.

Eden, C., 1988, Cognitive Mapping, *European Journal of Operational Research*, 36.

Firebaugh, M., 1989, *Artificial Intelligence: A Knowledge-Based Approach*, Boston: PWS-Kent.

Fletcher, D. and Goss, E., 1993, Forecasting with Neural Networks, *Information and Management*, 24 (3), March.

Galambos, J., Abelson, R. and Black, J., (eds.), 1986, *Knowledge Structures*, London, Lawrence Erlbaum Associates.

Garvin, D.A., 1993, Building a Learning Organization, *Harvard Business Review*, 78–91, July-August.

Gleick, J., 1988, *Chaos: Making a New Science*, London: Heinemann.

Haeckel, S. and Nolan, R., 1993, Managing by Wire, *Harvard Business Review*, September/October, 71 (5).

Hamel, G. and Prahalad, C., 1989, Strategic Intent, *Harvard Business Review*, May-June.

Hart, A., 1992, Using Neural Networks for Classification Tasks—Some Experiments on Datasets and Practical Advice, *Journal of the Operational Research Society*, 43 (3) March.

Hassard, J., 1993, *Sociology and Organization Theory: Positivism, Paradigms and Postmodernity*, Cambridge University Press.

Hassard, J. and Parkers, M. (eds.), 1993, *Postmodernism and Organizations*, London: Sage.

HNC, 1991, *Neurosoftware*, San Diego CA: HNC Inc.

Holden, A. (ed.), 1986, *Chaos*, Manchester: Manchester University Press.

Honey, P., 1991, The Learning Organisation Simplified, *Training and Development*, 9, 30–32.

Johansson, H., McHugh, P., Pendlebury, A. and Wheeler, W., 1993, *Business Process Reengineering—Breakpoint Strategies for Market Dominance*, Wiley.

Johnson-Laird, P.N., 1983, *Mental Models: Towards a Cognitive Science of Language Inference and Consciousness* Cambridge: Cambridge University Press.

Kaplan, R. and Murdock, L., 1990, Core Process Redesign, *The McKinsey Quarterly*, 2.

Keen, P., 1993, Information Technology and the Management Difference: A Fusion Map, *IBM Systems Journal*, 32 (1).

Kim, D., 1993, The Link Between Individual and Organizational Learning, *Sloan Management Review*, Fall.

Knorr, R., 1991, Business Process Redesign: Key to Competitiveness, *The Journal of Business Strategy*, November/December.

Kolb, D., 1984, *Experiential Learning: Experience as the Source of Learning and Development*, Englewood Cliffs: Prentice Hall.

Langton, C. (ed.), 1989, *Artificial Life*, Santa Fe Institute Studies in the Sciences of Complexity, Proceedings, 6, Addison Wesley, Redwood City, CA.

Leonard-Barton, D., 1992, The Factory as a Learning Laboratory, *Sloan Management Review*, Fall, 34 (11).

Lessem, R., 1991, *Total Quality Learning—Building a Learning Organisation*, Basil Blackwell, Oxford.

Lodewyck, R. and Deng, P., 1993, Experimentation with Back-Propagation Neural Networks, *Information Management*, 24 (1), January.

Niederman, F., Brancheau, J.C. and Wetherbe, J.C., 1991, Information Systems Management Issues for the 1990s, *MIS Quarterly*, December, 475–500.

Morin, E., 1990a, *Sciences avec Conscience*, Paris, Fayard.

Morin, E., 1990b, *Introduction à la Penséd Complexe*, Paris: Esf.

Nicolis, G. and Prigogine, I., 1989, *Exploring Complexity*, Freeman.

Nonaka, I., 1994, A Dynamic Theory of Organizational Knowledge Creation, *Organization Science*, 5 (1), February.

Nonaka, I., Byosiere, P., Borucki, C. and Konno, N., 1994, Organizational Knowledge Creation Theory: A First Comprehensive Test, *Annual Academy of Management Meetings*, Dallas, August.

Norden, P., 1993, Quantitative Techniques in Strategic Alignment, *IBM Systems Journal*, 32 (1).

Peppard, J. and Rowland, P., 1995, *The Essence of Business Process Re-engineering*, London: Prentice-Hall.

Peters, E., 1991, *Chaos and Order in the Capital Markets*, NY: Wiley & Sons, NY.

Prahalad, C. and Hamel, G., 1990, The Core Competence of the Corporation, *Harvard Business Review*, May-June.

Quinn, J., 1992, *Intelligent Enterprise*, Free Press, New York.

Ramaswami, S., Nilakanta, S. and Flynn, J., 1992, Supporting Strategic Information Needs: An Empirical Assessment of Some Organisational Factors, *Journal of Strategic Information Systems*, 1 (3).

Rockart, J. and Hofman, J., 1992, System Delivery: Evolving New Strategies, *Sloan Management Review*, Summer, 33 (4).

Rumelhart, D. and McClelland, J., 1986, *Parallel Distributed Processing: Exploration in the Microstructure of Cognition, Vol 1: Foundations*, Cambridge, MA: MIT Press.

Rumelhart, D. and McClelland, J., 1986, *Parallel Distributed Processing: Exploration in the Microstructure of Cognition, Vol 2: Psychological and Biological Models*, Cambridge, MA: MIT Press.

Santa Fe Institute, *Bulletin of the Santa Fe Institute*, 1987—present.

Scott Morton, M. (ed.), 1991, *The Corporation of the 1990s: Information Technology and Organizational Transformation*, New York: Oxford University Press.

Senge, P., 1990, *The Fifth Discipline*, New York: Doubleday.

Stacey, R., 1992, *Managing Chaos: Dynamic Business Strategies in an Unpredictable World*, London, Kogan Page.

Stacey, R., 1993, Strategy as Order Emerging from Chaos, *Long Range Planning*, 26, (1).

Swieringa, J. and Wierdsma, A., 1993, *The Learning Organization*, Reading, MA: Addison-Wesley.

Toffler, A., 1990, *Powershift: Knowledge, Wealth and Violence at the Edge of the 21st Century*, New York: Bantam Books.

Van der Linden, G., 1993, *Een Essay over en Empirisch Onderzoek naar Betekenissen van Loon en Beloning. Casus van een Postmoderne Visie op Bedrijfsbeheer*, Rijksuniversiteit Groningen.

Van Wezel, M. and Baets, W., 1995, Predicting Market Responses With a Neural Network: the Case of Fast Moving Consumer Goods, *Marketing Intelligence and Planning*, Autumn.

Venugopal, V. and Baets, W., 1994, Neural Networks and Statistical Techniques in Marketing Research: A Conceptual Comparison, *Marketing Intelligence and Planning*, Fall.

Venugopal, V. and Baets, W., 1995, An Integrated Intelligent Support System for Organisational Learning—A Conceptual Framework, *The Learning Organization*, 2 (3).

Wasserman, P., 1989, *Neural Computing: Theory and Practice*, New York: Van Nostrand Reinhold.

Widrow, B. and Stearns, S., 1985, *Adaptive Signal Processing*, Englewood Cliffs: NJ, Prentice Hall.

Yoon, Y., Brobst, R., Bergstresser, P. and Petersen, L., 1989, A Desktop Neural Network for Dermatology Diagnosis, *Journal on Neural Network Computing* 1(1), 43–52.

6
The Role of Learning in Information Systems Planning and Implementation

TAPIO REPONEN
Turku School of Economics and Business Administration,
Finland

INTRODUCTION

The aim of this chapter is to study the problem of creating implementable information systems (IS) strategies. The problem on which this chapter focuses is how to involve company management in planning and taking responsibility for IS issues. Strategic questions in IS are the same as in business planning in general. Planning and decision making require human deliberation, which thus needs to be made effective. This chapter presents ways in which interactive planning could be improved and the direction companies appear to be taking in this regard.

The conclusions presented here are drawn from previous cases and examples, in several large IS strategy projects over the last 10 years, and also from a literature review of the area. The starting point with regard to the latter is that the strategic use of information technology is a relatively well known area, and that readers will be familiar with the classical examples and current thinking in this area.

The concept of information systems strategy is multifaceted and the

Information Technology and Organizational Transformation. Edited by R.D. Galliers and W.R.J. Baets. © 1998 John Wiley & Sons Ltd

debate as to the strategic importance of information systems started early in the 1980s, the initial emphasis falling heavily on the competitive advantage to be gained. However, doubt has since arisen concerning the sustainability of any advantage gained from information technology.

Despite developments in the area, IS strategy has continued to be one of the most critical information management problems (Galliers et al, 1994), indicating that although the sustainability of competitive advantage through strategic information systems has been questioned, information as such has an essential role to play in future business operations. The myth of competitive advantage from strategic applications of information technology has been stronger in the US than in Europe. Generally speaking, European managers have been more circumspect as to what might be achieved through information technology. However, systems that improve competitive advantage have also been built in Europe, and the system base is very strong in many companies. The concern is now the same on both continents: are our information systems adequate to meet future demands?

This leads us to question how a purposeful state of information systems (IS) may be achieved in an organization. It has been clearly noted that real competitive advantage stems from an holistic view of utilizing information technology (IT) (Reponen, 1989; Galliers, 1994), not just from single applications, whether they are strategic or operational. This being the case, it is a responsibility of general management to ensure that this holistic picture exists. One way to do this is through an appropriate creation of an information systems strategy. Empirical evidence for this point is presented in the following.

The concept of an information systems strategy comprises different definitions and elements (Earl, 1990). The general aim, however, has been to link IS to business better than before. This has long been an aim, but has been emphasized during the current transformation stage. This section examines the utilization of IS from a general management point of view; an information systems strategy is a long-term precept for directing, implementing and supervising information systems (Reponen, 1994). Such a plan provides answers to questions like:

- Are our applications well linked to business?
- Is our application development well prioritized and managed?
- How much should we spend on IT?
- What kind of benefits can we expect from our projects?
- How should we organize our IS services?

Competitive advantage may be gained from both internal and external applications. In the 1980s, the significance of external links was emphasized, especially customer systems, but recent discussion about business process redesign emphasizes the simplification of internal processes and thus also draws the attention of general management to intraorganizational issues (Earl, 1993). Evaluation criteria for new projects are consequently in the process of changing from mainly increasing customer service to also considering price competitiveness. Cost savings are again relevant factors in deciding on IT investment.

The components of competition are price, quality and time. In the 1980s, the quality of products and services was stressed. The better and more extensive the service, the better the competitive advantage was seen to be. The economic realities of the 1990s, however, resulted in the necessity to pay more attention to costs and even undertake radical cost-cutting. However, successful competition requires effective control of each competition component. The price has to be competitive, quality very high and delivery time very short. All this means that linking IT to business and business to IT is now a necessity, not just an objective. This is possible only through the considerable involvement of all parties in thinking about the role of IT in the organization (Earl, 1990; Allen & Scott Morton, 1994). This involvement is a two-way process; the participants of an IS strategy process may contribute to the project but also learn from other participants' viewpoints.

The problems examined in this chapter are:

- How to create an implementable strategy?
- What constitutes the major elements of the strategy ?
- Who should create the strategy?
- What is the attitude of management and business representatives to the strategy process?
- How are the ideas of management and business representatives developing in relation to information management?

The aim is to present concrete evidence in favour of a participative strategy process. Strategic IS planning (SISP) literature is used as a starting point, which as such is assumed to be well-known and thus relevant references are used selectively.

STRATEGIC THINKING IN INFORMATION SYSTEMS PLANNING

There are several distinct schools of strategic planning (Mintzberg, 1989, 1990) which may be divided into three categories: prescriptive, descriptive and rescriptive (Carlsson, 1993). The prescriptive school represents the analytical and mathematical tradition of planning, seeing the strategy process as one of conceptual design and formal planning. It views strategy planning as an internal and external analysis, with the aid of which alternative strategies are created. The selection and implementation of the best strategy is the end result of the planning.

The descriptive school views planning as a mental, learning process that attempts to take into consideration the decision makers' values and their way of thinking. Several situational and random factors, which should be utilized for learning and action, are seen to affect the strategy. Here, the significance of understanding, learning and adaptation are emphasized (Dessler, 1980). The descriptive school comprises different sub-schools such as entrepreneurial (strategy as a visionary process), cognitive (a mental process), learning (an emergent process), and configurational (Mintzberg, 1990). The suggestion has come from this school that most strategies are emergent in connection with action and only a small proportion are intended and realized as a result of actual planning (Mintzberg, 1978). This would indicate that strategy planning would be of only minor significance.

The rescriptive school develops the line of the prescriptive school further, in such a fashion that the starting point lies in the knowledge and experience of experts and managers. This knowledge is then transformed into a representation suited to formal treatment in order to deal with management issues.

The nature of strategic planning has also been examined in the field of IS, for example as to whether IS strategy should be planned separately or whether it is a continuous process in which new ideas are born alongside operations. Our starting point here is descriptive thinking, in which the formulation of a strategy is seen as a cognitive learning process. The ideas of the descriptive school are transported to the area of SISP.

The fit between business and IT is changing and one key question is how to achieve a new fit. The research described here concentrates on the situations in which it is purposeful to perform the planning of a strategy as a separate project as, for example, an essential change in the competitive situation, a change in the software generation, architectural changes and so on. The basis for this choice is that more and more organizations are faced with situations in which great changes must be made at one go, and at which time it is worthwhile going through the entire organizational entity thoroughly. In the area of IS strategy, both one-time projects and continuous development are certainly necessary: neither of these suffices on its own.

The aim is to help management make IS plans that are well-suited to the organization's situation and objectives. This aim becomes increasingly important, as noted by Ciborra (1994) for example:

"... strategy formulation is bound to involve elements of surprise, sudden, radical shift in preferences, goals and even identity of the decision makers, as well as paralysing vicious circles that may stifle its development and implementation."

Strategies are thus formulated under different pressures for change, and involve a lot of political manoeuvring. In order to create an implementable strategy, business representatives must be involved in profound consideration concerning the opportunities to develop operations through IT. A strategy is formulated through initiation, thinking and maturation. This way, decisions are made during the process, in parallel with things seemingly becoming clearer.

A multitude of frameworks and methods have been developed for SISP (see e.g. Remenyi, 1991). The aim of all these is to bring business and IT closer. Different methods aid in the formulation of a strategy, but they are no more than a means of support. The actual formulation of a strategy is, after all, a mental process, which sets the basic aims for the operation.

On the basis of our studies, we have concluded that from the general management viewpoint the strategic planning of IS is an interactive learning process for the creation of a strategy for business process redesign and development incorporating IT (Reponen, 1993). A real IS strategy is something which is essentially a planning process in the minds of the decision makers, users and developers of the system. It is supported by written reports and plans, but they are of secondary importance.

Implementable IS strategies may be generated by a participative approach, where understanding about the use of IT will be increased. SISP is a cumulative learning process, where the participants possess the knowledge as to how best to utilize IT. If the same people who have planned the strategy are also in charge of its implementation, the strategy will be purposeful. If, on the other hand, totally different people are put in charge of the strategy implementation, the strategy will be little more than a report with—for them—an unclear purpose.

The success of a strategy is determined by how much impact the strategy process has had on the decision makers' thinking and, through this, their actions. The aim of this section is to outline the principles of strategy formulation and give practical examples of its implementation.

THE ROLE OF LEARNING IN THE IS STRATEGY PROCESS

Learning is a key concept in creating implementable IS strategies, that is, learning by doing. The ideal objective is to form a shared vision of how to use technology. Senge (1990) has put an interesting interpretation on the concept of shared vision:

> "When there is a genuine vision ... people excel and learn, not because they are told to, but because they want to ... What has been lacking is a discipline for translating individual visions to shared vision ..."

The problem is how to make people form and accept a shared vision. This can be promoted through cooperative learning efforts. Cooperative learning refers to learning environments in which small groups learn together to achieve a common goal. There are several different learning methods that have stemmed from two principal sources; one social and the other cognitive in emphasis (Light et al, 1992):

> "Educational sociologists assume that learning under 'positive contact conditions' can facilitate interpersonal relationships which in turn may have positive effects on (participants') motivation, self esteem, and academic learning.
> "Cognitive psychologists, on the other hand, emphasize the role of cognitive interactions in facilitating learning in small groups. According to this view, cognitive interactions can involve different features—all having positive effects on cognitive development. These include conflict resolution, cognitive scaffolding with no apparent conflict, reciprocal peer tutoring, overt execution of cognitive and metacognitive processes, and modelling."

Creating an IS strategy is usually a matter of team work involving representatives from different parts of the organization. The aim of the strategy is to cause learning. Action science offers one possible starting point for conceptualizing the interactive learning process in strategy generation. Argyris, et al (1985) state that:

> "Action scientists engage with participants in a collaborative process of critical inquiry into problems of social practice in a learning context. The core feature of this context is that it is expressly designed to foster learning about one's practice and about alternative ways of constructing it."

Action research is client-centered and contextual. The researcher who wishes to investigate an organization consults with its members. Research goals are negotiated between the client group and researcher. The research involves a learning cycle that is a continuous process resulting in outcomes acceptable to both client group and researcher

(Reponen, et al, 1992). Action research, therefore, aims pragmatically to produce practical outcomes for immediate use.

Its assumptions are that each social context is unique rather than an instance of a general case. It does not produce law-like generalizations about organizations in the same way as does positivism (Checkland, 1991; Wood-Harper, 1992). But in the practical work of planning IS strategies, action science-like procedures are exactly what is needed.

One of the main problems in IS strategy generation has been the "shelfware-effect": plans have been carefully developed but then stored and never actually used. This may be due to positivistic planning procedures, where planning results have been more important than their effectiveness. There are many different methods and frameworks for planning strategies; but methods do not plan, people do. Therefore, it is extremely important to have the key personnel highly involved in planning procedures (Earl, 1990, 1993). Their involvement makes implementable results much more likely.

Action science offers one possible scientific background for IS strategy generation and implementation. The role of the project manager is similar to that of an action scientist. The goals of the project should be negotiated from the users' point of view, the process should be an interactive learning cycle for all participants and the outcomes should be in the form of genuine, creative and innovative ideas from the interaction.

The data elements in action science are action and talk. There are different methods of collecting this data (Argyris, et al, 1985):

- observations accompanied by audio-taping
- interviews
- action experiments
- participant written cases.

The same methods may also be used in IS strategy formulation. The main objectives are to open the discussion, to offer new information and knowledge to participants, to influence the opinions of all participants and to try to find a common understanding as to what should be done. If IS strategy formulation is an interactive process with several participants, there will also be conflicting demands and opinions. According to the theory of action science, conflict situations are sources of new ideas and perspectives. Within certain limits they are essential parts of an interactive learning process, and the project leader should find ways to utilize their potential.

The key elements in action science-based planning are close interaction with all participants, multiple methods in collecting data, the requirement that all parties should learn, and the implementability of plans. In the following, these principles are applied to IS strategy formulation.

THE EVOLUTION MODEL FOR INFORMATION SYSTEMS PLANNING

The Evolution Model for Information Systems Strategy (EMIS) generation has been developed to meet the demands of creating implementable strategies (Reponen, 1989). It is based on using multiple methods (team-work, lectures, interviews, meetings, expert reports, drawing up plans) to promote mutual interaction between organizational actors. Each method should increase interaction between participants and act as a tool to support and develop each participant's personal skills and understanding of information management.

The skills, knowledge and views of organizational actors affect the way IS is managed and utilized. The human side of IS-related organizational maturity is understood here as a state of organizational learning, which consists of both management and user components (Auer & Ruohonen, 1994). The current state should be clearly understood before any new plans are made or implemented. Each organization has certain capabilities to use the systems they have; capabilities which are based on cumulative and past learning.

The objective of the IS strategy process is to establish the present state of learning and create ideas about how to utilize that state in the best way. An IS strategy is the product of the learning and planning processes, which include management vision and decisions about the planning, organization and control of IS resources (Earl, 1989). Personal perceptions, innovations and creative ideas play a highly relevant and significant role in this strategy process. The purpose of interaction is to increase business managers' ability to make IT decisions, to help IT professionals understand business needs better, and to increase users' efficiency in utilizing the technology.

The EMIS model has been created using the principles mentioned above and used in several large IS strategy planning projects, where it has been proven to work well. It is based on action science-like thinking, trying to root out even the most deeply held thoughts of participants and to find ways to improve the present situation. The intensity of global competition raises the need for redesign, and it is vitally important to find new and intuitive ways to use IT, both existing systems and new ones.

In the process of IS strategy formulation, the following questions should be answered:

- What is the link between business and IT? In which areas are we able to improve our productivity or services?
- Can we bring these improvements about by:
  - expanding the use of existing systems?
  - building new features into existing systems?
  - designing new applications?
  - a new software generation?
- What is the scope and nature of changes (radical-incremental)? Do these changes require a new architecture? How do we get there?
- Which kinds of investments are needed for realizing the improvements planned above? What are their expected benefits?
- How should we organize our IS services to make all the improvements happen?

Answers to these questions need expertise from many different areas, and consequently interaction with business people and IT professionals is fundamental. The plan states the key business areas: the possibilities to use present systems more effectively; the potential new application areas; and the resources needed to make the changes happen.

IS strategy as an holistic picture of the use of IT in the organization tries to find a balance between internal and external applications, existing and new systems, mainframe and client/server networks, and make/buy decisions. A tenet in the use of IT is that electronic links and automated processes are technically available solutions in almost any area. They can save a lot of manual work and make the processes faster; but when is the right time—from a competitive and economic perspective—to make each new investment?

General management has to solve the problems of timing and size of new investments. They also have to decide on the balance between using existing applications and building new ones. IS professionals then have responsibility for the technical realization of the plans. Gaining competitive advantage needs the involvement of different actors.

Information is one important source of productivity and competitiveness. It is a factor of production, but may also raise the productivity of other factors (Romer, 1990). Therefore, information may have both direct and indirect influences on the competitiveness of the organization. Its importance is growing as, increasingly, network organizations of knowledge workers become the norm.

One of the main questions is how to collect and select from the multitude of available information. This is a human process that requires a high degree of cumulative expertise in organizations, i.e. human capital. The dilemma is that the wider the diffusion of IT, the more human judgment is needed in what is crucial in using it. An organization needs both good business skills to understand how to use technology and technical skills to make it happen.

Avoiding the gap that has existed between business and IT groups is one of the great concerns in information management. Returning to the concept of learning, both parties—users and IS professionals—generally need education in utilizing IT in business. This is an organizational learning process, which has interconnections to individual learning in the following way (Kim, 1993):

> "Although the meaning of the term 'learning' remains essentially the same as in the individual case, the learning process is fundamentally different at the organizational level. A model of organizational learning has to resolve the dilemma of imparting intelligence and capabilities to a nonhuman entity without anthropomorphizing it ... The cycles of individual learning affect learning at the organizational level through their influence on the organization's shared mental models."

Organizational learning is dependent on individuals improving their mental models, and making those mental models explicit. The process itself allows organizational learning to be independent of any specific individual.

As stated above, competitive advantage may be gained through an holistic approach to the use of IT in business. The advantage originates from users' abilities to use the existing systems (Auer & Ruohonen, 1994), IS professionals' ability to serve the users, new creative ideas for using IT, and the success of development projects. Competitive advantage is a combination of several human and technological factors. The objective of an IS strategy is to promote each of these areas. Having said that, the creation of an IS strategy is easy compared to its implementation. We can help to realize an implementation with interactive planning processes, flexibility in the plans and well-defined responsibilities.

EMPIRICAL OBSERVATIONS ON THE IMPORTANCE OF LEARNING IN SISP

The EMIS model has been created on the basis of descriptive thinking, but its aim is to support separate SISP projects. A structure which creates the prerequisites for successful learning and, through this, for decisions, is necessary in the projects. Through the practical case examples documented below, it will be shown that systematic work facilitates the execution of intuitive processes and the realization of their results. This framework has been tested in several companies and in different situations. What is reported here is based on the insight provided into both the essential features of an SISP process and the prerequisites for its success, as acquired through these practical tests. The EMIS model has been tested in several case companies; some results have been reported in Reponen (1994) and in Galliers, et al (1994).

Almost all the projects have resulted in developmental steps in the organization concerned. From that point of view, the interactive planning processes have been successful. Interactive planning that is based on learning effects is, however, very sensitive to changes in personnel. Only those people who have been part of the planning process have the knowledge and understanding gained in the process. For outsiders the plan is just another piece of paper, with very little content and value. The best results may thus be achieved when the same people who have planned the strategy are those that implement it.

Although the results from interactive planning processes are very positive, there are some issues worth noting. The following views summarize current management perspectives of information management, based on this case company research.

- *Awareness.* General managers clearly understand and accept the strategic and competitive role of IT in their organizations, but have not to date been very active in taking any action in this regard. There are examples of many user-driven application development processes, but general involvement is low.
- *Desire to participate.* Top management feel a little let down by the unfulfilled promise of the 1980s regarding the strategic role of IT. Their attitude towards IS planning and decision making is thus somewhat indifferent. They have expectations that IS professionals are able to design and implement systems that fit the business strategy of the organization, with only limited involvement from users and managers. This would require new skills of IS professionals, namely that they should have a clear understanding of business processes. This view is contradictory to the general idea of integration and interaction, and if development is really taking such a course, IS professionals will surely need new training.
- *Interaction.* Interaction between business representatives and IS professionals is still fraught with difficulties. There has been some progress, however, and in tandem with the decentralization of

architectures, professionals have moved closer to operational processes. It would still appear to be the case, however, that in IS/business strategy processes, business people and IS professionals have very different goals and thinking.

- *Learning*. The aim of interactive planning is to lead to learning and thus to better decision making. The general opinion of project participants is that things have been clarified and knowledge has increased as a result. This means that learning has taken place. However, the difficulty still exists that people's opinions change slowly even through the acquisition of new information. During the process, the same views may keep recurring as at the beginning of the process, i.e. the process has not developed or changed people's basic mind sets. Some people are very stubborn in their way of thinking, in which case the role of project leader is essential in creating real change.

- *Human types*. Some testing of personality types was undertaken, and we then followed how different types of people behave in a project situation. It was apparent that personality has a distinct impact on behaviour. This should be taken into account in team work; it should thus be arranged in such a fashion that everyone will be able to make their best contribution. The same working methods do not suit everyone.

- *Project champion*. The case examples clearly demonstrate that the role of project champion is very significant at both the planning and implementation stages. In the organization, there must be a person or persons who really want to make changes and improvements. Resistance to change is usually quite strong, even in participative planning, thus increasing the significance of the project champion.

- *Decision making*. The formulation of an IS strategy should lead to decision making and actions. Ideation and planning, as such, are easy compared with implementation. Interactive planning very easily meanders in different directions: many ideas arise and different alternatives are considered. However, an IS strategy must lead to concrete suggestions for action and an implementation plan. It is thus necessary that the intuitive part of the process is ultimately made concrete in the form of plans. The planning process must proceed continuously from ideas to the concrete. On the systems side, solutions often have to be arrived at before the business side of the organization is ready or able to take them on board. This is unfortunate but often unavoidable.

- *Technology*. General managers often think that an IS strategy is the same as an IT strategy, i.e. that it mainly deals with hardware and software. So, in many projects, one often encounters the phenomenon that managers very quickly start talking about hardware and systems. One pedagogical contribution in an IS project might be that the aim is to bind technology and operation to each other; this is possible only through sufficient discussion about operation. Technical solutions can easily be left to the professionals.

These are excerpts of experiences drawn from case examples. In Finnish companies in general, the levels of systems and knowledge are high. Company management is surprisingly aware of the strategic role of IT. Projects no longer have to start from the basics, but can rapidly proceed to concrete work, i.e. to find out how possible it is in the currently tough competitive situation to improve operations through IT.

A relatively new concept, Business Process Re-engineering (BPR), has spread fast in recent years, emphasizing the need for radical change (Johansson, et al, 1993). It has influenced management thinking on how to compete and has also had repercussions on practical IS strategy work. It has proven to be difficult to find genuine, sizeable targets for re-engineering. It is possible to halve the cost or double the speed of operation in some areas, but as regards the whole organization, totally new models are difficult to find. BPR has drawn the attention of management to possible cost savings through restructuring operations, but there are some major issues here which are dealt with in Chapter 10.

It also appears that general managers' expectations for these kinds of project are constantly on the increase. IS strategy can no longer remain in the form of a superficial report on potential new application targets, but has to be a relatively concrete and costed presentation of what must be done next in the context of business aspirations and goals

FUTURE CHALLENGES IN SISP

Interactive, learning-based IS planning has been described above, and it has been noted—based on practical experience—that a working model of this nature has clear effects on the operation of an organization. At the same time, however, the case companies have given some indication as to what changes are required and the problems encountered: organizational changes are so great that they also clearly impact on the IS base. Where organizations are restructured, the essential growth in the effectiveness of work is a simultaneous aim. As a result, personnel see a rise in the complexity, versatility and range of their tasks. At the same time, pressure of work rises and the use of time becomes very tightly controlled.

In such an environment, participation in IS development projects is very difficult: there is neither enough time nor the mental agility for such investments. Despite the fact that everyone recognizes the import and usefulness of IS, running or participating in development projects easily becomes burdensome. Such a situation leads to a growing demand for IS professionals to be capable of more independent construction of systems that match the needs of the organization. Demands for decentralization and independence remain the same, however.

This situation is, of course, in stark contrast with developments in recent years that have emphasized user participation in and responsibility for systems—developments that have achieved many good results. It appears, however, that there will also be task decentralization such that IS professionals will in the future be responsible for a greater proportion of tasks than at present in the IS area. This of course requires a sound knowledge of the operation of the organization on the part of IS professionals. At the same time, however, the need for general management and user input will be greater than at present in the area of strategic applications.

Research has also shown that individuals do not make good use of what they know and master, for several reasons (Salomon & Globerson, 1987; Nissbett & Ross, 1980; Glaser, 1984; Gick & Holyoak, 1983). There is evidence that many individuals operate for much of the time under the simple impression that what they do is correct because it makes sense (Perkins, 1985), on the basis of the least-effort principle. Langer (1985) terms this "mindless behavior". Salomon & Globerson (1987) argue that there is a gap between what learners could do in terms of the skills, strategies and knowledge they have already acquired, and what they actually do under normal, nontrivial learning conditions, and that the gap can be narrowed by increasing mindfulness. Mindfulness is a state of mind that is defined as the "volitional, metacognitively-guided employment of non-automatic, usually effort demanding processes."

This is certainly a key strategic question with regard to IS: how do we get the whole organization to build and use systems in a mindful way, through which true competitive advantage might be gained? One barrier is management's and users' somewhat evasive and superficial attitude towards systems as an essential part of work. Work and its IS tools are often still seen as separate components, despite all the arguments for their integration.

Differentiation from other organizations may be achieved through the use of systems; in other words, systems will have been well tuned to the needs of the organization and people can use them effectively. Learning is needed both in the areas of system construction and in their use.

It is necessary to some extent to develop new operational models in which previous experience may not be directly usable due to a new competitive environment. A special problem is how to manage the change to the new competitive situation. Operational models may require quite large-scale changes, in which case systems development should support these changes. But even in a new situation, the cumulative know-how of the organization is a means to a competitive edge being created.

It may be noted, however, that business people are actually enlightened strategic IS thinkers. A company's operation, its processes and competitive opportunities, etc. are actually quite well known. On occasion it even seems as though researchers expect the level of knowledge to be lower than it actually is. In joint projects and training situations the standard has risen quite considerably, particularly in recent years. We are arriving at a situation where basic company issues with regard to information streams are at least logically under control. There is thus an awareness of what should be done, but implementation naturally takes time.

IS strategy research thus faces new challenges. We should now be able to see where the next competitive advantage is to be found. The building of a good IS entity is already in progress in companies, as well as the construction of interorganizational links. In many organizations, internal processes have also been made essentially more effective. In a sense, IS becomes more uniform in companies, as everyone has similar systems at their disposal. At the same time, public services are being constructed in communications, for example, and this helps the standardization process.

Now seems to be an opportune time for true intuitive thinking, with which we search for opportunities to make ourselves different from others. This work requires interactive, participative planning. We have arrived at a situation where IT is used to such an extent that it is no longer easy to differentiate oneself through it. Consequently, differentiation has to be realized through people's skills—in other words, what we actually do with systems.

REFERENCES

Allen, T.J., and Scott Morton, M.S., 1994, *Information Technology and the Corporation of the 1990s: Research Studies*, Oxford University Press, Oxford.

Argyris, C., 1990, *Overcoming Organizational Defenses: Facilitating Organizational Learning*, Allyn and Bacon, a Division of Simon & Schuster, Inc., Needham Heights, MA.

Argyris, C., Putnam, R. and McLain Smith, D., 1985, *Action Science*, Jossey-Bass Publishers.

Auer, T., Ruohonen M. and Reponen T., 1993, Joint Learning as a Solution to Create Implementable Information Systems Strategies, Proceedings: 16th Information Systems Research Seminar in Scandinavia, Copenhagen, 7–10 August, 770–781.

Auer, T. and Ruohonen, M., 1994, Organizational Maturity in the Context of IS Management and Use. Proceedings: Information Resources Management Association International Conference, IDEA Group Publishing.

Carlsson, C., 1993, Knowledge Formation in Strategic Management, in C. Carlsson (ed.), *Knowledge Formation in Management Research*, IAMSR, Abo Akademi.

Checkland, P., 1991, From Framework through Experience to Learning: The Essential Nature of Action Research, in: H.E. Nissen, H.K. Klein and R. Hirschheim (eds.), *Information Systems Research*, North-Holland.

Ciborra, C., 1994, The Grassroots of IT and Strategy, in C. Ciborra and T. Jelassi (eds.), *Strategic Information Systems*, Wiley, Chichester.

Dessler, G., 1980, *Organization Theory, Integrating Structure and Behavior*, Prentice-Hall, Englewood Cliffs, N.J.

Earl, M.J., 1989, *Management Strategies for Information Technology*, Prentice Hall, London.

Earl, M., 1990, Approaches to Strategic Information Systems Planning, Proceedings: 11th International Conference on Information Systems, Copenhagen.

Earl, M., 1993, Experiences in Strategic Information Systems Planning, *MIS Quarterly*, 17, March.

Galliers R.D., 1993, IT Strategies: Beyond Competitive Advantage, *Journal of Strategic Information Systems*, 2 (4).

Galliers R.D., Pattison, E.M. and Reponen, T., 1994, Strategic Information Systems Planning Workshops: Lessons From Three Cases, *International Journal of Information Management* 14, 51–66.

Gick, M.L. and Holyoak, K.J., 1983, Schema Induction and Analogical Transfer, *Cognitive Psychology*, 15, 1–38.

Glaser, R., 1984, Education and Thinking: The Role of Knowledge, *American Psychologists*, 39, 93–105.

Johansson, Henry, J., et al, 1993, *Business Process Re-engineering: Breakpoint Strategies for Market Dominance*, John Wiley & Sons, Chichester.

Kim, D.H., 1993, The Link Between Individual and Organizational Learning, *Sloan Management Review*, Fall, 35 (1).

Langer, E.J., 1985, Playing the Middle Against Both Ends: The Usefulness of Adult Cognitive Activity in Childhood and Old Age, in S.R.Yussen (ed.), *The Growth of Reflection in Children*, Academic Press, New York.

Light, Paul, H., Mevarech, Z.R. and Zemira R., 1992, *Cooperative Learning with Computers: An Introduction, Learning and Instruction*, 2.

Mintzberg, H., 1978, Patterns in Strategy Formation, *Management Science*, 24 (9), 934–948.

Mintzberg, H., 1989, Strategy Formation: Ten Schools of Thought, in J. Fredricson (ed.), *Prospectus on Strategic Management*, Ballinger, New York.

Mintzberg, H., 1990, The Design School: Reconsidering the Basic Premises of Strategic Management, *Strategic Management Journal*, 11, 171–195.

Nisbett, R. and Ross, L., 1980, *Human Interface: Strategies and Shortcomings of Social Judgement*, Prentice Hall, Englewood Cliffs.

Perkins, D.N., 1985, The Fingertip Effects: How Information-Processing Technology Shapes Thinking, *Educational Researcher*, 14, 11–28.

Remenyi, D.S.I., 1991, *Introducing Strategic Information Systems Planning*, NCC Blackwell Limited.

Reponen, T., 1989, Aligning Information Systems Strategy to Business Strategy, Case Finnpap, Liiketaloudellinen Aikakausikirja 4/89, Helsinki, 360–373.

Reponen, T., 1990, *Information Systems Strategy Evolution Process. A Case Example*, Turku School of Economics and Business Administration, Discussion and Working Papers Series, 8.

Reponen, T., 1992, The Role of Information Technology, in M. Jahnukainen and A.P.J. Vepsäläinen (eds.), *Joining the Global Race: Redesign of Business Processes and Logistic Capabilities*, Publications of the Helsinki School of Economics, Series F, 20–26.

Reponen, T., 1993, Information Management Strategy—an Evolutionary Process, *Scandinavian Journal of Management*, 9 (3), 189–209.

Reponen, T., 1993, Outsourcing or Insourcing?, Proceedings: International Conference on Information Systems (ICIS), Orlando, Florida, December 5–8.

Reponen, T., 1993, Strategic Information Systems—a Conceptual Analysis, *The Journal of Strategic Information Systems*, 2 (2), 100–105.

Reponen, T., 1994, Organizational Information Management Strategies, *Journal of Information Systems*, 4, 27–44.

Reponen, T., Wood-Harper, T., and von Hellens, L., 1992, Action Research as a Bridge between Academic World and Business Life, manuscript, The Turku School of Economics Business Administration.

Romer, P.M., 1990, Endogenous Technological Change, *Journal of Political Economy*, 98 (5), 71–103.

Salomon, G. and Globerson, T., 1987, Skill May Not Be Enough: The Role of Mindfulness in Learning and Transfer, *International Journal of Educational Research*, 11, Pergamon Press, 623–638.

Senge, P.M., 1990, *The Fifth Discipline: The Art and Practice of the Learning Organization*, Century Business.

Wood-Harper, T., 1985, Research Methods in Information Systems: Using Action Research, in E. Mumford, R. Hirschheim, E. Fitzgerald and T. Wood-Harper (eds.), *Research Methods in Information Systems*, North-Holland.

Wood-Harper, T., 1992, Action Learning in Context, in L. von Hellens (ed.), *Action Research in Management information Systems*, Publications of Turku School of Economics, Series A-3.

Part 3
INNOVATION, NETWORKS AND CORPORATE IDENTITY

Having looked at the nature of strategic information systems and the way we communicate and work together in Part 1, followed by a consideration of learning in order to make best use of our IT investments in organizations in Part 2, we now turn to wider questions of innovation, interorganizational systems and IT architectures that may support and enhance an organization's development.

First, in Chapter 7, Johannes Pennings explores the issues of technological innovation by recounting the disruptive impacts that technology can have on organizations. Citing empirical research on the topic, he demonstrates the impacts of IT investments and the time taken for benefits to be felt. Implications for our treatment of measuring the effects of IT initiatives are proposed as a result of Dr Pennings' analysis.

Chapter 8 widens our consideration of the topic of IT and Organizational Change in another dimension, namely interorganizational systems. Here, our understanding of the nature of boundaries between legal corporate entities requires reconsideration given the wide-ranging impacts on such collaborating organizations. In it, Ramon O'Callaghan looks at the question of Electronic Data Interchange (EDI) and provides us with case study evidence of the impacts of this technology on logistics and corporate strategy. As a precursor to Part 4, he also touches on the question of Business Process Re-engineering (BPR), given the need to revisit core processes when introducing systems which cut across organizational boundaries.

Part 3 is brought to a close by a chapter by Walter Baets and V. Venugopal. In it they focus our attention on the different IT architectures that might be utilized to enhance an organization's development potential. Following a review of the existing IT tools that may be used in this way, they go on to develop a conceptual framework of an intelligent system for supporting organizational transformation, and show how such thinking is being used in a large European financial holding.

7
Innovations as Precursors of Organizational Performance

JOHANNES M. PENNINGS
The Wharton School, University of Pennsylvania, USA

INTRODUCTION

In this chapter, we examine the effect of three types of innovations on the performance of commercial banks. Commercial banks constitute a big component of the service sector—a sector whose growth continues to outpace the industrial sector such that more than 80% of the US labor population is now employed in services and less than 20% in manufacturing. The financial services industry is among the fastest growing components of the service sector.

Innovation is crucial for preserving a firm's competitive advantage. In the banking industry we can distinguish various classes of innovations. They include information technology, product innovations and administrative innovations. Information technology is probably the most ostentatious one. The rise of electronic networking, office automation and computerization of service delivery render banks among the most prominent users of information technology. These technologies embody significant investments. Compared to product and administrative innovations, adoption of information technology is costly and difficult to implement. Information technology also alters the architecture of service production and service delivery dramatically. Product innovations are often stand-alone and can be delivered with-

Information Technology and Organizational Transformation. Edited by R.D. Galliers and W.R.J. Baets. © 1998 John Wiley & Sons Ltd

out major intrusions in the organization's functioning. Likewise, many administrative innovations can be implemented without affecting significant parts of the organization.

This chapter describes research that examined the effect of these types of innovations on the bank's bottom line. We asked the question, does it pay to invest in innovations, and if so what is the magnitude of the effects? The results show innovations to have a negative immediate effect on profitability (net income and cash flow), but a more positive effect when we shift the focus to one year later. Apparently the beneficial effects do not materialize until the firm has ironed out the problems. Our research also shows marketing and product innovations to have a positive effect, particularly for banks whose strategy is slanted toward retail banking.

The findings regarding information technology are the most problematic in that the initial drain on earnings is substantial. Over time, benefits do surface, but the results clearly show that organizations investing in information technology should expect delayed benefits. This observation has been made earlier, when authors commented on the impact of electric power replacing steam power during the heydays of the industrial revolution. Information technology requires not only substantial investments, but also a time window that is large enough for the firm to absorb the technology. Innovation is therefore intimately intertwined with organizational learning. The full benefits of information technology might require a time window that far exceeds the 11 years (1977–1987) of this study and, in any event, will be dependent on the firms' ability to manage the benefits.

BACKGROUND

Research on the consequences of innovation is fairly scant—even more so when the focus is on service organizations. Much of the research to date has dealt with manufacturing organizations, and these organizations continue to receive most attention among innovation researchers. Presumably, manufacturing organizations have high levels of capital assets and produce tangible output so that innovations involving capital goods and associated outputs are more visible and tangible, and more amenable to empirical research. Service organizations are labor, rather than capital intensive, and their outputs are abstract, nonphysical and cannot readily be gauged. Compare a cochlea implant, video recorder or chip with community mental care, wine futures trading or debit card services. These innovations not only differ in their sheer tangibility, but the resources necessary for producing them differ likewise with respect to their physical, capital intensive nature.

Yet the manufacturing sector is on the decline in much of the Western world. This decline is demonstrated by changes of the relative proportion in the labor force or share of GNP. Therefore organizational research on service organizations merits more attention, is timely and socially desirable, and will satisfy our need to understand how or whether their performance can be attributed to innovation.

This chapter considers the question of whether innovation is conducive to superior organizational financial performance. The importance of innovation for individuals, organizations and societies has been the centre of debate, yet our knowledge about its role as a precursor of organizational effectiveness has never been fully resolved. Much of the relevant literature deals with antecedents of innovation (e.g. Kamien & Schwartz, 1982; Mohr, 1982; or Scherer, 1982). There is no well-developed theoretical argument, nor is there a well established empirical link between the innovation's costs and benefits.

There is no denying that since the onset of the industrial revolution, social scientists, historians and philosophers have stressed the role of technological advancement in stimulating economic growth and development. Among the early observers Marx and Schumpeter stand out. Marx fulminated against the alienating consequences of technological progress yielding efficiencies at the expense of meaningful relations between humans and their work. Technological change in the means of production leads to a specialization of the workforce and obsolescence of skills, while at the same time providing for more rationalized and more productive systems of production. Schumpeter, in contrast, was more optimistic in his assessment of technological advancement. Innovations and the associated entrepreneurship are the engine which drive societal progress. Entrepreneurs contribute to the creative destruction of existing order, and create the seeds of a higher, more advanced new order, with concomitant additions to the welfare of society and its members.

The contributions of Marx and Schumpeter, however, have limited value for the organization theorist who is interested in the effectiveness and consequences of innovation. They have not only covered a much higher level of analysis, but have also been speculative rather than empirical in their assertions. Yet their work has been a major impetus for organizational research in general, and organizational innovation in particular. This is particularly the case for information technology, whose current "sweep" mirrors the revolutionary impact which the steam engine and later the electric dynamo had on firms, industry and society.

ORGANIZATIONAL INNOVATION

It is beyond the scope of this chapter to review the concept of innovation in an elaborate way. Here, it is treated as an adoption of technology that has performance implications. The adoption can be construed as an event, a "jolt" that ripples through the organization. We could contrast development with diffusion, i.e. whether the innovation adoption involves a first mover, or whether adoption is a manifestation of diffusion of an existing innovation which is still new to the adopting organization. In this chapter we do not make this distinction. However, as we will indicate, some innovations, especially marketing ones, in the services sector can often be copied quickly. For competitive reasons alone, its firms have little choice but to mimic each other's behavior. The implication is such that diffusion of discrete innovations resembles a process of institutionalization (DiMaggio & Powell, 1983) at the industry level of analysis. At the firm level, innovation too can be viewed as either an event or as a process leading up to the event. Here, we treat it as an event, and disregard the sequence of its antecedents.

At the organizational level, industrial economists have examined the performance consequences of R&D expenditures (e.g. Mansfield, 1980; Scherer, 1982; Kamien & Schwartz, 1982). In general the impact of such expenditures on subsequent performance is quite strong and clearly attests to the comparative advantage of firms in investing in R&D. The limitations of these studies, however, is that measurement of innovation is done at a high level of aggregation. A common proxy for innovation is corporate R&D expenditures, or employment of scientists and engineers (e.g. Scherer, 1970).

R&D expenditures cover a myriad of projects, some of which may be totally new, while others may involve some adoption of new ideas developed elsewhere. They are measured at the firm level and therefore present major problems, particularly in highly diversified firms where R&D expenditures cannot be identified with respect to various lines of business. Even in highly specialized, single product firms, R&D expenditures can involve a wide range of activities, some of which never culminate in full commercial application. Furthermore, over time R&D expenditures cannot readily be tied to income streams if the lag is too short, or if the latency from expenditures to actual adoption is extensive. Finally, much of the R&D expenditure literature deals with product innovations, much less with modifications in the manufacturing process. Both types of innovation may have performance advantages. R&D expenditures might not always separate the two, tending not to differentiate between invention and innovation.

Invention can be defined as the creation of a new idea, product, system, structure or procedure, while innovation constitutes its actual adoption, regardless of whether the idea originated inside the organization or was acquired elsewhere. Innovations can then be classified in numerous ways; among the best known typologies are "product" and "process" or technological (e.g. Abernathy & Utterback, 1987), and "technical" and "administrative" (e.g. Daft, 1978). These distinctions are useful for the development of a framework on innovation and performance.

A Framework

Innovation can be viewed as the adoption of an idea which is new to the adopting organization. This may include new products or services, new technologies for producing or delivering the product or service, and new procedures, systems and social arrangements. The emphasis is on ideas which are new to the organization, so that the distinction between invention and innovation can be bypassed; the literature has overwhelmingly converged on innovation (e.g. Daft, 1978). In this chapter we consider adoptions as well.

Innovation Types

We classify adoptions respectively into product, process and administrative innovations. Product innovations involve the introduction of a new product or service, including new applications of existing products, or diffusion to new sets of customers. Process innovations are those that affect the production process in all its ramifications, including the transformation from raw material to end products and all the support activities associated with them. In the service sector, these innovations entail primarily those that we would subsume under the broad label of *information technology*. They include automated teller machines, magnetic code reading, electronic networking and back office automation for example. Administrative innovations are those that involve the administrative component and impact the social system of an organization, which includes social structure or design, rules, procedures, reward and information systems and communication/authority structures that govern the relationships among members.

The relationship between these three types of innovations has been the subject of a considerable amount of debate. Some authors do not distinguish between output (or product) and process innovation, and refer to them both as "technical innovations". These are typically contrasted with "administrative innovations", the prevailing idea being that some balance and complementary lag between the two is imperative (e.g. Daft, 1978). The adoption of information technology will often trigger administrative innovations—for example, adoption of programmable numerical control necessitates formation of autonomous work groups, or performance appraisal systems. Information technology also triggers many product innovations, perhaps because the distinction between the production and delivery of services is overlapping. The client participates in the production of a service so that any process innovation has profound implications for how the client perceives the product, its quality and its delivery. Job-design changes, the creation of a new and stand-alone department and other administrative innovations may conversely facilitate the adoption of programmable automation. Other examples are automotive assembly islands and team structures or prepaid medical care delivery and health maintenance organizations.

Users of the administrative-"technical" distinction skirt the issue of how process innovations relate to product innovations, or whether either of the two relates differently to administrative innovations. There is an increased interest in whether the adoption of product innovations is conditioned by administrative innovations. It has been argued that firms ought to set up "skunk works" (Peters & Waterman, 1982), internal ventures and other local arrangements in order to enhance product innovations (e.g. Burgelman, 1983). Others have pointed to organization-wide administrative innovations, including boundary spanning mechanisms, matrix-like structures, and group-based compensation plans such that a firm's research, sales and manufacturing functions become sufficiently meshed in order to introduce product innovations successfully (Dougherty, 1990). Such alternative administrative changes are illustrated by Ford and General Motors respectively, with the former employing a matrix-like structure for its Taurus car and the latter adopting a stand-alone, internal venture for its Saturn product.

In contrast, the distinction between administrative and product/process innovations seems rather straightforward. They may be mutually conducive for adoption. Several studies show a correlation between these types of innovation (e.g. Damanpour, et al, 1989; Nord & Tucker, 1987). These latter authors found, for example, that technological innovations—e.g. the introduction of the NOW account by commercial banks—will be adopted to the extent that organizations have the administrative capacity to do so. New processes may necessitate the erection of new organizational arrangements (e.g. Pennings & Harianto, 1990) such as liaison roles, team-oriented cost accounting systems and internal corporate ventures. Process and administrative innovations may have unique performance implications, but it is plausible to argue that jointly these implications are even more pronounced.

While it may be fairly easy to distinguish between administrative as against the other two innovation types, it is somewhat problematic for authors like Daft (1978) to separate product innovations from process innovations. Altering, refashioning and automating a production line compared to designing a new product involves wholly different sets of skills and is governed by rather divergent routines. Therefore among engineering-oriented researchers this distinction is well-established now, particularly since the publication of papers by Utterback & Abernathy (1985, 1987). In their developmental model, product and process innovations evolve as successive movements around "musical chairs". When process innovations show diminished productivity or efficiency increments, conditions for new products emerge. The new product will receive growing market acceptance, culminating in a dominant design, but initially remaining still quite expensive and saddled with many design flaws. Eventually the process improvements and associated price reductions stimulate demand until the market is saturated; only those firms which then innovate in their technology can survive the inescapable shake-out, and the musical chair scenario repeats itself. A well-known example is Ford's Model-T, with its subsequent assembly line, illustrating product and process innovations respectively. The two types of innovations can be examined from the producer's standpoint although it is not uncommon to examine process innovations in conjunction with the adopter of capital goods, i.e. the user and product innovations from the producing organization's vantage point.

For innovations to be successful, user acceptance is crucial. Marketing research on consumer behavior has emphasized the factors which explain consumer behavior. In organizational research, the inquiry has typically emphasized product innovations from the producer's standpoint and process innovation from the user's standpoint. Compare innovations such as CAD/CAM versus compact disk. The former are typically researched in conjunction with manufacturing organizations, while the latter involves inquiries such as competitive timing, lateral engineering, licensing, product standardization, and so forth. These somewhat gross generalizations are analogous to "market push" and "market pull" respectively, (e.g. Braun & McDonald, 1982; Urban & von Hippel, 1988). In recent times such distinctions are not very tenable, particularly among service organizations where distinctions between product and process innovations are blurred.

Manufacturing versus Service Organizations

For manufacturing organizations where the production process is sharply segregated from the recipients of outputs, product-process distinctions appear very useful. Except for some capital goods markets, the customer has little awareness of the technology required to produce the output. In contrast, service organization clients are often intimately exposed to the rendering of outputs, and might be drawn into the role of co-producer. In the service sector the distinction might therefore be less adequate. Service firms typically integrate the customer into the service rendering and delivery process. In libraries customers take the books from the shelves and check them out; in medical centres they interact with physicians and nurses in order to receive medical care; and when visiting a bank branch they communicate with officers to process a loan, or to research the balance of their account. Innovations in these sectors often impart a blend of output and technology transformations. Thus, in libraries patrons have access to computerized, on-line, real-time retrieval systems; in health care patients can purchase pregnancy or disease detection kits and abortion medication. Banking has introduced credit cards and smart cards, automated teller machines and home banking, again illustrating innovations that embrace both the production of a service and the use function for its customer. The role of the recipient can vary on dimensions, such as amount of contact with the organization, degree of delegation of service production or the amount of time the customer is included in the organization. Yet the very dimensions of these product innovations are very much conditioned by the process through which they are generated.

The implications of these observations are profound. Information technology innovations, for example, may foster product or service differentiation, alter the distribution logistics of the firm and render certain established products obsolete. On the other hand, product innovations such as the pregnancy testing kit and home banking can result in extensive cost savings and other process improvements, and might result in the partial elimination of out-patient clinics or retail bank branches respectively.

Innovation and Performance

The relationship between innovation and performance also merits reflection. Performance may either be a precursor to or the result of innovation. For example, the adoption decision may be triggered by a so called "performance gap" (Daft, 1978; Zaltman, et al, 1973), the implication being that adoption satisfies a specific unmet need. In other cases superior performance generates slack, which allows an organization to experiment with new ideas, while inferior performance makes an organization austere and less amenable to experimentation. When considered jointly, the three types of innovation may differ in the way they impact on performance. The effect may be deferred, depending on how long it takes for the adoption to have an impact, if any. It is conceivable that process and administrative innovations are prone to having a more immediate effect. Product innovations entail some level of diffusion among customers and are therefore partially contingent on factors beyond the control of the organization. The innovation's impact should be isolated in order to determine its latency. Here, both the individual and joint effects of different innovation events are explored.

The rationale for innovation to affect performance is ill-understood. The Boston Consulting Group has popularized the growth-share matrix with the well-known postulate that firms need to preserve their long term profitability by balancing their portfolio. Some established, mature products generate a stable earnings stream, part of which can be diverted to finance new projects that provide for future cashflow. Firms should upgrade their product offerings since, following the product life-cycle notion, the decline of older products should be off-set by newer, emerging products. Innovating firms are more likely to avert obsolescence of their product offerings. They do so by broadening their existing product offerings, or by redesigning existing products. By way of pertinent illustration, in the financial services sector, commercial banks have realized that the conventional bread and butter services of loans and deposits have become a near-commodity, and that alternative ventures such as home banking, credit and debit cards, retail brokerage and mutual funds might forestall decline and even organizational mortality.

While organizations have little choice in generating new products, they also face major risk in their quest for innovation. Estimates of failure rates have ranged from 30 to 60% (e.g. Mansfield 1977). In the service industry the risks might even be higher since imitation can be done precipitously. One would expect innovators to resemble "hares", rather than "turtles" (Pennings, 1993). The implication is that unlike many industrial firms, many service sector firms may earn profits which are disproportionate to their cost of innovation.

Fairly recently, evidence on the innovation-performance relationship has been provided by Chaney, Devinney & Winer (1989). These authors explored the presence of abnormal stock returns as a function of the announcement of a firm's new product. This event history research is analogous to other studies which employ the capital asset pricing model for identifying a stock price's sensitivity to unusual events such as an acquisition, sudden executive succession or an abrupt increase in corporate earnings. The detection of abnormal returns in the case of new product announcement is extraordinary because unlike precipitous incidents such as an executive's death, press releases announcing a new product would appear to be superfluous. Knowledgeable external observers have already anticipated major new product development activities, while its announced realization signals already a high probability of success, compared to innovations that await full realization. In spite of this caveat, the presence of the observed effect is significant as the study is the first of its kind in relating product innovations to performance.

Information technology has performance implications, and this too has been spelled out through simple, parsimonious concepts, particularly that of organizational learning. When firms expand investments in technology, they often enjoy diminished costs per unit, partly because the firm has been able to fine tune its routines in producing the good or service (Cohen & Levinthal, 1990). Finally, administrative innovations are not only necessary for the successful implementation of product and process innovations, but also for enhanced rationalization of the process. A study by Damanpour, Szabat & Evan (1989) regarding public libraries showed administrative innovations to have a positive correlation with performance in a later time period (as well as with "technical" innovations); performance was measured by circulation as a proportion of inventory.

Ultimately, the adoption decision is a matter of expected returns. For example, if a service innovation increases a firm's income stream, or information technology investments enhance productivity and efficiency, the incentive for innovation is bound to be strong. However, when the expected benefits are dubious, the adoption decision is more difficult to justify. When the adoption of product innovation necessitates the adoption of process and administrative innovations, conditions arise which render the adoption more radical and considerably more uncertain. The more radical the innovation, the lower the adoption probability, and the higher the chance of failure.

The significance of administrative innovations is more enigmatic, and theoretically speaking, even less well developed. Apart from the debate on the so-called structural lag, in which organizations require extra time to catch up with information technology innovations, there appears not to be general awareness of the issue. Presumably, organizational innovation *per se* is disruptive, transforms the use of current routines, evokes anxiety, stress and distraction and could therefore have a deleterious effect on performance. However, changes in organizational routines are often induced by some unmet need—for example, a novel personnel training programme, the merging of two complementary departments, or adoption of a new compensation system. Their adoption should therefore promote individual or corporate performance, particularly after the organization has been able to absorb the adoption's disruptive effects.

PERFORMANCE IMPLICATIONS OF BANKING INNOVATIONS

Here these issues are examined with respect to the banking industry in the United States. Particularly in this sector we witness the simultaneous rather than sequential occurrence of process and product innovations. This phenomenon is manifest in the adoption of information technology, which pervades both the processing of transaction activities and the creation of new services. True, there are still product innovations whose adoption did not require process innovations, or vice versa. For example, banks have refashioned cheque clearing procedures to reduce their lost availability (i.e. the opportunity costs associated with the "float" whenever cheques against other banks are not processed sooner). Likewise, numerous product innovations among banks have been extensive; they range from asset management, NOW accounts, small gift inducements and certificates of deposit. Similarly decentralization of back room operations and formation of interstate banking structures amount to administrative innovations that in themselves had no direct connection with process and product innovations. These innovations are comparatively trivial compared with those involving information technology, whose arrival in the financial services sector has been phenomenal (e.g. *The Economist*, 1989); Mohr (1987) refers to a micro-electronic "sweep."

As implied earlier, information technology innovations have both process and product elements. Consider for example automated teller machines (ATM) or smart cards, which could be labeled as product innovations, yet these very adoptions do not exclusively represent opportunities for product differentiation, increased customer deposits and occasions for cross selling. Obviously, computer based information and telecommunication technologies have been major ingredients in a bank's ability significantly to expand the scope and competitiveness of its services. They furnish new opportunities for product differentiation and market segmentation. However, these very same innovations also provide many opportunities for process improvements as indicated by the time reduction for processing a transaction, by diminishing the number of transactional errors, or by the abatement of slack human resources. Indeed, the very elements for product differentiation and service expansion have created major improvements in processing banking services that have enabled banks to cope with increases in data processing; increases which are huge by 1970 standards (*The Economist*, 1989), while accumulating slack for new marketing strategies.

The conventional wisdom, as portrayed in *The Economist* (1989) suggests that the above mentioned "sweep" does not allow banks much discretion as regards the extent of their innovation. Failure to join the bandwagon with respect to IT innovation is a strategic necessity, rather than a move to implement advantageous competitive choices. A bank would isolate itself if it were to refrain from joining an ATM network. Increased interdependence in financial transactions requires a merging of their hardware and the elimination of incompatible software features. Banks parallel airlines, trading services and insurance firms in adopting new technologies to manage their interdependencies. Such interdependencies also create conditions that are optimal for copying innovations, which are easy to imitate in the service industry as we have seen before. The implication is that innovation benefits might vary from those of the manufacturing sector.

The mere fact that imitations are abundant renders diffusion of innovation in the financial sector prototypical of "institutional isomorphism" (DiMaggio & Powell, 1983). Widespread mimicking suggests that first mover advantages might be small, that adoption is motivated not only for the quest of product or service differentiation but also for signaling conformity to widely held beliefs about banking services. The technological networking of banking services through micro-electronic resources fosters inter-firm communication and co-ordination and augments the rise of institutional isomorphism.

The *American Banker* (1987) estimates that the banking system will save between $6 to $8 million per year if only 50% of wholesale cheques were to be transacted electronically. Due to float reductions, there could be cost and time savings for the customer as well; in the aggregate, these amount to tens of billions of dollars, but ironically these efficiency improvements do not translate into incentives for banks. These organizations stand to forgo sizable amounts of revenue if paper mediated transactions are substituted by electronically mediated transactions. It is one manifestation of how the arrival of information technology is affecting the shape of today's financial market place.

Following this discussion on various types of innovations and their adoptions' performance implications, we will now present the empirical findings arising from our research. The findings involve product, process and administrative innovations. It is hypothesized that the rate of adoption in each of these innovation classes is conducive to organizational performance. Product innovations improve revenue, process innovations diminish the costs for generating revenue and administrative innovations might improve revenue through more customer-responsive structures and procedures, or by refashioning the internal efficiency enhancing social arrangements. However, this latter class of innovations might also affect performance negatively, as we have seen.

Research Methodology

The Sample

The hypotheses were tested with a set of 125 banks, drawn from a list of approximately 250 banks as reported by *The American Banker*. This listing includes most of the larger banks, many of which have both consumer and commercial banking operations. The loss of observations is due to several factors. Since the data collection window comprises 11 years, several banks disappeared from the listing as a result of mergers, acquisitions and death. Others were deleted due to lack of data. The sampling proceeded retroactively, where as many banks as possible were included. Some reduction in loss of data was accomplished by interpolation of missing firm years. Great effort was expended here to have as many observations as possible. Over 20% of the observations had to be deleted because two or three firms' years on a particular variable were missing. In the event a single year observation was absent, it was filled through interpolation or extrapolation.

The data cover the period 1977–1987 and originate from various sources. They include *Predicast Index, The American Banker, FDIC Directories, Moody's Financial Directories, Annual Reports* and *Electronic Fund Transfer Directories*, complemented with telephone interviews among about 30% of the firms involved. Additional information is reported in Pennings & Harianto (1990).

The Design

Cross-sectional pooled time series regression was conducted. Two dependent variables were sequentially examined on their susceptibility to innovation. The model included three innovation variables, as well as several organizational and environmental variables. Additionally, 124 dummy variables to control for firm-specific correlates of performance were included in the estimation. This procedure yields results that are conceptually similar to aggregating the regression effects from each of the 125 banks. Both the simultaneous and lagged effects of innovation on performance have been examined. Since the causal model may not apply to all banks in the sample, results on subsets will be presented as well.

The Variables

Figure 7.1 presents a listing of the variables, their measurement and their source. As indicated, the data originate from a variety of sources.

The innovation variables represented cumulative frequency of adoptions of any of the three types, i.e. process, product and administrative innovations. As we have argued, since customers are often co-producers of the services rendered, process innovations have profound implications for how the customer perceives or uses the services. Therefore, process innovations in banking include a significant marketing dimension and are often highly visible in the packaging of existing products in a novel way. Product or marketing innovations include new financial services as well as implementation of new marketing instruments such as promotion campaigns, distribution channels and advertising. For the sake of classification we exclude innovations involving micro-electronics, which are relegated to the class of process innovation. This permits us to explore the relative significance of innovations with and without a micro-electronic component. Process innovations comprise those involving hardware, software and telecommunications, and might also constitute major elements in a bank's delivery of transaction services. Finally, administrative innovations comprise reorganizations, adoption of new compensation plans or employee training programmes. Examples include the following:

Product (and Marketing) Innovations
- Undertakes major image-building ad campaign following recent renaming.
- Offers financial futures advisory services, including new client data.
- Opens branch exclusively for small business customers.
- Offers discount brokerage services through Fidelity Brokerage Service.

IT Innovations
- Continental Illinois jointly links automatic teller operations for nationwide banking.

Variable	Description
Performance:	
Profitability	net income after interest and taxes (NIAT) (Annual Report)
Cashflow	actual cashflows + loan loss provision and depreciation (Annual Report)
Innovation:	
Product and marketing	cumulative number of product and service innovations (Predicast Index, 1977–1988)
Administrative	cumulative number of structural, procedure and system innovations (Predicast Index, 1977–1988)
Information Technology	cumulative number of telecommunication and computer hardware/software innovations (Predicast Index, 1977–1988)
Organization: Consumer Loans Strategy	ratio of consumer loans to total loan portfolio (Annual Report)
Size	size of bank as measured by log of total assets (Annual Report)
Diversification	scope of services (Moody's, 1978–1988)
Debt-equity ratio	financial leverage (Annual Report)
Environmental:	
State banks	log (number of banks in the state) (FDIC, 1977–1988)
State deposits	log ($ consumer loans in the state) (FDIC, 1977–1988)

Figure 7.1 *Description of the Variables*

- Wang Laboratories' word processing network improves information flow.
- Renews commitment to consumer banking with new POS services for retailers.
- New electronic settlement service to allow paperless deposits.

Administrative Innovations
- Beneficial offers executive termination protection to 250 officials.
- Commerce Bankshares cuts holdings to 26 banks by switching state-chartered banks to national charters.
- Aims to control health care costs by using Health Wise Program.
- Will consolidate its 11 banks under the same name and logo.

The organizational and environmental variables are included to control for factors which traditionally have been associated with innovation research (e.g. Bantel & Jackson, 1990) or which are important correlates of performance (e.g. Scherer, 1970).

Results

Table 7.1 provides descriptive statistics on the sample of 125 commercial banks during the 11 year period. By way of comparison several macro-economic indicators are included as well. Table 7.1 shows that changes in stock prices, interest rate and inflation follow conventional business cycles, with indications of the onset of a recession in 1987. By 1985 several of the multi-national banks initiated extensive write-offs of Third World debt. While only a comparatively small proportion of banks in the sample had far-reaching involvement in Third World borrowing, in the aggregate they suppress the earnings of the financial services sector as indicated in this sample.

The entries in Table 7.1 are intended to provide a developmental picture of the US banking industry against the backdrop of the US economy. Within this window, the presence of business cycles is clearly discernible. For example, inflation is relatively high during the years 1978–1981 after which it begins to drop toward a very low level in 1986. The US T-bill rate is a proxy for risk-free investment return which typically lags inflation by one or two years.

Without imputing causality, it can be pointed out that commercial banks witness major losses at the end of this 11 year window. Net income after tax (NIAT) is on the average −30%. This loss can be attributed to the large reserves that some banks have set aside to finance "non-performing assets"—a euphemism for loans to Third World countries that are unlikely to be repaid. The aggregate increase in loss

Table 7.1 Summary Statistics of Economic Conditions during the Period Observed

	BANKING INDUSTRY							THE ECONOMY		
YEAR	IT	Admin	Product	NIAT	Cashflow	Losspr	ROE	S&P 500	US T-Bill	Inflation
1977	0.0726	0.0726	0.0323	28.620	51.016	15.914	13.34%	−7.18%	5.12%	6.77%
1978	0.0323	0.0484	0.0161	35.407	58.446	16.070	12.63%	6.56%	7.18%	9.03%
1979	0.0081	0.0565	0.0484	42.337	66.445	16.413	13.48%	18.44%	10.38%	13.31%
1980	0.0242	0.2177	0.0403	45.357	73.659	19.677	12.82%	32.42%	11.24%	12.40%
1981	0.0726	0.1129	0.0242	48.328	80.919	22.168	11.89%	−4.91%	14.71%	8.94%
1982	0.0565	0.2581	0.0565	53.205	100.02	34.845	12.44%	21.41%	10.54%	3.87%
1983	0.0645	0.1694	0.0323	61.355	117.76	41.052	11.94%	22.51%	8.80%	3.80%
1984	0.1210	0.2258	0.0645	60.207	143.52	63.912	11.74%	6.27%	9.85%	3.95%
1985	0.0887	0.2984	0.1210	80.670	193.20	86.562	13.20%	32.16%	7.72%	3.77%
1986	0.0887	0.3871	0.2903	84.047	226.80	114.00	12.76%	18.47%	6.16%	1.13%
1987	0.1935	0.4435	0.5242	−30.02	235.01	232.06	1.768%	5.23%	5.47%	4.41%

provisions is particularly noticeable during the years 1986 and 1987. These increases are concentrated in the large, multi-national banks which had altered their strategy during the late 1970s; they had diversified away from retail banking and other domestic business activities.

The three measures of innovations represent the average number of adoptions per year, while the four financial measures—net income after taxes (NIAT), cashflow, provisions for non-performing loans and return on equity (ROE)—are ratios. Both NIAT and ROE show 1987 to be a dismal year, but as the cashflow and loan-loss provision variables suggest, the declining productivity should be attributed to depreciation. If their performance is gauged by cashflow, these firms enjoyed a stellar year. In the analysis to be reported both profitability and cashflow variables were included.

Table 7.2 presents the results of the time series regression analysis. For obvious reasons, the results indicate the effect of innovation on performance while controlling for firm-specific trends. The effects of the dummy variables are not included. The results pertain to net income after taxes (NIAT) and cashflow. In addition to the simultaneous effects, we include also the one year lagged effects of the three types of innovation. The analysis is conducted to determine whether innovations will result in superior performance.

For the non-lagged analysis, the results show that the NIAT coefficients for IT and administrative innovations are negative, and highly significant ($p < .001$). Similar results were obtained when the innovation variables are lagged one year. As suggested before, NIAT may not be a good measure of performance, and the window of 1977–1987 may not be an optimal time period, as many banks set aside huge reserves to shield themselves against defaulting Third World debts.

The next two columns of Table 7.2 present the results with cashflow as the dependent variable. As mentioned before, cashflow measures net income plus depreciation and loan loss provisions. This performance indicator may be superior since these latter two additions represent accounting or non-cash charges. The results are much more in line with the hypothesis: IT innovations have a positive effect on performance. When the lagged effects are considered the administrative innovation variable also turns positive, although it is not significant.

More enigmatic is the result involving product innovations. The effects are weak, negative and/or insignificant, except for the cashflow analysis, where the findings are consistent with expectations. This in itself is not conclusive. An interaction effect involving product innovations and level of consumer loans proportion is also examined in the model. This interaction effect is strong, positive and highly significant, for both net profits and cashflow (with $p < .001$ and $.01$ respectively).

Table 7.2 *Pooled Cross-Sectional Time Series Regression of Financial Performance Dependent Variable: Net Income (Model 2.1 and 2.2) after Taxes and Cashflow (Model 2.3 and 2.4)*

	Model 2.1 Current	Model 2.2 One-Year Lag	Model 2.3 Current	Model 2.4 One-Year Lag
Independent Variables				
Intercept	−574.59***	−621.71***	−273.41+	−360.02*
	(160.07)	(182.28)	(162.56)	(173.13)
Process Innovations	−53.63***	−69.78***	99.22***	81.84***
	(9.77)	(11.47)	(10.21)	(11.49)
Administrative Innovations	−63.00***	−38.94***	−37.99***	7.396
	(6.32)	(7.702)	(6.59)	(7.705)
Product Innovations	11.41	−21.29+	−21.59	30.97**
	(16.53)	(11.36)	(17.24)	(11.35)
Organizational Attributes				
Consumer Loans	30.47	8.322	262.19***	470.08***
	(63.87)	(86.59)	(66.30)	(84.98)
Size	196.12***	206.44***	74.33***	85.36***
	(27.24)	(31.25)	(22.44)	(22.78)
Diversification	−19.28	−9.470	−0.0449	−1.735
	(62.96)	(69.89)	(65.85)	(70.23)
Debt Equity Ratio	−1.44	−1.843	1.693	20.025
	(1.97)	(2.391)	(2.058)	(2.400)
Environmental Attributes				
State Banks	−0.0884+	−0.1123+	−0.119*	−0.08166
	(0.0456)	(0.05362)	(0.0476)	(0.05380)
State Deposts	−0.000257+	−0.000647***	0.00196**	0.002312***
	(0.000133)	(0.0001706)	(0.000135)	(0.0001631)
Interaction				
Product* Consumer loans	71.76	108.49**	278.34***	189.79***
	(75.67)	(39.47)	(78.85)	(38.87)
N (firm years)	1364	1240	1364	1240

Note:(1) Significance Levels: $= p < .10$; * $p < .05$; ** $p < .01$; *** $p < .001$

Commercial banks gravitating toward consumer banking and higher frequencies of product and marketing innovations display disproportionate high degrees of profitability and cashflow.

Table 7.3 presents comparable results for net income after taxes when seven commercial banks with heavy loan losses are omitted from the

Table 7.3   Polled Cross-Sectional Time Series Regression of Financial
Performance Dependent Variable: Net Income after Taxes [Excluding banks
with heavy losses]

Independent Variables	
Intercept	−353.90***
	(182.28)
Process Innovations	−7.000
	(6.404)
Administrative Innovations	−7.735*
	(3.220)
Product Innovations	−83.45***
	(8.228)
Organizational Attributes	
Consumer Loans	−10.05
	(21.77)
Size	120.14***
	(9.655)
Diversification	−3.136
	(20.96)
Debt-Equity Ratio	−0.700
	(0.659)
Environmental Attributes	
State Bank	−0.0784***
	(0.0191)
State Deposits	−0.000116*
	(0.0000575)
Interaction	
Product* Consumer Loans	361.91***
	(33.42)
N = 1288	

Note: (1) Significance Levels: $£ = p < .10$; $* \ p < .05$; $** \ p < .01$; $*** \ p < .001$
(2) Standard errors are in parentheses

data set. This sample reduction was predicated on the assumption that
the causal relationship between innovation and performance might not
apply to these large multi-national banks; the effects in Model 2.1 and
2.2. may be skewed by banks saddled with extensive Third World debts
and comparatively small emphasis on retail banking, where the reli-
ance on IT is comparatively more prominent. Thus exogenous
conditions in the period 1985–1987 in developing countries render our
results biased. Clearly, by omitting these seven banks the regression
analysis results of net profit after taxes are consistent with the hypoth-

eses, provided we assume a one year lag. The effect of administrative innovations is not significant however. The removal of banks with heavy loan loss provisions, and *ipso facto* the deletion of several of the more innovating banks has the effect of diminishing the variance in innovation. Innovation frequency is Poisson distributed and a decrease of significance levels is to be expected in Table 7.3.

Finally, it may be noted that organizational size has a positive and significant effect on performance. Larger banks enjoy economies of scale and scope and therefore enjoy disproportionately higher levels of performance. In the case of cashflow the effect is larger when the analysis is lagged by one year. In contrast, environmental attributes have only a minor effect. Number of competing banks and level of state deposits are proxies for competition and size of demand, but they appear to have some negative effect. As with the earlier cases the effects are stronger when the performance variables are lagged.

DISCUSSION

The research described in this chapter has attempted to identify the performance impact of three types of innovation in the financial services sector. It found innovation adoption to have a positive effect on two financial performance indicators, although the expected effect was most pronounced for product and IT adoptions. Administrative innovations tended to have a small effect if the sample was adjusted for period idiosyncratic or firm idiosyncratic elements.

It should be pointed out that we aggregated innovation adoption events for each year. Unlike R&D expenditures, these adoption events are more immediate to the subsequent outcomes, particularly those that are within the control of the focal organization. Most notable are IT and administrative innovations. In several cases more than one innovation event in a particular year materialized; their separate effects were not analyzed, but it can be assumed that in such cases the effects on performance are equally likely.

With so many events, and a sample of 125 organizations, it would be interesting to examine the interaction effects between the three types of events, particularly because it would furnish a more robust test of what Damanpour, et al, 1989 call "technological lag." Such analysis is not practical here, but could certainly be explored in case studies which resolve the question of whether a firm's capacity to adopt IT is conditioned by its administrative proclivity. IT has altered the vertical and horizontal relationships between people groups and departments, and it is therefore obvious that ensuing social changes are forthcoming. IT pushes the formation of a "virtual organization" (*Business Week*, 1993) and the rise of horizontal networking, thereby eroding the jobs of managers (Kanter, 1989).

The results are limited to financial returns, not so-called "social" returns which are probably significant (Mansfield, 1977). Social returns include improved quality of service, customer satisfaction, and cost and time savings for banking customers. In view of the earlier distinction between product and process innovation and the associated role of being a producer or user of innovation, it would be most desirable to determine these social returns. These returns might be at variance with the firms' returns because, as we have seen, the diffusion of micro-electric technology may generate customer savings which occur at the expense of their banks, for example, the float elimination.

The moderate, but delayed effect of IT innovations suggests that there are considerable advantages for banks in the adoption of new technology. Many banks have been laggards, postponing the acquisition of hardware and software. As the popular business press (e.g. *The Economist*, 1989) has pointed out, banks have little choice in whether or not to adopt such new technology. It is equally clear that new technology has generated surplus earnings for those banks which do. This new technology provides not only private returns to the bank, but also enhances the bank's ability to differentiate its products. While these externalities were not included in the examination of IT innovations, it is plausible to assume that they are prevalent.

We should also emphasize that IT investments are surrounded by a productivity paradox (compare David, 1990). Many people have been disappointed with the computer revolution and the emergent "information age", as the financial or productivity benefits have not materialized in a way that technical progress would imply. The implementation of IT innovations takes time, and time compression is often neither feasible nor desirable (Dierickx & Cool, 1989). Organizations learn over time, and the implementation of IT innovations represents a form of learning: "learning by using". This learning by using has been amply demonstrated with the introduction of steam power and electric dynamo. Designing interfaces between the human organization and these technologies requires experimentation and calibration. There are, of course, important differences between steam power and IT. Information flows much more freely, both in the manufacturing and service sector (compare *The Economist*, 1994). The interface between man and computer is also much more subtle, tacit and complex. Mapping IT onto economic benefits might be tenuous. Its costs are also difficult to isolate. Information flows are subject to bottlenecks, overload perhaps because information is free, travels freely and multiplies freely. The required screening by employees, customers and managers of high quantities of information taxes their cognitive individual and collective capacity. The structures and procedures that are created to diffuse and screen information present challenges that we are only now beginning to comprehend.

Product innovation effects seem more unequivocal. An interesting result was the strong positive interaction effect of consumer loan proportion and product innovations. If we view the first variable as a proxy for the bank's market strategy, we may conclude innovation benefits are contingent on strategy. Even for the largest of commercial banks, the return from the Third World debt experience has resulted in the retrenchment toward retail banking, but some of them continue to be comparatively less involved in consumer business. They stand to gain less from the diffusion of product innovations. Indeed it is among the more heavily oriented retail firms that we see the profound benefits of product innovations.

The findings regarding administrative innovation remain somewhat enigmatic. Some would question whether drastic reorganizations and other administrative changes deserve the label innovation. Some reorganizations might have been triggered by poor financial conditions, motivated by the desire to avert decline or even bankruptcy. The negative effect of administrative innovation could thus be interpreted as steps for arresting the decline of financial losses. In the absence of more qualitative information this remains highly speculative, however.

It goes without saying that a full examination of administrative innovations has to be examined in conjunction with IT innovation. The arrival of computers, local area networks and human-computer interfaces requires considerable reorganization, with changes in the design, control and reward systems. The emergence of the *virtual organization* with its networking, mutuality and trust among the interdependent actors has been facilitated by the arrival of IT. Banks, along with construction firms, publishing houses and film producers appear to be the very first firms that had virtual features. Joint ventures, clearing houses and electronic consortia induced banks into networking to coordinate their interfirm relationships. This networking is now extended to suppliers and clients. It renders boundaries between banks more permeable. Boundaries among units within the bank also become permeable, with widespread information availability among departments and levels. In short, the arrival of IT reverberates throughout the banks and their external relationships. The implication is that IT creates pressures to reconfigure organizational structure and other design elements.

In this chapter an important service industry was examined. The financial services sector is a prominent component in western economies, and understanding the role of innovation for improved financial and social returns will become an increasingly important concern. Unlike in manufacturing, in many service industries R&D expenditure is absent or minimal. Traditional industrial settings have yielded insights about innovation and performance which have therefore little relevance for the service industry. The study of diffusion of innovations acquires additional significance. We trust that this chapter has shown that innovation returns in the service industry can be substantial.

ACKNOWLEDGMENT

This research has been supported by National Science Foundation grant # SES 8909674. Leng Kean Meng provided research assistance in data collection and data analysis.

REFERENCES

Abernathy, W. and Utterback, J. 1987, 'Patterns of technological innovation,' *Technology Review*, 80, 40–47.
American Banker 1977–1988 *Annual Survey*. Washington D.C. The American Banker.
Bantel, K. A. and Jackson, S. E. Top Management and Innovations in Banking: Does the Composition of the Top Team Make a Difference? *Strategic Management Journal*. Summer 1989, 10, 107–124.
Ben-Zion, U., 1984, The R&D and Investment Decision and its Relationship to the Firm's Market Value: some Preliminary Results, in Z. Griliches (ed.) *R&D, Patents and Productivity*, Chicago: University of Chicago Press, 299–312.
Braun, E. and MacDonald, S., 1982, *Revolution in Miniature*, Cambridge: Cambridge University Press.
Burgelman, R. A., Managing the New Venture Division: Research Findings and Implications for Strategic Management. *Strategic Management Journal*. January/March 1985, 6(1), 39–54.
Business Week, 1993, The Virtual Organization, *Business Week*, January 18.
Chaney, P.K., Devinney, T.M. and Winer, R.S., 1989, The Impact of New Product Introductions on the Market Value of the Firms, working paper, Cambridge, MA: Marketing Science Institute.
Cohen, W. M. and Levinthal, D. A. Absorptive Capacity: A New Perspective on Learning and Innovation. *Administrative Science Quarterly*. March 1990, 35(1), 128–152.
Daft, R. L., 1978, A dual core model of organizational innovation, *Academy of Management Journal*, 21, 1978, 193–210.
Damanpour, F., Szabat, K.A. and Evan, W.M., 1989, The Relationship between Types of Innovation and Organizational Performance, *Journal of Management Studies*, 26, 587–601.

David, P.A., 1990, The Dynamo and the Computer: an Historical Perspective on the Modern Productivity Paradox, *American Economic Review*, papers and proceedings, 355–361.

Dierickx, I., Cool, K. and Barney, J. B. Asset Stock Accumulation and Sustainability of Competitive Advantage: Comment; Reply. *Management Science*. December 1989, 35(12), 1504–1514.

DiMaggio, P. and Powell, W. W. 1983 The iron-cage revisited: Institutional isomorphism and collective rationality in organizational fields. *American Sociological Review* 48: 147–160.

Dougherty, D. Understanding New Markets for New Products. *Strategic Management Journal*. Summer 1990, 11, 59–78.

The Economist, 1989, Metamorphosis: a Survey of International Banking, *The Economist*, March 25.

Erickson, G. and Jacobson, R., 1989, Gaining Comparative Advantage through Discretionary Expenditures: the Return to R&D and Advertising, working paper, Seattle: University of Washington.

Harianto, F. and Pennings, J.M. 1989, Technological Innovations Through Interfirm Linkages, in L. Gomes and M. L. Lawless (eds) *Managing the High-Technology Firm*. Greenwich, CT: JAI Press.

Harianto, F. and Pennings, J.M., 1990, Technological Innovations Through Interfirm Linkages, in L. Gomes and M. L. Lawless (eds.), *Strategic Management in High Technology Firms*. Greenwich, CT: JAI Press, 1990, 15–42.

Jaffe, A.B., 1986, Technological Opportunity and Spill Overs of R&D: Evidence from Firms' Patents, Profits and Market Value, *American Economic Review*, 76, 984–1001.

Kamien, M. I. and Schwartz N. L. 1982, *Market Structure and Innovation* New York: Cambridge University Press.

Kanter, R.M., 1989, The New Managerial Work, *Harvard Business Review*, November/December, 85–92.

Mansfield, E., 1977, Social and Private Rates of Return from Industrial Innovations, In E. Mansfield (ed.) *The Production and Appropriation of New Industrial Technology*, New York: Norton, 144–166.

Mansfield, E., 1980, Basic Research and Productivity Increase in Manufacturing, *American Economic Review*, 863–873.

Mohr, L.B., 1982, *Explaining Organizational Behavior*. San Francisco: Jossey Bass.

Mohr, L.B., 1987, Innovation from the Vantage Point of New Electronic Technology in Organizations, in J. M. Pennings and A. Buitendam, (eds.,) *New Technology as Organizational Innovation*, 13–34, Cambridge, MA: Ballinger Publishing.

Nord, W. R. and Tucker, S., 1987, *Implementing routine and radical innovations* Lexington Books:.

Pennings, J.M., 1993, The Strategic Role of Timely Innovations. *Holland Management Review*, 37, 104–111.

Pennings, J.M. and Harianto, F., 1992, The Diffusion of Technological Innovation in the Commercial Banking Industry. *Strategic Management Journal*. January, 13(1), 29–46.

Peters, T.J. and Waterman, R.H., 1982, *In Search of Excellence*, New York: Harper.

Ravenscraft, D. and Scherer, F.M., 1982, The Lag Structure to Research and Development, *Applied Economics*, 14, 603–620.

178 *J.M. Pennings*

Sayrs, L.W., 1989, *Pooled Time Series Analysis*, Newbury Park, CA: Sage.
Scherer, F.M., 1970, *Market Structure and Industrial Performance*, Chicago: RandMcNally.
Scherer, F.M. 1982, Firm Size, Market Structure, Opportunity and the Output of Patented Inventions, *American Economic Review*, 19, 1097–1125.
Urban, G.L. and von Hippel, E., 1988, Lead User Analysis for the Development of New Industrial Products, *Management Science*, 34, 569–582.
Zaltman, G., Duncan, R., and Holbek, J., 1973, *Innovations and Organizations*, New York: Wiley.

8
EDI, Organizational Change and Flexible Strategies

RAMON O'CALLAGHAN
School of Economics, Tilburg University

BACKGROUND

Over the last decade or so, IT applications involving the exchange of information between organizations have proliferated. For many companies, the adoption of such systems has had far reaching effects. These firms have not only redefined their transactions with customers and/or suppliers, but have also undergone significant changes within the organization itself.

Electronic Data Interchange (EDI) is a particular type of interorganizational system that involves the exchange of structured information (typically business documents) between companies, from computer to computer and in a standard format. Interorganizational systems, and EDI in particular, have been reported to have a wide range of impacts on organizations (Barber, 1991; Benjamin, et al, 1990; Buffkin, 1991; Callahan, 1987; Cash et al, 1988; Dearing, 1990; Emmelhainz, 1987, 1991; Gupta & Neel, 1992; Holland, et al, 1992; O'Callaghan, et al, 1992). While EDI obviously affects interorganizational relations, the focus of this chapter is on its *intraorganizational* effects.

At the lowest level, when an EDI transaction is introduced, the first impact is technical. It involves the integration into existing computer applications that must either generate or accept the data. At a higher

Information Technology and Organizational Transformation. Edited by R.D. Galliers and W.R.J. Baets. © 1998 John Wiley & Sons Ltd

level, significant organizational changes are undoubtedly also required. EDI may affect operating procedures and even the definition of how the work is accomplished.

Changes in business processes are the most cited effects of EDI (Callahan, 1987; Emmelhainz, 1987; Gupta & Neel, 1992). Processes must change to conform with EDI messages and to take into account new procedures in communication patterns, report formats, and internal controls. In turn, the shift in the underlying business processes may bring changes in the skills and responsibilities of employees and, in some cases, new roles. There may even be an impact on the basic attitudes that have existed internally, among business functions, which now must work closely together. When used in a key business function, EDI may imply changes not only in skills and organization structure but also in business strategy (Cash & Konsynski, 1985). The impact of EDI can thus ripple through the entire organization.

ORGANIZATIONAL IMPACTS FRAMEWORK

Different frameworks have been proposed to classify the wide range of impacts. The 7S framework (Athos & Pascale, 1982), despite its critics, can be used to categorize the internal changes triggered by inter-organizational systems. Cash et al (1988) regroup the 7S impacts and consider three levels: (1) systems (procedures and processes), (2) skills and staff, and (3) style, structure and strategy. In a similar way, Barber (1991) classifies the effects of EDI in four major categories: people (skills, leadership style), management practices (tasks, operating procedures), support structures (information systems, organizational structure) and corporate culture (shared beliefs and assumptions). Holland, Lockett & Blackman (1992) describe the internal effects of EDI on organizational structure and process (individual roles and tasks, size and productivity of staff, new organizational units). In her study of EDI applications in Purchasing, Emmelhainz (1991) discusses three internal effects: (1) procedures (purchasing process), (2) workload (productivity, staffing), and (3) buyer attitudes. MIT's "Management in the 1990s" Framework (Scott Morton, 1991) can also be used to categorize EDI impacts along the following areas: management, technology, strategy, structure, individuals and roles.

Whatever the classification scheme, the different taxonomies suggest various interrelated levels of impact. On the one hand, impacts can be assessed for different "units of analysis," such as individuals, departments, or whole business units. On the other hand, the impacts can be experienced at different levels along a "scope" dimension (e.g. changes

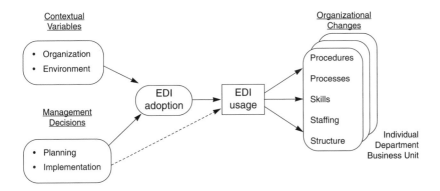

Figure 8.1   *Framework for EDI impact analysis*

in procedures, staff or organizational structure). Figure 8.1 presents a framework that incorporates these different levels and dimensions of change.

Implicit in the framework is a process view of EDI; i.e. the process of the EDI adoption decision and its subsequent effects. This process involves the following stages: (a) pre-existing organizational and environmental context, (b) planning and implementation decisions, (c) EDI adoption and usage, and (d) organizational changes. "Context" refers to anything which is important in understanding the setting in which EDI is adopted, e.g. type of company, general awareness of EDI, competitive situation, motivation to adopt new technologies and so on. The adoption decision is made at the "Planning" stage, and then the potential EDI applications are analyzed and prioritized. "Implementation" is seen as the onset of organizational change, in a combination of technical, human, and organizational decisions intended to stimulate the proper use of EDI by the organization. Finally, the use of EDI should lead to the desired organizational changes which, ultimately, should improve business performance.

The framework assumes that these organizational changes are intended, and that they are beneficial for the organization (i.e. will contribute to increase the value of its products and services, or reduce operating costs). Through changes to business processes, EDI permits companies to save both time and money because the data is transmitted rapidly, requires no additional data entry, and has been generated by an application (a computer program). Additionally, it can greatly reduce the order cycle and/or payment period, which in turn allows a company to reduce its inventory levels and improve cashflow. For most companies, these potential benefits constitute the major reasons for the adoption of EDI.

The link between organizational change and business performance is therefore implied. The framework suggests that effective EDI planning is the planning of organizational change. For many companies, however, this is not easy. The organizational consequences of EDI are not always well understood. In these companies, changes are not planned, they just happen (i.e. the opposite of what the Re-engineering pundits would advocate).

The question is thus how to plan for EDI. Next, EDI planning, its implications, and the less tangible organizational impacts are discussed and some research propositions are suggested.

Planning and Organizational Change

In the above framework, the changes at the different levels can be analyzed in conjunction with the attitude of the firm towards EDI. The sequence of intraorganizational impacts (internal changes) can be hypothesized to vary depending on the proactive/reactive posture of the firm (EDI Planning)—i.e. whether an organization is reacting to an EDI implemented by another company or whether it is the initiator or implementer of the system (Cash & Konsynski, 1985). The logic is as follows: if a company joins an EDI project proposed by another organization, general management is much less likely to have participated in the earlier decision-making process, and will neither explicitly plan nor consider the implications of the system. Changes will occur first in business processes, then in skills and staff, and later, perhaps, in organizational structure. Eventually, the company may be forced to reassess its business strategy. On the other hand, if the organization is the initiator (has a proactive attitude), EDI will then be an enabling tool for changes in strategy. It can be hypothesized that the system will be better planned and the order of impacts will be the reverse: first, strategy and organizational structure; then, selection and training of staff; and finally, business processes.

Strategic Intent and Degree of Change

Similarly, the extent of intraorganizational impact can be hypothesized to vary with the initial motive to adopt EDI; i.e. whether the firm pursues a strategic objective (e.g. competitive advantage), or an operational objective (e.g. direct cost savings). For the reasons mentioned above, if EDI is an element of a broad strategic plan, one would expect EDI to be associated with changes at many levels: strategy, structure, staff, skills and business processes. If EDI is an element of a narrower objective (e.g. direct cost reduction), one would expect EDI to be associated with changes at the lower levels such as the business processes directly involved, and fairly minor concomitant changes to skills and/or staff.

Effects on the Individual

The literature on the impacts of IT on individuals has traditionally concentrated on jobs, skills and employment. (Adler, 1986; Kelley, 1989; Osterman, 1986, 1991; Salzman, 1985; Zuboff, 1988). Changes to job descriptions are often suggested: Will work become more or less skilled, broader or narrower? Will jobs be lost? How will the organizational transformations feed back upon careers? These are some of the classical questions, and they, too, apply to EDI.

There is a debate underlying these questions. Some believe that IT will have negative consequences for individuals, in terms of employment loss (Osterman, 1986) or degradation of skill and job quality (Kelley, 1989). Others believe that creative use of IT can expand employment opportunities (Lynch & Osterman, 1989), expand the demand for workers with new and high skills (Spenner, 1987), and open up possibilities for creative expression and satisfaction at work (Salzman, 1985). This debate can be applied to EDI as well. Thus, on the one hand, EDI can be hypothesized to cause unemployment and de-skilling, while on the other, EDI can be hypothesized to increase job content and skills requirements, or even create new employment opportunities.

The rationale for increased skill levels implies moving away from manual skills and towards working with data and knowledge (as discussed in Chapter 1, for example). This aspect is at the heart of Zuboff's (1988) distinction between "automate" and "informate". She argues that IT will distance workers from the physical "feel" and will require instead that they learn the meaning of data generated by computers. In this context, training becomes key. An important element of new skills is responsibility. In most instances the system may perform well on its own, but the importance of spotting and understanding malfunctions increases sharply (Hirschhorn, 1984). These arguments can be extrapolated to the EDI. By automating the routine tasks of data entry, EDI frees clerical time that can now be spent in more valuable tasks that imply more responsibility. Thus, EDI can be hypothesized to foster more autonomy and responsibility.

Group Work and Organizational Structure

IT can reshape work beyond its impact on specific jobs. The way jobs link together may change and new forms of work organization may emerge. For example, work teams, in which job boundaries are diffuse, are more productive than traditional arrangements (Katz, et al, 1987; MacDuffie & Maccoby, 1986).

Because of its multifunctional nature, EDI can be hypothesized to affect the social relations of individuals within the firm, and the way their jobs interrelate. By extension, EDI can also be hypothesized to affect organizational structure, for example, in making it flatter and more decentralized.

SUMMARY OF RESEARCH PROPOSITIONS

This introduction has illustrated how EDI can affect an organization in ways other than the obvious changes to the processes directly involved in EDI transactions; in summary these are:

1. The sequence of intraorganizational impacts (internal changes) can be hypothesized to vary depending on the proactive/reactive posture of the firm. For example: if the organization has a passive attitude (e.g. merely joining a system developed by another company), the technical changes will occur first and the organizational changes will only be "experienced" subsequently (with some being unplanned); whereas if the company is more proactive, strategy changes and BPR will precede the technical changes.
2. The extent of intraorganizational impact can be hypothesized to vary with the initial motive to adopt EDI; i.e. whether the firm pursues a strategic objective (e.g. competitive advantage), or an operational objective (e.g. direct cost savings).
3. EDI can be hypothesized to cause unemployment for certain job categories (e.g. data entry work).
4. EDI can be hypothesized to increase job content and skills requirements, or even create new roles and opportunities.
5. EDI can be hypothesized to foster more autonomy and responsibility.
6. EDI can be hypothesized to affect the social relations of individuals within the firm and the way jobs interrelate.
7. EDI can also be hypothesized to affect organizational structure (e.g. flatter and more decentralized structures).

FLEXIBILITY, EDI AND ORGANIZATIONAL CHANGES: THE CASE OF ALCATEL BELL TELEPHONE

Alcatel Bell Telephone is Belgium's most prominent and dynamic exporter of telecommunications equipment and systems for both public and private networks. The company's broad range of activities includes system studies, R&D, production, installation, training, technology transfer and turnkey projects in the fields of both public and private telecommunication, data-communication, end-user systems, space and defence. The company is heavily oriented toward export activities: more than 50% of its turnover comes from sales to other countries.

A detailed case description of Alcatel Bell Telephone (ABT) can be found as part of a study of the TEDIS II programme (O'Callaghan, 1995). The study illustrates a company (ABT) that was able to take advantage of market niches and business opportunities requiring flexibility and short lead times. To increase flexibility towards customers, ABT also needed flexibility and short lead times from suppliers. Given that purchases constituted 60% of the cost of goods sold, procurement then became the critical business process.

The case discusses the redesign of the Procurement organization and the role played by EDI. The redesign of business processes allowed the company to go directly from the MRP system to the suppliers by automatically generating the purchase orders and sending them to the suppliers via EDI.

Re-engineering the Purchasing Process

The changes to the purchasing process occurred in several steps. In the early days, buyers got requisitions on paper, they studied the materials, and entered the data from the requisition on to a purchase order. If everything was in order, the purchasing department approved the purchase order (PO), and the next day, the paper documents and a number of copies were produced. Next, in order to reduce lead times, the PO was automatically faxed overnight and later confirmed by paper documents; but the ordering process was still work intensive. Finally, the raising of the PO was automated and the PO was sent by EDI to the supplier.

Regardless of whether the order was sent by fax or by EDI, the key point was that the processes between the MRP and the purchasing system had been automated. A description of the steps that were taken in order to automate the process follows.

For every component covered by a single Frame Agreement and coming out of the MRP system, the supplier was known. In a first stage, the system automatically created proposals for purchase orders, which went to the corresponding buyer, who checked and eventually modified them. At that stage, however, the buyers still had to intervene. Sometimes they had to correct data, like minimum order quantities. Later, algorithms were incorporated in the system that verified and changed order quantities. By building in all these rules, the intervention needed by the buyer was so drastically reduced that the order proposals were no longer required. The next step was the automatic generation of POs (with automatic approval). For many materials this was accomplished and, therefore, no manual intervention was required. In addition to the automatic generation, the transmission of these orders via EDI has finally created a "buyerless" buying process. The goal is to go from the MRP to the supplier "in one shot" for routine orders of production materials and components.

These changes are considered essential pre-requisites to achieve the benefits of EDI. In essence, ABT wants to automate the whole chain: from the MRP system to the customer order processing system of the supplier. To achieve it, ABT has created the right environment for EDI: accurate data, a high level of in-house automation, a good supply plan. As a result, the orders can be sent directly overnight independent of the presence or absence of a buyer. By so doing, the administrative lead time has been reduced to one day. In the past, between MRP and the supplier, it took days or weeks before the order got into his system. Now it takes one day, always one day. Each time an order is generated, it is no longer necessary to check that the vendor part-number is correct or that the price is correct, for example. Everything has been dealt with up-front.

Higher Level Changes

Beyond the direct changes to the purchasing processes, the implementation of EDI has had implications at other levels: changes to the tasks of buyers, reductions in head count, shorter lead times and lower inventory levels, greater data accuracy and fewer errors, more cooperative relations with suppliers, increased business with them, single sourcing for individual components, and a flatter organizational structure in the Procurement section.

This case supports several of the research propositions that have been summarized above. For example, proposition 1 and proposition 2 are both supported. At ABT, EDI is viewed as an element that contributes to that aspect of ABT's strategy concerned with flexibility. EDI planning was proactive: top management participated in the decision-making process, and the implications of the EDI were considered ex-ante. ABT used EDI as an enabling tool for strategy and EDI was planned in addition to other changes. The order of changes was first, strategy and organization structure, and then staff and business processes. Overall, the extent of change was far greater than the cases of other companies that were just responding to EDI initiatives launched by a trading partner.

The changes to the tasks of buyers, reduction in headcount, the more cooperative relations, and a flatter organizational structure in procurement provide support for propositions 3, 6 and 7, as discussed in more detail below.

Redesign of the Procurement Organization

Along with the changes to the purchasing processes, the Procurement organization was also redesigned; the reorganization created three employment categories: Procurement Engineers, Advanced Procurement Engineers, and Logistic Buyers.

The main task of the Procurement Engineers is the negotiation with suppliers; e.g. prices, delivery, quality and service levels, as well as the legal and financial details of the purchase agreements. One of their objectives is to reach a "Frame Agreement". During the term of the Frame Agreement, ABT should purchase from the supplier and the supplier should sell and deliver to ABT, the products at the terms and conditions as specified in the agreement.

Advanced Procurement Engineers constitute a link between engineering and the suppliers, increasing the effectiveness and freedom of procurement. They are technologically and product oriented, and are familiar with R&D. They keep abreast of market information, perform cost analysis, vendor rating and write a design guide. Their objectives are to avoid "backdoor selling" and to promote the use of market standards.

Logistic Buyers are responsible for handling the call-offs, i.e. orders generated automatically from the information contained in the Frame Agreements. Logistic buyers have to follow up these call-offs and take care of any incidents, such as goods refused. They also handle exceptions not contemplated in the Frame Agreements; e.g. phoning a supplier to ask for overnight delivery of urgently needed components.

In summary, the focus of Procurement has shifted upstream from downstream in the procurement life-cycle. Whereas in the past buyers used to concentrate their efforts on the ordering and follow-up phases, now there is more emphasis on activities that take place at earlier stages (e.g. at the time of product design) such as the selection of components, rating of vendors, and reaching Frame Agreements. ABT claims that this new procurement organization is more "process oriented" and "flat" than the previous one. This would seem to support proposition 7.

Changes to the Work of Buyers

Before its implementation, EDI entailed the streamlining of procedures and the "cleaning" of the data. In addition, by eliminating data re-entry, EDI has reduced data errors. However, not all errors have disappeared. Although infrequent, errors still occur when entering data into systems. From ABT's perspective, errors are unlikely because the correct codes and part numbers are already in the system (and have been cross-checked between the two parties), the price is fixed, the minimum and multiple quantities are also in the system. What the company sends out is correct. Errors are more likely at the supplier end because some still retype orders into their systems, and may either read the wrong code number or mix up quantities.

A logistic buyer talked about her experience with this kind of problem:

> "I had this last week. I ordered 1000 pieces of LM258 (by fax) from a distributor and they delivered LM358. The girl who received my order had to order the pieces to their headquarter office in Munchen and probably they made a mistake there. It could also have been a picking error (picking and delivering cannot be done by EDI!). It was clearly their fault.
>
> "Solving these problems is part of the job. I hope that EDI will not solve all the problems—everything can't be done with EDI . . . that otherwise we'll no longer be necessary! (laughing). Well, in fact (speaking with a more serious tone), for the job I do now, there used to be four buyers three years ago. We were four people to purchase the same quantities from the same number of suppliers as today. Now, I'm alone. A dramatic reduction in manpower!"

Several reflections are worth mentioning here:

- EDI did not eliminate all errors, and therefore
- EDI did not eliminate the need for a buyer to follow up orders. Yet,
- EDI reduced the need for the total number of Logistic buyers, and,
- the work of the buyer changed (from "routine ordering" to "exception handling").

With all the "up-front" changes in procedures and the implementation of EDI, ABT has been able to achieve a "buyerless" process for routine purchase orders. The logistic buyers have not totally disappeared, but compared with the situation some years earlier, their number has been considerably reduced: from 12 in 1985, down to only three. This clearly supports proposition 3 (about EDI leading to unemployment in certain jobs).

Interestingly, however, the remaining logistic buyers had a positive attitude towards EDI. A logistic buyer said that, before automatic call-offs and EDI were implemented, she was unable to perform her job well (in her own words "there was too much to do!"). With EDI, her workload diminished and now she can take a Monday off if she needs to. (This was something she could never do before because the MRP was run during the weekend and the results came out on Monday.) She discussed how EDI affected her job:

> "Before, we had to call the supplier every time for the prices. This is all under the Frame Agreement now, and I do not have to bother. Now my orders are made during the weekend by the computer. Even if I am not here on Monday, my order will be delivered to the supplier on Tuesday. I do not have to intervene any more. I deal with 3000–4000 part numbers and 35–40 frames every week. 99% of the calls are in Frame Agreements, and everything that is in a frame goes automatically to EDI.
>
> "Most materials have a six week lead time, but sometimes production needs the pieces immediately. If so, the supplier has 48 hours to answer yes or no (i.e. can or can't deliver). However, they may say: you will have the pieces in two weeks. Then it is my job to decide whether two weeks is acceptable or not. If two weeks is not acceptable, then I have to find an alternative supplier.
>
> "Each week, we place between 700 and 800 orders, and there are always three or four orders where the supplier will say: sorry, I can't deliver. If a supplier fails to deliver a component in time, I don't take the component out of the Frame Agreement for that supplier, because his failure to deliver is perhaps an exception. I then track his performance and follow up if subsequent deliveries are on time. I will definitely take it out of the Frame Agreement if production has technical problems with the component (e.g. reliability, quality). All this is my job now. I concentrate more on problem solving."

This qualitative change in the nature of the buyer's work seems to support proposition 5 (EDI leading to more autonomy and responsibility). Indeed, the changes to the ordering process have brought more responsibility to the buyers. On one hand, the automation of the buying process and the reduction of administrative lead times implied that human intervention be kept to a minimum. Yet, on the other hand, this has meant getting rid of former controls and thus empowering the people that raise the POs in the first place. The buyer explained:

> "Before EDI, POs had to be authorized. Today, I may raise a PO binding the

company for $500 000 and no control is necessary; whereas, in the past, a $10 000 order needed the signature of somebody else. It's a different world that we're living in."

New Responsibilities, New Job

Changes in work and responsibilities may lead to new skills, and even new employment opportunities. At ABT, for example, EDI created new job requirements and roles. The EDI start-up of new suppliers and/or messages is carefully planned and monitored. This new activity affected the job of the person in charge of the Systems Function, whose main responsibility is to ensure the quality of the data contained in the respective databases and who now has become the EDI administrator. He explained the impact of the implementation of EDI on his job:

> "Before a first test message can be sent to a new EDI supplier, the EDI flag in various databases has to be put in. The system must be told that the supplier, the proper Frame Agreement and the relative part numbers become part of our EDI program. Test messages to check the end-to-end communications link must be built, exchanged and compared with the paper documents sent in parallel. Different controls have to be executed: for example, you can't take it for granted that an inexperienced partner will always deal with the messages sent to him within 24 hours of receipt in his mailbox."

This supports proposition 4 (increase in job content and skills requirements, or even the creation of new employment opportunities).

Better Relations

Although there is no direct evidence in the ABT case that EDI has affected the social relations of the individuals within the firm and the way their jobs interrelate (proposition 6), the relations with trading partners are reported to have changed. In particular, some suppliers using EDI experienced an increase in business. This was seen as a consequence of the closer cooperation between ABT and its suppliers. The EDI project manager made the following remarks:

> "EDI links have fostered better relations between trading partners. As a result you are more willing to cooperate ... It is only natural: you sit together, you discuss business details, you discover problems and work out solutions together. EDI is a synonym of 'partners willing to cooperate in logistics'.
> "It's the result of a natural process ... we start to know each other ... we feel there is an opportunity for a 'win-win' and everybody becomes less like

buyer and seller, more like partners. You tend to go to the people you know, the people who cooperate, the people who are willing to help you."

By extension to the intraorganizational environment, this experience would seem to support proposition 6.

CONCLUSION

A framework has been presented to study the organizational impacts of EDI. The starting point is a process view of the EDI adoption and implementation decisions. Based on the literature, the framework suggests a taxonomy along two dimensions: organizational unit, and scope of change. The framework thus proposes different areas and levels of impact. The process view of EDI (context, planning, implementation and impacts) has been used to derive a series of research propositions linking the adoption of EDI and organizational changes. The ABT case has been used to illustrate with empirical evidence most of the research propositions. This exercise can, of course, be extended to other cases in order to increase the external validity of both the framework and the associated research propositions. The framework can thus be seen as a tool for analysis (as a lens for an in-depth clinical case study) but also as a model to be refined and potentially enhanced.

It is also worth commenting on a paradox associated with the proposed framework. On the one hand, the framework seems to imply a somewhat myopic (or passive) view of the links between EDI adoption and organizational changes (i.e. that after EDI is adopted, there is uncertainty about its effects, and thus we need research to assess these effects). However, the real value of the framework lies precisely on the opposite, more proactive view. This implies starting with the outcome of the process and then working backwards (just as the pundits of re-engineering would advocate). In this regard, an empirical validation of the model on a larger scale will constitute the basis for a normative model linking EDI and organizational change. In other words, once the effects of EDI are known with some certainty, EDI can be used more proactively, as a tool to enable or support some desired changes in organization and strategy. This is precisely one of the messages of the ABT case.

It should be pointed out that ABT always viewed EDI as an element of the whole logistic chain and, as such, the benefits of EDI have come from its contribution to the flexibility objectives of the firm. The major conclusion from the ABT case is thus that EDI cannot be treated in isolation. The planning of organizational changes and the redesign of business processes are essential prerequisites. In this regard the ABT case provides an interesting link between the management of EDI (i.e. EDI planning) and BPR (Davenport, 1993; Hammer & Champy, 1993), of which, much more in Chapter 10.

REFERENCES

Adler, P., 1986, New Technologies, New Skills. *California Management Review* 29 (1), Fall, 9–28.

Athos, A. and Pascale, R.J., 1982, *The Art of Japanese Management*, Warner Books.

Barber, N.F., 1991, Implementing EDI beyond Connectivity: The Management Challenge of the '90s, in *EDI Forum*, 4, The EDI Group Ltd.

Benjamin, R.I., de Long, D.W. and Scott Morton, M.S., 1990, Electronic Data Interchange: How Much Competitive Advantage? *Long Range Planning*, 23(1), 29–40.

Bjørn-Andersen, N., Eason, K. and Robey, D., 1986, *Managing Computer Impact: An International Study of Management and Organizations*, Ablex Publishing Corporation, Norwood, NJ.

Buffkin, R., 1991, EDI at CIBA-GEIGY Corporation: A Catalyst for Change and Improvement in Purchasing, in *EDI Forum*, 1, The EDI Group, Ltd., 80–83.

Callahan, D.K., 1987, The Impacts of Electronic Integration on Buyers and Suppliers, *Master's Thesis*, Sloan School of Management, MIT, Cambridge, MA., May.

Cash, J.I., Jr. and Konsysnki, B.R., 1985, IS Redraws Competitive Boundaries, *Harvard Business Review*, March-April, 134–142.

Cash, J.I. Jr., McFarlan, F.W., McKenney, J.L. and Vitale, M.R., 1988, *Corporate Information Systems Management*. Irwin (second edition), 209–213.

Davenport, T.H., 1993, *Process Innovation: Re-engineering Work through Information Technology*, Harvard Business School Press, Boston MA.

Dearing, B., 1990, The Strategic Benefits of EDI, *The Journal of Business Strategy*, January-February.

Emmelhainz, M.A., 1987, "The Impact of Electronic Data Interchange on the Purchasing Process," (2 vols.) *Working Paper 87–3*, The Center for Business and Economic Research, School of Business Administration, University of Dayton, Dayton, OH, February.

Emmelhainz, M.A., 1991, EDI: Does it Change the Purchasing Process? in *EDI Forum*, 4, The EDI Group, Ltd., 158–161.

Gupta, P.Y. and Neel, G.A., 1992, The Origin of EDI and the Changes Associated with its Implementation, *Industrial Engineering*, August.

Hammer, M., 1990, "Re-engineering Work: Don't Automate, Obliterate", *Harvard Business Review*, July-August.

Hammer, M. and Champy, J., 1993, *Re-engineering the Corporation: A Manifesto for Business Revolution*, Harper Business.

Hirschhorn, L., 1984, *Beyond Mechanization: Work and Technology in a Post-industrial Age,*. Cambridge, MA: MIT Press.

Holland, C., Lockett, G. and Blackman, I., 1992, Planning for Electronic Data Interchange, *Strategic Management Journal*, 13, 539–550.

Katz, H., Kochan, T. and Keefe, J., 1987, Industrial Relations and Productivity in the US Automobile Industry, *Brookings Papers on Economic Activity*, Special Issue on Microeconomics, 3, 685–728.

Kelley, M., 1989, Unionization and Job Design under Programmable Automation, *Industrial Relations*, Spring.

Lynch, L. and Osterman, P., 1989, Whatever became of the Wichita Lineman? Technological Change in the Telecommunications Industry, *Industrial Relations*, Spring.

MacDuffie, J.P. and Maccoby, M., 1986, The Organizational Implications of New Technologies: Remote Work Stations at AT&T Communications, Harvard University, Kennedy School of Government, Discussion Paper 154D, September.

McKersie Robert, B. and Walton Richard, E., 1991, Organizational Change, in Scott Morton, (ed.), *op cit.*, 245–277.

O'Callaghan, R., 1995, EDI in Procurement and Flexibility Strategies: the Case of Alcatel Bell Telephone in Belgium, in N. Bjørn-Anderson, H. Krcmar and R. O'Callaghan (eds.), *EDI in Europe*, John Wiley, Information Systems Series, Chichester.

O'Callaghan, R., Kaufmann, P. and Konsynski, B., 1992, Adoption Correlates and Share Effects of Electronic Data Interchange Systems in Marketing Channels, *Journal of Marketing*, April.

Osterman, P., 1986, The Impact of Computers upon the Employment of Clerks and Managers, *Industrial and Labor Relations*, January.

Osterman, P., 1991, Impact of IT on Jobs and Skills, in M.S. Scott Morton (ed.), *op cit.*, 221–243.

Salzman, H., 1985, The New Merlins or Taylor's Automatons? The Impact of Computer Technologies on Skill and Workplace Organization, Center for Applied Social Science, *Working Paper 85–5*, Boston University, May.

Sanders, N.R., 1992, Merging EDI with JIT: The Impact on US Manufacturing, *Journal of Applied Business Research*, 8, Spring, 133–137.

Scott Morton, M.S. (ed.), 1991, *The Corporation of the 1990s: Information Technology and Organizational Transformation*: Oxford University Press Oxford.

Spenner, K., 1987, Technological Change, Skills Requirements, and Education, *Mimeo*, Department of Sociology, Duke University, July.

Walton, R.E., 1989, *Up and Running: Integrating Information Technology and the Organization*, Harvard Business School Press, Boston, MA.

Whisler, T.L., 1970, *Information Technology and Organizational Change*, Wadsworth Publishing Co., Belmont, CA.

Zuboff, S., 1988, *In the Age of the Smart Machine: The Future of Work and Power*, New York: Basic Books.

9
An IT Architecture to Support Organisational Transformation*

WALTER BAETS[1] AND V. VENUGOPAL[2]
[1]Euro Arab Management School, Granada, Spain and
[2]Nijenrode University, The Netherlands Business School

OVERVIEW

In the current global competitive environment, if an organization is to be successful, it has to be a learning organization, as discussed in Part 2. Organizations learn from their internal dynamics and their assertive and adaptive interaction with the environment. Organizational learning needs to be supported as external environments and internal dynamics of organizations become more complex. This chapter draws consequences for the IT architecture of different learning processes and gives an overview of the existing IT tools which can support and enhance the company's leverage. The chapter proposes a conceptual framework of an integrated intelligent system for supporting organizational transformation. Finally, an example is provided of a large financial holding which is experimenting with these concepts and this architecture.

---

*An earlier version of a part of this chapter has been published in *The Learning Organization*, 2 (3) 1995 under the title "An Integrated Intelligent Support System for Organizational Learning—A Conceptual Framework", MCB University Press.

Information Technology and Organizational Transformation. Edited by R.D. Galliers and W.R.J. Baets. © 1998 John Wiley & Sons Ltd

INTRODUCTION

In today's competitive world, no organization can afford to stand still. Organizational success in the global competitive race depends on the knowledge of its members and their ability to make the right business moves to cope with the environment, as argued in Chapter 5. Organizations not only need knowledge; they also need the skills dynamically to update and put knowledge into practice. This results in the need for organizations to learn continuously and to look for continuous improvement in their actions through the acquired knowledge. Hence, to survive in the global competitive environment, organizations transform themselves into learning organizations (cf. Chapter 4).

A learning organization enables each of its members to learn continually and helps in generating new ideas and thinking. By this process, organizations continually learn from their own experience and that of others and adapt themselves so as to improve the chances of achieving their goal. In a way, learning organizations aim at converting themselves into "knowledge-based"' organizations by creating, acquiring and transferring knowledge so as to improve their planning and business activities.

To create a learning organization, companies should be skilled at systematic problem solving: learning from their own experience, and from others' transferring knowledge quickly and efficiently through the organization, and experimenting with new approaches (Garvin, 1993). Developments in IT make it increasingly possible to achieve these competitive needs and skills as has been argued throughout this book. Intelligent IT tools which are capable of supporting certain aspects of learning processes are now widely available commercially.

The objective of this chapter is to develop a conceptual framework for integrated intelligent systems which can support organizational transformation. Many of the organizational issues discussed thus far in this book have consequences for the IT architecture and system of a company. In the subsequent sections, we briefly summarise organizational learning as a concept followed by a discussion of different learning processes and the available support from IT. Towards the end of this chapter, a conceptual framework of an integrated support system for organizational learning is presented together with an example of a particular company's application of the framework.

ORGANIZATIONAL LEARNING

Extensive literature (e.g. Argyris & Schön, 1978; Daft & Huber, 1987; Dixon, 1992; Garvin, 1993) indicates that there is no clear unique definition for "organizational learning". Most of the definitions proposed, however, project organizational learning as a dynamic process of creating, acquiring and transferring knowledge (Garvin, 1993) which leads to a "knowledge-based" organization (Drucker 1988; Applegate, et al, 1988; Quinn 1992; Shukla, 1994), as discussed in Chapters 4 and 5.

A "hunger" for knowledge is an initial precondition for learning. Without knowledge and the capability to update it and put it into practice, it is difficult to live up to the expectations in the changing environment. Lessem (1991) has defined organizational learning-constructs, viz. knowledge origination, knowledge development, knowledge refinement, knowledge promotion, knowledge adaptation, knowledge implementation (dissemination), and knowledge application, and has suggested organizations build on these constructs to become a learning organization. According to Lessem, knowledge origination is the process which opens up entirely new fields of knowledge. Knowledge development is the process which uncovers potential for the application of newly discovered knowledge across a wide diversity of fields in the organizations. Within organizations, both knowledge origination and development take place in the Research and Development activity since these two processes are becoming increasingly important if organizations are to keep pace with the technological innovation.

Knowledge refinement is the process which refines the originated and developed knowledge into systems, policies, routines and procedures. For instance, marketing analysts would refine and specify the system required for the introduction of a new product. Knowledge promotion is the process of promoting the knowledge so that it can be used by others. Promotion does not involve any original or developmental activity other than customization of knowledge. Knowledge adaptation is the process of adapting the knowledge which is specific to a situation/field to solve an *analogous* problem. Such a process is conventionally used in management services. Knowledge implementation (dissemination) is the process of ensuring that the knowledge physically reaches the right place at the right time. IT plays a major role at this stage. Knowledge application is the process of putting the acquired knowledge into action.

Learning from a knowledge-based perspective is one of building up these processes, all of which can be classified into two categories, viz. knowledge acquisition and knowledge management. When knowledge is generated within the organization or from outside the organization, learning is said to occur. To be specific, learning in the context of organizations occurs when individual members:

- *form* their views/knowledge ("mental models") on the action-response of organization and environment (Lee, et al, 1992)
- *share* their knowledge and form a pooled knowledge
- *update* their knowledge in a changing environment.

Organizational learning is inherently a collective and shared individual learning and the process of learning is depicted in Figure 9.1.

Interorganizational learning involves learning from other companies and competitors. Interorganizational IT like EDI (see Chapter 8) is one of the most important technologies here. Intercompany learning takes place as the members of the organization meet business partners, suppliers, customers and competitors. Learning occurs in particular when a company watches and uses the experience of another firm in resolving a problem. Learning can occur between organizations due to joint-ventures and through benchmarking (Pedler, et al, 1991).

Learning may take place within the organization due to *internal information exchange* (Chapter 4), *participative policy making* (Chapter 2) and a *learning approach to strategy formulation* (chapter 6). *Internal information exchange* and *participative policy making* leads to learning as they enable members of the organizations to share their knowledge and values. In a *learning approach to strategy* formation of strategy, its implementation, evaluation and improvement are consciously treated as a learning process as it enables companies to interrelate their performance and anticipated environmental changes. In practice, certain organizations consider planning as a learning process. For instance, at Shell "Planning means changing minds, not making plans" (de Geus, 1988). *Needless to say, a part of intercompany and intracompany learning takes place during the planning process.* This chapter discusses some of the learning processes that may be translated into an integrated IT architecture.

LEARNING PROCESSES AND INFORMATION TECHNOLOGY SUPPORT

"Creating a learning/knowledge-based organization is simple but not easy" (Honey, 1991). A new wave of IT can support the creation of a knowledge-based/learning organization. New developments in IT such as Case-Based Reasoning Systems (CBRS), Expert Systems (ES), Group Decision Support Systems (GDSS), Cognitive Mapping and Artificial Neural Networks can support some aspects of organizational learning processes and organizational transformation. This section overviews different learning/change processes, and the corresponding IT support tools.

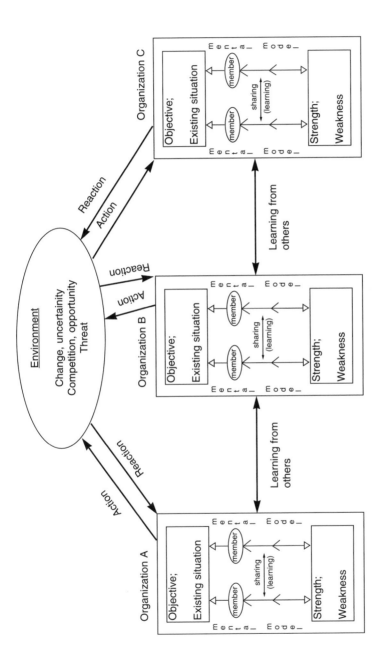

Figure 9.1 *Some Aspects of Organizational Learning*

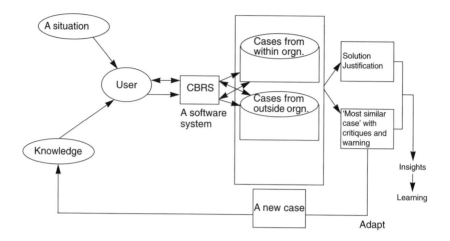

Figure 9.2   *Case-Based Reasoning System*

Learning through Cases (LC)

Human beings find it easy to use cases/analogies in handling uncertain situations in a complex and dynamic environment. In the context of organizations, managers are often interested to know how other companies approach certain problems. Especially while making strategic decisions, managers often look for a similar case from other industries to get an idea or insight into the experience of one firm in resolving a particular problem. The objective here is not to follow a "Me too" strategy but to look for an "analogous" strategy. When managers do not find a similar case, a "most similar" case is identified and adapted so as to establish a strategy or solution that is relevant and feasible (Sullivan & Yates, 1988). Even when they do not find "most similar" cases, the process generates new ideas and facilitates "learning from the experience of others". The ability to use and manipulate cases is important for learning organizations. A Case-Based Reasoning System (CBRS), a recent development in Aritificial Intelligence (AI), is a tool that can support the learning processes through cases.

Case-Based Reasoning Systems—A Tool for LC

A Case-Based Reasoning System (CBRS) essentially consists of a case library and a software system for retrieving and analysing the "similar case" and its associated information. A pictorial representative of a simple CBRS is shown in Figure 9.2.

The case library may have cases covering a broad range of ideas across different industries and business functions. Each case may contain a description to capture the underlying competitive situation, the environmental condition, management priorities, experience, values that allowed a certain strategy to succeed. A software system helps indexing each case in such a way that a search yields a modest number of "analogous cases". The system can supply a complete explanation of reasoning leading to each recommendation (Sullivan & Yates, 1988).

Given a problem situation as an input, a CBR system will search its case library for an existing case that matches the input specification. If there is a case that exactly matches the input situation/problem, then it directly gives a suggestion with appropriate explanation. If there is no case that "exactly" matches the given situation, then it selects the "most similar" case. Then, CBR modifies that portion of the retrieved case that does not match with the input specification. An adaptation procedure can be encoded in the form of adaptation rules. Even if the cases cannot be adapted by the CBR system, at least the system provides a significant starting point for analysis. The result of the case adaptation is a completed "solution" but it also generates a new case that can be automatically added to the case library. Learning is a basic part of a CBR system's architecture. So, if the same problem is given at a future point, the system will "solve" the problem without any effort.

A CBR system can support some aspects of both intercompany and intracompany learning. For instance, when a company is involved in launching a new product, it could use prior cases of other companies for the prediction and situation analysis. In such situations, a case in the CBR system could be a record giving knowledge on industry type, company, company strategies, information on competitors, economic factors, and company/industry success factors. Likewise, suggestions and feedback from users, marketing, manufacturing and testing departments of the same organization would be a useful source even in future (Kolodner, 1991) and would facilitate intracompany learning. Cases in the CBR system can be indexed in such a way that it would help easy retrieval and decision making by employees.

Exposure to prior cases/experiences and the steps taken to arrive at a decision can often be richer and more useful as the CBR system encodes the important learning and thinking that went into the decision. As CBR can generate details regarding justification for particular decisions and explanations for failures, it could be a support tool for a learning organization. Most of the existing CBR systems have the ability to retrieve cases, to give warning of potential problems and to help in critiquing. The potential uses of case-based reasoning are in the areas of planning, situation analysis, policy interpretation and argument, projecting the effects of a plan or decision, justification of a decision, diagnosis and classification, legal reasoning, component design and scheduling.

One may question the extent to which it is likely that adequate cases from other companies/industries can be found. In a learning environment, companies would share information for mutual learning—and this does happen. For instance, Rank Xerox has a slogan "come and steal shamelessly from us" (Pedler, et al, 1991). Cases/information can be gathered by members who have been in contact with external customers, clients, suppliers, companies and so on. At Rank Xerox, sales people are seen as information gatherers just as much as product sellers.

CBRS—Existing Support and Commercial Experience

In general, case-based systems are easy to build and maintain. Efforts to build commercial CBR shells are also under way at Cognitive Systems and Inference Corp. Examples of currently available CBR tools include *CBR Express* and *Case point* from Inference Corporation, *REMIND* from Cognitive Systems and *ESTEEM* from Esteem Systems. CBR industry applications are being built and used in several industries such as Lockheed, GTE, DEC, and Boeing. For instance, Compaq's customer service department uses a CBR system, called SMART. SMART is an integrated call-tracking and problem resolution system that contains hundreds of cases related to diagnostic problems arising in the use of Compaq products. Incoming customer problems are presented to SMART, which retrieves the most similar cases from its case base and presents them to the customer service analyst, who then uses them to resolve the problem. The percentage number of problems solved on the first call increased from 50% to 87% due to SMART (Acorn & Walden, 1992; Allen, 1994) *which can be treated as an indicator for learning*. Other examples of CBR systems are SQUAD at NEC Corporation (Kitano, et al, 1992), QDES at Nippon Steel (Iwata & Obama, 1991) and CLAVIER at Lockheed's Sunnyvale plant (Hennesy & Hinkle, 1992). SQUAD is a corporate-wide system that captures and distributes quality control knowledge. QDES and CLAVIER are case-based design and configuration systems that support the reuse and modification of standard designs.

Knowledge-Based Systems—Another Tool for LC

As knowledge-based organizations also rely on their specialists, replacement of the specialist often causes difficulties due to the nature

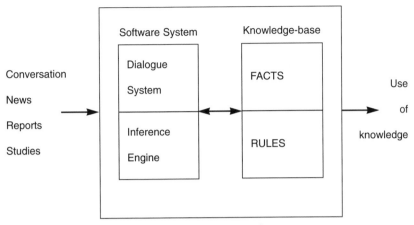

Figure 9.3   *Knowledge-Based Systems*

of the work. Intelligent systems such as a *Knowledge-Based System* (*KBS*) /*Expert System* can serve as "knowledge-base" or "organizational memory" to counteract their dependency on the expertise of individual members. Expert systems differ from CBRS with respect to knowledge representation, inference and control.

A general structure of a Knowledge-Based System (KBS) is shown in Figure 9.3. The knowledge-base and the software system are the two main components of KBS. Experts' knowledge in terms of a set of classification rules can be extracted manually and stored in the knowledge-base. Software systems basically consist of a dialogue system and an inference engine. The dialogue system facilitates a better dialogue between the user and the system, and the inference engine infers the knowledge. Certain systems infer the knowledge and provide explanation also. This in total supports the learning activity.

KBS—Existing Support and Commercial Experience

Hundreds of knowledge-based systems have been developed and deployed in industrial and commercial settings. Some of the systems which are relevant here are ORGEN, ORSYS and VIPS. The ORGEN (Organization GENerator) and ORSYS (Organizational Structuring System) assist in attempting to isolate and classify the parameters of an organizational structuring (Lehner, 1992). VIPS interactively accesses an electronic organization handbook and supports the planning of new procedures. Besides these, expert systems are available for planning activities such as resource planning and project planning.

KBS have been used in major companies all over the world especially in the US, Europe and Japan. Organizations such as Digital, Shell, Canon, Boeing, American Express, and Coopers & Lybrand are some of the companies which use knowledge-based systems in their planning process. Digital Equipment Corp. uses expert systems to support sales planning (Hayes-Roth & Jacobstein, 1994). Canon's optex camera lens design system is helpful to lens designers. ExperTAX system at Coopers & Lybrand has increased its quality of service.

Learning through Participative Strategy Formation (LPSF)

Changes in organizational culture have led to increased use of participatory management methods. For instance, Japanese management methods stress the importance of management by consensus. As a result, organizations form committees or working groups in which members of the organizations meet and share their knowledge so as to solve complex and ill-structured problems. Due to the uncertainty and complexity prevailing in the environment, sometimes even a "normal" well-defined problem requires participative/group decision making. Hence, it is a common phenomenon in a contemporary organization.

Participative strategy formation constitutes a learning process as there are always differences in perceptions and understanding among various interest groups in organizations. Some group members may have more knowledge, competence and experience. Group learning occurs as the interaction among members takes place. As one shares knowledge with the other members in the organization, they gain information/knowledge but their feedback instantly adds value for the sender. As each group learns and creates from its new knowledge base, the base itself grows. Exponential growth occurs in the value of each sharing group's knowledge base (Quinn, 1992).

Sometimes, participative/group planning fails due to a lack of proper participation, communication and understanding among the members in the group. Recent developments in IT have provided systems such as Group Decision Support Systems (GDSS) which can support participative/group planning. These systems are certainly not a cure for all afflictions in participative/group planning, but there is a growing interest in their use (Richman, 1987).

Group Decision Support System (GDSS)—A Tool for LPSF

A GDSS is a computer-based system consisting of software, hardware, language components, procedures and tools (Huber, 1984) which can support participative strategy formation. There could be many differ-

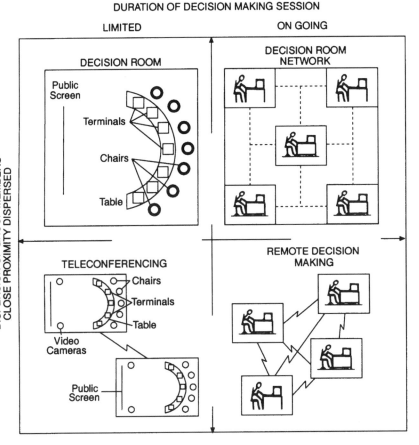

Figure 9.4 *A Configuration of GDSS*

ent configurations of a GDSS. One such typical configuration of GDSS is shown in Figure 9.4.

A GDSS enables a group of people to work interactively and simultaneously using networked hardware and software to complete various aspects of the planning process. For example, automated brainstorming tools can be used to address the question, "what should the company do to become a knowledge-based/learning company in the next five years?". Using the system, group members can interact to generate and evaluate relevant ideas from their terminals. The group facilitator can then prioritize the ideas they have generated and can select one for further electronic discussion. Finally, the group can work together using a text editor to formulate a policy statement regarding the goal they have selected. This is how a GDSS can support a learning process (Jessup & Kukalis, 1990).

The capabilities of existing GDSS vary. Essentially, they reduce communication barriers by providing technical features such as the display of ideas, voting compilation, anonymous input/interaction, decision modelling and electronic mail. Also, they act as group expert by providing advice in selecting and arranging the rules to be applied during the decision making process. The ultimate aim of this technology is to bring people together and facilitate efficient and effective interactive sharing of information among group members.

GDSS—Existing Support and Commercial Experience

Software is available to facilitate group learning. "Groupware", a computer-based system that supports groups of people engaged in a common task by providing an interface to a shared environment, is increasingly being used in commercial environments. Groupwares such as *Co-ordinator, Conversation Manager, Higgins, Lotus Notes, Participate* and *Syzygy* improve communication within teams and facilitate the execution of day-to-day operations (McConnell & Hodgson, 1990).

Some systems are intelligent in the sense that they are capable of summarizing and directing a rambling conversation on strategic planning concepts. For example, *Consensus Builder* is an Intelligent GDSS designed to assist decision making under conditions where individual members frequently experience difficulty in achieving agreement or taking prompt action. The difficulties usually occur because the committee members represent different interests or points of view. *Consensus Builder* weighs each person's judgements in accordance with their own personal standards, capabilities, biases or other unique characteristics. The system provides feedback to users concerning personal standards or biases, and the consistency of their point of view. Many users of *Consensus Builder* have said how useful this feature is, given that it can be understood by the group, thus making the resulting decisions more acceptable. Some of the other notable GDSS are *CaptureLab* and *ForComment*.

In general, GDSS have been used for a variety of planning tasks such as idea generation and evaluation, setting goals and objectives, evaluation of alternative strategies, stakeholder analysis, identifying assumptions and voting.

Some of the GDSS currently being used are COLAB in Xerox Parc, and CaptureLab at EDS Corp. COLAB has various tools such as PLEXSYS and COGNOTER which can guide participants toward group consensus (Stefik, et al, 1987). COLAB supports simultaneous action,

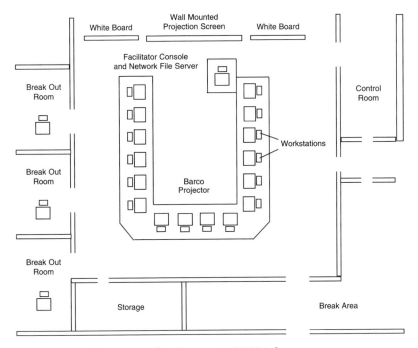

Figure 9.5 *Plex Center—A GDSS Laboratory*

allowing group members to work in parallel on shared objects. For further information on these GDSS, readers are refered to Nunamaker (1989).

Burr-Brown Corporation, a Tucson based international electronics company, has used one of the GDSS laboratories at the University of Arizona. Configuration of one such laboratory is shown in Figure 9.5. During three days of continuous sessions in the laboratory, the company was able to develop five year plans for several divisions and related one year action plans. The CEO of the company commented that the use of GDSS improved the understanding of those participating in the planning process (Jessup & Kukalis, 1990): "... there is a strong sense of understanding and agreement among the employees. A lot of education happened that previously hasn't happened . . ".

IBM has successfully used GDSS to address strategic planning needs (Nunamaker, et al, 1989). Participants appreciated and commented upon the effectiveness of GDSS. One such comment was: "I see several advantages ... open participation, the way that personalities are taken out of the process so that the process becomes more rational, and the amount of data which is automatically captured."

Learning through Sharing Individual Knowledge (LSIK)

It goes without saying that no one has perfect and complete knowledge about the large and complicated world in which we live. Each member of an organization has their own views/knowledge/mental models about the happenings in the organization and its business environment. Expertise from each member is limited in both quality and scope. Hence, sharing and updating of knowledge is essential. This shared and pooled knowledge can be viewed as the knowledge corpus for the organization and could be useful in many ways (see Chapter 5). When the knowledge is stored in an appropriate medium, sharing of knowledge can take place with few problems, but pooling knowledge is not without its problems and support tools are helpful here. Such a tool is a Cognitive Mapping System.

Cognitive Mapping System—A Tool for LSIK

A Cognitive Map (CM) is a representation of relationships that are perceived to exist among any attributes and/or concepts such as the approach proposed in Chapter 10. It is a tool which can be used to represent the thinking, knowledge and mental model of different individuals. The components of cognitive maps are nodes and signed directed arcs. Nodes represent concepts or variables. Signed directed arcs represent causal relations between concepts/variables. The sign "+" in the directed arc represents a direct relation and the sign "−" represents an inverse relation. The process of constructing cognitive maps for a given environment is called cognitive mapping. Cognitive mapping has been employed in different fields such as cognitive science and decision analysis, and could be used to analyze organizational policy (Hall, 1984). We now proceed to demonstrate the role of cognitive maps in organizational learning.

For illustrative purposes, let us consider the pooling of knowledge pertaining to a specific organizational problem. When a company wants some fresh insights into aspects of its plan—say, improving net profit, cashflow and return on investment—company employees may be asked to give their ideas on this issue. Quite different ideas are likely to arise. For example, one employee may have the belief that reducing the price of the product may improve the net profit of the company under certain assumptions. Another may have a view that reducing inventory would increase cashflow and return-on-investment. Yet another may suggest that decreasing inventory would lead to a decrease in operating expenses, which would lead to increased profit. These ideas (mental models) can be captured in the form of a cognitive map, as shown in Figures 9.6, 9.7 and 9.8.

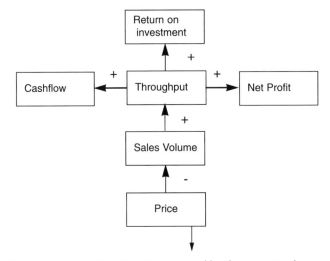

Figure 9.6 *Cognitive Map Constructed by the First Member*

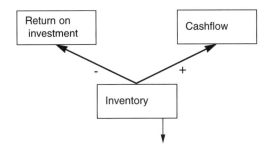

Figure 9.7 *Cognitive Map Constructed by the Second Member*

This knowledge can be pooled and, in this case, pooling results in the cognitive map shown in Figure 9.9. This pooled knowledge brings out the indirect relationship between inventory and net profit.

A computerized cognitive mapping system can provide further support to the pooling process. Figure 9.10 provides a general architecture of a such a system. The "mapping system" interactively gathers knowledge from members and forms the map. Representation of knowledge (maps) may differ from system to system. For instance, MIND (Ramprasad & Poon, 1985) represents elements and relationship in the form of a matrix. The "pooling system" analyzes common and unique concepts and their relationship, and joins them. As it is possible for

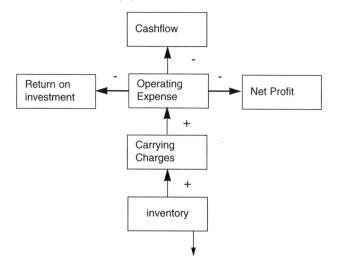

Figure 9.8   *Cognitive Map Constructed by the Third Member*

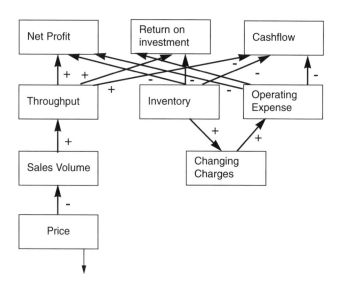

Figure 9.9   *Pooled Cognitive Map of Three Members*

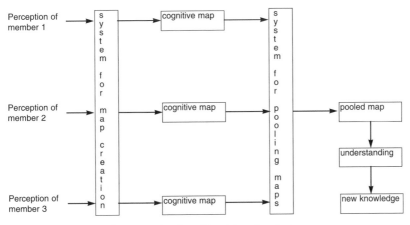

Figure 9.10 *Cognitive Mapping System*

members to use different terms for the same concept, some systems also use a dictionary (Lee, et al, 1992).

Existing Support and Commercial Experience

Computer software, such as COPE, can record, represent and analyze maps. It accepts concepts and their relationship through controlled dialogue and offers a number of different ways for analyzing maps. Lee, et al (1992) have developed a prototype system COCOMAP for forming and pooling cognitive maps. Other similar software includes DESIGN, VENSIM, ITHINK and STELLA (Peterson, et al, 1990; Richmond, et al, 1990). Companies are in the process of introducing this kind of software, with Shell International, for example, using STELLA and SODA in their planning process (Eden, 1990).

Dynamic Learning of the Relationship between Organizational and Environmental Factors (DLROF)

In a learning environment, if an organization has to be adaptive and responsive, it has to sense the present situation and predict the future environment both inside as well as outside the organization. For predicting the future environment, organizations have dynamically to learn the relationship among several factors and business processes. The dynamic learning of the relationship between business processes and other factors is essential for various purposes such as strategic planning and bench marking. Often, top management has found that strategic planning has created problems which have arisen due to the assumption that there are specific and identifiable relationships among the factors. For instance, use of quantitative models for long range forecasting make the simplifying assumption of linearity in their underlying structure, which enable models to be built more easily. But, linear models are not good at absorbing turning points in the business processes. It is no longer advisable to make assumptions about the relationship between various factors and business processes; it is better to "learn" the relationship. Neural Networks offer exciting possibilities for "dynamically learning" the relationship between various factors and business processes (as demonstrated in Chapter 5).

Artificial Neural Networks for DLROF

Artificial Neural Networks (ANNs) are a new information processing paradigm which simulates the living human brain. When knowledge is in the form of quantitative information, ANNs play the role of Case-Based Reasoning Systems. ANNs consist of many simple elements called nodes. The nodes are densely interconnected through directed links. Nodes take a number of information inputs and combine these in a particular way for reasoning purposes. The power of neural computing comes from connecting artificial neurons into artificial neural networks. The simplest network is a group of neurons arranged in a layer. Multilayer networks may be formed by simply cascading a group of single layers. Figure 9.11 shows a three-layer neural network: an input layer, an output layer, and between the two a so-called hidden layer. The nodes of different layers are densely interconnected through directed links. The nodes on the input layer receive the signals (values of the input variables) and propagate concurrently through the network, layer by layer.

ANNs have the ability to learn and identify complex patterns of information and to associate these with other information. ANNs can recognize and recall information in spite of incomplete or defective input information. They can also generalize learned information to other related information. These abilities form the basis for supporting learning about the relationship among business factors and processes. For instance, ANNs could be used in "learning" the relationship between factors such as the company's product complexity in technical terms, the market need, product uniqueness, marketing and managerial synergy of the company. This learning could be useful for predicting the success of the company's product. Likewise, the learning of the relationship among factors such as cashflow, return on assets, capitalization, cash turnover, inventory turnover, sales, total assets and the other business processes is a critical requirement in learning organi-

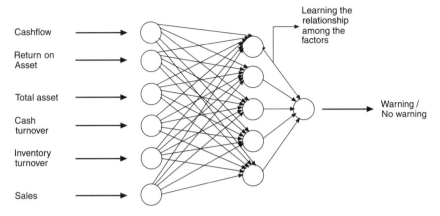

Cashflow

Return on Asset

Total asset

Cash turnover

Inventory turnover

Sales

Learning the relationship among the factors

Warning / No warning

Figure 9.11 *ANN for Predicting Corporate Failure*

zations for monitoring organizational performance. ANNs (Figure 9.11) can take such information from corporate databases and can help in learning the relationship. Once the relationship is learned, it could be used as an early warning system to guard against corporate failure. Though statistical tools could also be used for this purpose, they are constrained by their assumptions.

Though ANNs lack the ability to provide explanations at intermediate stages, integrating them with expert systems would remove this deficiency to some extent and hence they could support the learning process. Efforts are being made both academically and commercially towards this end.

ANN—Existing Support and Commercial Experience

Tools for developing and programming ANNs are available on the market. Some of the tools worth mentioning here are *ExploreNet* from Hecht-Nielsen (USA), *Explorer Neuralworks* from NeuralWare (USA) and *Neuroshell* from Ward Systems Group (USA).

The use of ANNs in the corporate world is increasing daily. Several banks and credit card companies such as American Express, Mellon Bank and Chase Manhattan Bank of New York use ANNs to study the patterns of credit card usage and to detect fraudulent transactions. In addition, banks use ANNs to identify and verify hand-written signatures and to evaluate corporate loan risks. Volvo Corporation of Sweden uses ANNs for audio analysis of engine sounds and visual analysis of paint finishes in its Göteborg plant. A UK financial institution uses an ANN for segmentation purpose.

INTEGRATED INTELLIGENT SUPPORT SYSTEM FOR LEARNING: A CONCEPTUAL FRAMEWORK

From the above, it is clear that different IT tools can independently support different organizational learning processes. For instance, some aspects of interorganization learning and intraorganization learning can be supported by CBRS. Similarly, GDSS supports learning through participative policy-making. As organizational learning is viewed as integrated and collective learning, it is necessary that existing IT tools should enlarge the scope of their supporting roles and have greater capability or they should be integrated in an appropriate way so as to support organizational learning.

Intelligent support tools such as CBRS, KBS, COMS, GDSS, ANN together with a knowledge-base, case library and database can be loaded on to a fileserver which is connected to other computers/ terminals through a local area network where all members have equal access to the different tools and are able to communicate freely. New technologies such as electronic brainstorming, group consensus and negotiation software and general meeting support systems can be integrated in the GDSS to provide support for group learning. Computer mediated communication systems and wide area networking would enable the companies to store, process and retrieve external information, and provide an electronic learning environment where all members can communicate freely. Technologies such as voice mail, e-mail and video conferencing can be made available for efficient and effective communication. All these together can serve as environmental scanners. Companies can be networked through wide area networking with a relevant external system. Thus, remote access to business environmental knowledge can be made available within the company at any time. Figure 9.12 gives a conceptual framework for integrating these intelligent tools which could facilitate efficient and effective learning processes. However, in line with much of what has been said throughout this book, it should be noted that the implementation of any such prototype integrated system would require a fundamental rethinking of the organizational design and transactions.

CONCLUSION

Global competition forces organizations to convert themselves into learning organizations. But, creating a learning organization is not that easy. As the dynamics of the learning process become more complex, they need to be supported. IT, as described in the earlier chapters of this

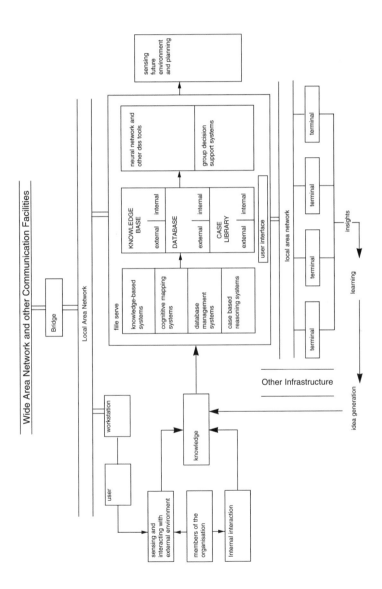

Figure 9.12 *The Conceptual Framework of the Integrated Intelligent System for Organizational Learning*

book, can contribute considerably to this process. Developments in IT make it increasingly possible to support some aspects of organizational learning. Intelligent tools such as Case-Based Reasoning Systems, Knowledge-Based Systems, Cognitive Mapping Systems and Neural Networks are potential tools for supporting organizational learning. When these tools are integrated and made available together with other advanced IT tools, they can support and enhance some of the organizational learning processes. It can be expected that in the coming years, these tools, together with management's commitment, will play a central role in supporting organizational learning.

Companies have already started experimenting with this kind of alternative IT architecture and approach. They have tended not to replace systems, rather they build new systems based on new techniques and architectures utilizing information made available from existing systems. This decreases the risk of translating badly documented programs. If this trend continues, IS may look rather different in companies in the decade to come.

In the last part of this chapter, we will briefly describe the experience of a particular company with this new type of architecture and the use of some of the above mentioned tools. This section does not claim general validity, it is provided merely as an illustration of what is possible.

THE EXPERIENCES OF A MAJOR FINANCIAL HOLDING

The Company

Achmea Holding is a financial company which has its main activities in the insurance business. It undertakes a number of different insurance activities such as general risks, life insurance, pension funds and medical care insurance. It has different brands in each of the activities and each activity in itself has a legal corporate structure. In addition, it provides banking services, and has companies running large financial portfolios. Its total annual revenue is around 10 billion Dutch guilders and assets are valued at 4 billion. Achmea employs 6700 people. Over the past 10 years, this holding was very active in acquisitions, which partly explains the existence of the large number of branded products. There has been no attempt to integrate and rationalize the newly acquired companies. Achmea has almost a 10% market share which makes it the second largest insurance company in The Netherlands: the largest having a 20% market share.

The market can be characterized by growing inability, which implies stronger competition, a growing number of mergers and less profitable companies leaving the market. Efficiency is a major issue strengthened by the Third European Guideline on Deregulation of the insurance sector. As compared to other insurance companies, Achmea relies heavily on direct writing. Whereas the market norm is 22% direct writing and 50% via intermediaries, Achmea's numbers are 86% direct writing and only 10% via intermediaries. In view of a total number of clients of around 2.5 million and the large number of different brands, the IT architecture for Achmea is of paramount importance.

The Management Culture

The Achmea structure and philosophy is based on the "fleet" philosophy. The *ship* is the business unit. The *captain* is the manager who has overall responsibility. The *admiral* of the fleet is the executive board and the management board. They determine the overall strategy. The *course* is set out by each individual business unit. They have their own agreed targets. Mutual competition is allowed, but conflicts are not. This is to prevent *collision* problems while at sea. The *fleet* itself is characterized by a "small is beautiful" and "big is strong" philosophy. However, in the maritime insurance business they are not so strong and this is probably why this metaphor is used by the company.

This vision leads to decentralization and delegation, within a networked organizational structure. Synergy is not achieved through integration but through cooperation, with the holding giving due importance to interface management. Japanese innovation strategies are what Achmea is interested in, with co-ordination taking place at the product platform level, thus allowing the holding to retain its unity within diversity.

Clearly, in this industry and with this management culture, many of the classical approaches would fail. Therefore, Achmea has experimented with alternative approaches, but while IT plays an important role in the process, the underlying philosophy is one which is very much in line with the ethos of this book in that, while highly important, IT is by no means the only consideration.

Achmea's Experiments

Figure 9.13 gives an overview of how Achmea considered trends inside the company and trends in the overall environment.

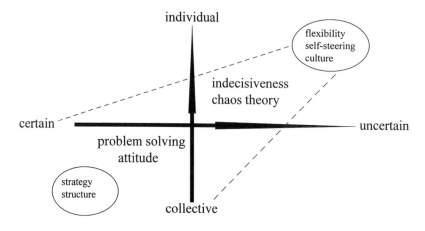

Figure 9.13   *Previously: Internal Focus*

The focus of the company had mainly been internal up to now. This fostered flexibility and a self-steering culture where the individual was confronted with uncertainty. This led in certain cases to indecisiveness. The managerial attitude might be identified as one of problem-solving, with importance being given to what is known as chaos theory. This approach has led to a dilemma between flexibility and synergy. On the flexibility side they have chosen multi-labelled products via multi-distribution channels, with management control being decentralized. They have given flexibility a decisive role, unless arguments in favour of synergy alter the balance: low cost strategies and economies of scale being most significant in this context.

In order to solve this dilemma they have chosen the approach which is illustrated in Figure 9.14. They refocused the company to become more outward looking. In the individual-uncertain quadrant they fostered a best practices approach and gave their employees additional training in order to make them aware of the crucial importance which managerial competencies play as a support for each individual as a manager. They chose a networked organization and gave due attention to the managerial process in the many cases of uncertainty. They introduced team technologies, scenario planning and programme management. The rationale of the company had become too focused on the individual. Team building was fostered, together with enhanced mobility. Simulation techniques allowed employees to be an active part of the definition of the corporate purpose itself. Where before strategy and structure were in place to manage the "collective certainty", almost no importance is given to this today: processes and competencies are

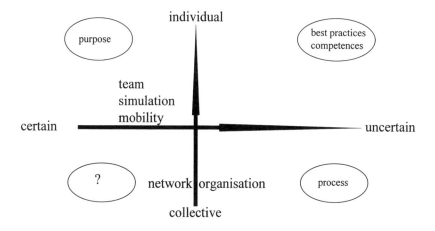

Figure 9.14   *Now: External Focus*

where attention is now focused. It is this new approach which necessitated a creative use of IT in the manner described earlier in this chapter.

Their IT Approach

Achmea explored a number of IT developments, positioning what is available against the added value and the maturity of the technology. Their analysis of IT technologies for distribution is summarized in Figure 9.15.

In relation to the distribution of services and product innovation they have been exploring those mature techniques promising high added value. But in order to support the new managerial focus described above and illustrated in Figure 9.14, team technologies in particular had to be introduced. In the new network environment experiments are taking place today with a number of those technologies which have been described earlier in this chapter, such as group decision support, team memory, knowledge networks, neural networks and data warehousing. A personal workspace concept supports these experiments. The impacts have been felt as regards certain competencies of course and new IT skills have had to be acquired in respect to client-server architectures, Groupware, office automation, data mining, multimedia and neural networks, for example.

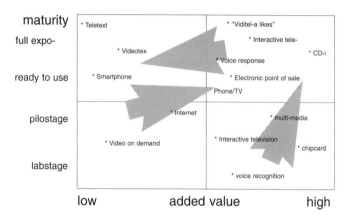

Figure 9.15   *IT: Distribution and Product Innovation*

All this has resulted in a number of remarkable changes in the IT management of Achmea itself. A convergent IT infrastructure has emerged and within the *fleet*, economies of scale and synergies are used more efficiently, as demonstrated by vendor management, pick and mix strategies and shared development of many applications. IT entrepreneurship and IT management are located within the operating companies. IT performance reports have been established. IT strategic platforms for co-ordination and overall prioritizing include members of the Executive Board, IT directors and group information managers. In a completely different way, IT service centres are now empowered. Needless to say that this has created a much more stimulating climate for the IT professionals with considerably more team working and staff exchanges.

The overall message, though, is one that demonstrates a *role* for IT in this organizational change, while reinforcing the range of other factors requiring active consideration.

REFERENCES

Acorn, T. and Walden, S., 1992, SMART: Support Management Automated Reasoning Technology for Compaq Customer Service, in Proceedings of the 4th Innovative Applications of Artificial Intelligence Conference.

Allen, B.P., 1994, Case-Based Reasoning: Business Applications, *Communications of the ACM*, 37 (3), 40–42.

Applegate, L.M., Cash, J.I. and Quinn Mills, D., 1988, Information Technology and Tomorrow's Managers, *Harvard Business Review*, 66, 128–36.

Argyris, C. and Schön, D.A., 1978, *Organizational Learning: A Theory of Action Perspective*, Reading, MA: Addison Wesley.

Daft, R.L. and Huber, G., 1987, How Organizations Learn: a Communication Framework, in *Research in Sociology of Organizations*, S. Bucharach and N. Ditomaso (ed.), 5, JAI Press, Greenwich, CT.

De Geus, A.P., 1988, Planning as Learning, *Harvard Business Review*, March-April, 70–74.

DeSanctis, G. and Gallupe, B., 1985, Group Decision Support Systems: a New Frontier, *Database*, Winter 3–10.

Dixon, N.M., 1992, Organizational Learning: A Review of the Literature with Implications for HRD Professionals, *Human Resource Development Quarterly*, 3 (Spring), 29–49.

Drucker, P.F., 1988, The Coming of the New Organization, *Harvard Business Review*, January-February, 45–53.

Eden, C., 1990, Strategic Thinking with Computers, *Long Range Planning*, 23 (6), 35–43.

Garvin, D.A., 1993, Building a Learning Organization, *Harvard Business Review*, July-August, 78–91.

Hall, R.I., 1984, The Natural Logic of Management Policy Making: its Implications for the Survival of an Organization, *Management Science*, 30, 905–927.

Hennesy, D. and Hinkle, D., 1992, Applying Case-Based Reasoning to Autoclave Loading, *IEEE Expert*, 7 (5).

Hayes-Roth, F. and Jacobstein, N., 1994, The State of Knowledge-Based Systems, *Communications of the ACM*, 37 (3), 27–39.

Honey, P., 1991, The Learning Organization Simplified, *Training & Development*, 9, 30–32.

Huber, G.P., 1984, Issues in the Design of Group Decision Support Systems, *MIS Quarterly*, 8, 195–204.

Iwata, Y. and Obama, N., 1991, QDES: Quality Design Expert System for Steel Products, in Proceedings of the 3rd Innovative Applications of Artificial Intelligence Conference.

Jessup, L.M. and Kukalis, S., 1990, Better Planning Using Group Support Systems, *Long Range Planning*, 23 (3), 100–105.

Kitano, H., et al, 1992, Building Large-Scale and Corporate-Wide Case-Based Systems: Integration of Organizational and Machine Executable Algorithms, in Proceedings of the 10th AAAI Conference, AAAI, San Jose, CA.

Kolodner, J.L., 1991, Improving Human Decision Making through Case-Based Decision Aiding, *AI Magazine*, 12 (2), 52–68.

Lehner, F., 1992, Expert Systems for Organizational and Managerial Tasks, *Information & Management*, 23, 31–41.

Lee, S., Courtney, J.F. and O'Keefe R.M., 1992, A System for Organizational Learning Using Cognitive Maps, *OMEGA*, 20 (1), 23–36.

Lessem, R., 1991, *Total Quality Learning—Building a Learning Organization*, Basil Blackwell, Oxford.

McConnell, D. and Hodgson, V., 1990, Computer Mediated Communication Systems (CMCS)—Electronic Networking and Education, *Management Education & Development*, 21(1), Spring.

Nunamaker, J.F., 1989, GDSS: Present and Future, *IEEE*, November, 6–16.

Nunamaker, J.F., et al, 1989, Group Support Systems in Practice: Experience at IBM., Proceedings of the Twenty-second Annual Hawaii International Conference on Systems Sciences, Vol.III, R. Blanning and D. King (eds,), IEEE Computer Society Press.

Pedler, M., Burgoyne, J. and Boydell, T., 1991, *The Learning Company—A Strategy for Sustainable Development*, McGraw Hill, London.

Peterson, B., Richmond, B. and Boyle, D., 1990, *STELLA II Documentation*, High Performance Systems, Hanover, NH.

Quinn, J.B., 1992, *Intelligent Enterprise*, The Free Press, New York.

Ramprasad, A. and Poon, E., 1985, A Computerised Interactive Technique for Mapping Influence Diagrams (MIND), *Strategic Management Journal*, 6, 377–392.

Richman, L.S., 1987, Software Catches the Team Spirit, *Fortune*, June.

Richmond, B., Peterson, S. and Charyk, C., 1990, *ITHINK Documentation*, High Performance Systems, Hanover, NH.

Shukla, M., 1994, *Knowledge-Based Organizations : how Companies use Knowledge as a Strategic Leverage*, Unpublished manuscript, XLRI Jamshedpur (India)/ ESADE (Barcelona).

Stefik, M., et al, 1987, Beyond the Chalkboard: Computer Support for Collaboration and Problem Solving in Meetings, *Communications of the ACM*, 30 (1), 32–47.

Sullivan, C.H. and Yates, C.E., 1988, Reasoning by Analogy—A Tool for Business Planning, *Sloan Management Review*, Spring, 55–60.

Part 4

IT AND ORGANIZATIONAL CHANGE

Part 4 attempts a synthesis by reinforcing the messages and utilizing some of the material introduced in the preceding chapters of the book in order to refocus our attention on our main topic of Information Technology and Organizational Change.

In Chapter 10, Bob Galliers casts a critical eye over the subject of Business Process Re-engineering (BPR), IT and organizational change, by reviewing some of the hard-won lessons in this area from such fields as strategic management, socio-technical systems and the management of change. Questioning calls by the proponents of BPR for the "obliteration" of existing processes and truly radical change—often made in the same breath as supporting the kind of organizational learning initiatives which were the subject of Part 2—he points out the apparent contradiction here and suggests a more balanced approach by focusing attention on the implementation of realistic strategies for change.

This is followed by a chapter written by Jon Turner in which he draws together a number of examples whereby IT may support the organizational change process. In many ways, this chapter complements Chapter 9, but here the focus is on such technologies as EDI (cf. Chapter 8) and CSCW (cf. Chapter 2) in addition. A key message, central to the book as a whole, is that while IT may be an important enabler of organizational change, it should not be viewed as the single, key component of the change process.

Part 4 ends with Chapter 12, written by Peter Meester and Jan Post. In it they describe a real live business process change project—called

LUCIA—for which they have been responsible in the Dutch PTT. Their experiences have led to the creation of a consulting arm of the company, through which these experiences are now shared with a number of other companies in a range of industries. The chapter brings further balance to our treatment of the subject by reflecting on an actual change project, and it again reinforces the message that such change can indeed be brought about with only minor attention being paid to IT. As such, it presents a useful introduction to Chapter 13, which brings the book to a close.

10
Reflections on BPR, IT and Organizational Change[1]

BOB GALLIERS
Warwick Business School, University of Warwick, UK

INTRODUCTION

Contrast, if you will, the views expressed by proponents of Information Technology (IT) enabled business process redesign (BPR) or business innovation and those successful chief executive officers (CEOs) who have set in place the vision and strategy to achieve major change and improved results for their companies—sometimes quite dramatically—in the global market place. The contrast is an enlightening one which should help us to understand the crucial issues associated with strategy formation and implementation—the management of change in other words—and to locate the role of IT in that change process.

In an interview with the Whirlpool CEO David Whitwam, (Maruca, 1994), the major components of change in "going global" are identified as defining and communicating a vision, objectives and market philosophy into a unifying focus worldwide, leading to common processes and systems; a focus on the customer; a realization that were we to stick "to the path we were on, the future would be neither pleasant nor profitable" (*ibid.*, p.137), and a *slow* process of communication and persuasion

---

[1] An earlier version of this chapter appears under the title "IT and Organisational Change: Where does BPR fit in?" in G. Burke & J. Peppard (eds.) *Examining Business Process Reengineering: Current Perspectives and Research Doctrines*, Kogan Page, London 1995, pp. 117–134 Published with permission.

Information Technology and Organizational Transformation. Edited by R.D. Galliers and W.R.J. Baets. © 1998 John Wiley & Sons Ltd

to get managers to buy into globalisation—"thinking global but acting local":

> "You can't expect it to happen overnight. Bear in mind that we have many, many employees in our manufacturing plants and offices who have been with us for 25 or 30 years. They didn't sign up to be part of a global experience ... Suddenly we give them new things to think about and new people to work with. We tell people at all levels that the way of doing business is too cumbersome. Changing a company's approach to doing business is a difficult thing to accomplish in [a single country], let alone globally." (*ibid.*, pp. 139–140)

Ways of achieving such major change include helping employees own both the change itself and the process of change, by giving them authority and responsibility to see through aspects of the overall change, and to compensate them based on their performance in so doing.

Note that the emphasis is on understanding customer requirements, defining a new vision, and communicating and implementing it through people. Changed processes and systems in all the different company locations—greater commonality—are part of the process (and an integral part at that), but the focus is on people. There is hardly a mention of IT in the whole interview.

Contrast this with the following extracts from Davenport's (1993) book *Process Innovation. Re-engineering Work through Information Technology*. While acknowledging that "information and IT are rarely sufficient to bring about process change; most process innovations are enabled by a combination of IT, information and organizational/human resource changes" (*ibid*, p.95), the central role of IT in the process is virtually unquestioned. For example, "... the use of IT for process innovation [is] a virtual necessity" (*ibid.*, p.44) and "Although it is theoretically possible to bring about widespread process innovation without the use of [IT], we know of no such examples. IT is both an enabler and implementer of process change" (*ibid.*, pp.300–301).

This chapter attempts to locate an appropriate role for IT in organization change. While recognizing that it may well have a role to play, along with other drivers for change, this chapter questions IT's centrality in the process. For BPR to be taken seriously, for the proportion of BPR success stories to improve from the current reported low level of 30% or so, a more balanced, holistic stance has to be taken. This is the contribution that this chapter attempts to make: to present a case for a more holistic and even-handed stance on BPR which sees, as we argued in Part 2, the process as a learning experience requiring on-going assessment and review, which emphasizes the need to develop and communicate a shared vision, leading to a review of existing structures and processes, but which takes account of customer requirements and the values, expectations and viewpoints of those whose job it will be to implement the change.[2] In a nutshell, the argument is for a refocusing of our attention from strategy formulation to strategy implementation and from IT-induced business change to the *incorporation* of IT considerations, in a more balanced way, into that change process.

The chapter looks first at the question of radical versus incremental change and places BPR in the context of developments in our thinking regarding business strategy. Given the much vaunted radical new thinking which underpins BPR, or so it is claimed, the outcome of the following analysis may come as a surprise. Our analysis suggests that BPR, as currently practised and discussed in the literature, far from being a new departure, is in fact a reversion to the classical school of strategic thinking popularised in the 1960s.

In line with the above arguments, the chapter then presents an holistic framework for BPR which incorporates IT considerations but does not place IT centre stage. As a result of this analysis, it presents a process by which business innovation may be achieved. The process should not be seen as a prescriptive methodology, but is introduced more as an *aide memoire* for the kind of considerations that should be incorporated into change projects of this kind. Any thought that all innovation should take precisely the same route should be banished from one's thinking at the outset. Each situation we face is unique and should be treated as such. The kind of issues we need to incorporate into our treatment of the topic can be identified, however, and this chapter aims to do just that.

RADICAL *VERSUS* INCREMENTAL CHANGE

Davenport (1993), in arguing for radical change rather than incremental change, suggests that this is the only means of obtaining the order-of-magnitude improvements necessary in today's global marketplace. In the face of intense competition "... quality initiatives and continuous, incremental improvement, though still essential, will no longer be sufficient" (*ibid.*, p.1). In addition, he discounts existing approaches as being unable to deliver the scale of improvement necessary: "Existing approaches to meeting customer needs are so functionally based that incremental change will *never* yield the requisite interdependence" (*ibid.*, p.4, emphasis added).

---

[2] This argument is echoed by Julian Watts in an editorial to the journal *Business Change & Re-engineering* (Watts, 1993).

Table 10.1   The characteristics of process improvement and process innovation compared

	Improvement	Innovation
Level of change	Incremental	Radical
Starting point	Existing process	Clean slate
Frequency of change	One time, continuous	One time
Time required	Short	Long
Participation	Bottom-up	Top-down
Typical scope	Narrow, functional	Cross-functional
Risk	Moderate	High
Primary enabler	Statistical control	IT
Type of change	Cultural	Cultural, structural

(source: amended from Davenport, 1993, p.11)

Both these central tenets of his argument are highly contentious, as we shall see. First, let us consider the question of radical versus incremental change. Davenport (*ibid.*, p.11) provides a summary of what he sees as the key distinguishing features of the two philosophies. This is reproduced as Table 10.1.

The first point of contention is the starkness of the contrast presented by Table 10.1. One could certainly question whether it is indeed the case that all incremental change is characterized by a focus on existing processes, a short period of intervention and a bottom-up, functionally-based approach, all informed by statistical data and motivated by a perceived need for greater control. Quinn's (1980) theory of logical incrementalism, for example, suggests that while we need to take account of the current circumstances in effecting change (as does BPR for that matter), we do not have to use as a basis for our analysis existing processes or structures.

Similarly, Checkland's (1981) soft systems methodology enables us to base our analysis on the processes (he uses the term activities) that are required to achieve a defined objective (formulated in what he terms a root definition) which can represent a minor or major departure from the current situation, depending on what is perceived as relevant and appropriate. In addition, it is often the case that the scope of the analysis is broad and almost certainly cross-functional because, almost by definition, a narrowly-focused, functionally-based analysis is likely to be asystemic!

In addition, Senn (1992) reminds us that it is often the case that, in situations where IT has been the catalyst for change, radical improvement in competitive standing may have arisen from *incremental* change in *existing* information systems (IS) or their application. Clemons (1986) questions the sustainability of any competitive advantage that may have been brought about by IT, unless it is accompanied by improved skills and knowledge on the part of the firm concerned, with the IS being embedded into new business practice, thereby rendering it more difficult for competitors simply to replicate what has been achieved.

A second point of departure from the analysis of many an advocate of BPR is that radical change will be required in every case. Notwithstanding evidence that suggests radical improvements can be achieved through incremental change (Senn, 1992), it appears to be almost self evident that periods of change need to be followed by periods of relative stability during which time the change is being put into effect. Lewin's ("unfreezing", "change", "refreezing") analysis is apposite in this context (Lewin, 1951). This is not to say that no change should occur in the refreezing era; organizations will always need to adapt to the changing circumstances and environments in which they operate.

But there is an even more subtle, but no less crucial, point about the nature of change and stability that seems to have been overlooked in the rush to BPR:

"Change is ubiquitous. Or is it? In the micro-events which surround our particular lives and in the daily trumpetings of the media change has an ever-present illusion of reality. Yet observe other men consciously attempting to move large and small systems in different directions, or attempt it yourself, and one sees what a difficult and complicated human process change is. And there is the problem of perspective. Where we sit not only influences where we stand, but also what we see. No observer of life or form begins with his mind a blank, to be gradually filled with evidence. Time itself sets a frame of reference for what changes are seen and how those changes are explained. The more we look at present-day events the easier it is to identify change; the longer we stay with an emergent process and further back we go to disentangle its origins, the more we can identify continuities. Empirically and theoretically, change and continuity need one another ... Change and continuity, process and structure, are inextricably linked." (Pettigrew, 1985, p.1)

BPR IN THE CONTEXT OF BUSINESS STRATEGY

In one of the more thoughtful contributions to the topic of business strategy, Whittington (1993) identifies four major schools of thought which have characterised developments in our understanding of the topic since the 1960s. These he labels *classical, processual, evolutionary* and *systemic*. He locates the four generic approaches on the kind of two-by-two grid (Figure 10.1), now all too familiar to us all.

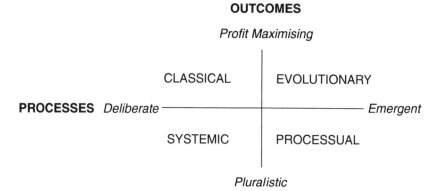

OUTCOMES

Profit Maximising

CLASSICAL | EVOLUTIONARY

PROCESSES *Deliberate* —————————————— *Emergent*

SYSTEMIC | PROCESSUAL

Pluralistic

Figure 10.1   *Four approaches to business strategy*
Reprinted from *What is Strategy—and Does it Matter?* by Richard Whittington,
p 3. Copyright 1993 by Routledge.

The underlying philosophy of the *classical* approach is the kind of self interest first identified by Adam Smith in his *Wealth of Nations*. Formal, deliberate plans are the result of rational analysis. Competition is the watchword. Similarly, the *evolutionary* approach has as its objective, survival in the jungle that is the marketplace. It takes a more fatalistic view of the world: organizations are unable to anticipate and respond to environmental changes, it is the market itself that makes the choices. The best one can hope to do is optimize the current fit between one's organization and the business environment, and hope that this will lead to survival. The *processual* school also takes a fairly pragmatic view of the world. Here, the argument is that strategy emerges, not from the marketplace, but as a result of individual actions, which are themselves a series of compromises. Given the complexity of the environment, all that one can hope to do is to adapt to changing circumstances and to pursue an objective of satisficing. The *systemic* school of thought is more recent, and more optimistic in its outlook. While it recognizes the plurality in desired outcomes, it also recognises that these are sociologically sensitive, that cultural influences will play a major part in their determination. Table 10.2 provides an overview of the key features of the four generic approaches to strategy.

If we analyze the underlying philosophy of BPR, we can see immediately that it fits most closely with the classical school. Profit maximization is the key; little thought is given to more pluralistic outcomes; there is little concern for cultural, contextual issues other than to deal with them as obstacles to change; the process is a deliberate one—a rational analysis (undertaken by senior executives) of the key

Table 10.2 *Key aspects of the four schools of strategic thought*

	Classical	Processual	Evolutionary	Systemic
Strategy	Formal	Crafted	Efficient	Embedded
Rationale	Profit maximization	Vague	Survival	Local
Focus	Planning	Internal politics	Environment	Culture, society
Processes	Analytical	Bargaining, learning	Keep options open	Social fit
Key influences	Economics	Psychology	Economics, Biology	Sociology
Key Period	1960s	1970s	1980s	1990s

Reprinted from *What is Strategy—and Does it Matter?* by Richard Whittington, p 40. Copyright 1993 by Routledge.

business processes in line with a shared business vision that meets customer requirements.

It seems, then, that our radical new departure from the staid approaches of yore is in fact more of a rerun of the classical approaches of the 1960s! And given that the major features that distinguish BPR from existing approaches, or so it is claimed, turn out to be not so clear cut after all, one is left to ponder whether there is anything special or even helpful about the process, especially when so little is provided in terms of advice regarding the *implementation* of the (radical) change.

BPR IN CONTEXT: TOWARDS AN HOLISTIC FRAMEWORK

But let us not "throw out the baby with the bathwater". If we take into account its limitations and place BPR in the context of current thinking on both strategy and change, we can utilize the most useful features of the approach to good effect. If, at the same time, we remember to incorporate information and IT into our consideration of the topic, we might avoid the myopia that all too often exists when treating strategy and change from the sole perspective of marketing and strategic management on the one hand, or organizational behaviour on the other.[3]

---

[3] It is so often the case that our treatment of the subject of strategy and change is considered from the perspective of a particular discipline only. We seem to be imprisoned in our own disciplinary base. Strategy is, or so it is often argued, the domain of Marketing; change, that of Organizational Behaviour. In addition, when reading any well-known text on strategy or organizational change, how often do the topics of information and IT get considered? And if they are considered, the treatment is likely to be either superficial or, at the other extreme, filled with hyperbole, with IT being seen as the key to organizational success! A more balanced, multidisciplinary view (something that the BPR literature is beginning to hint at) is rare indeed.

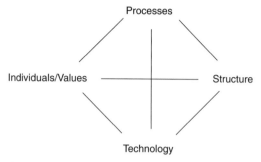

Figure 10.2   *An amended version of Leavitt's "diamond"*
(source: amended from Davis & Olson, 1984, p.355)

One way of placing BPR in this broader context is to reflect on the lessons brought to us by the socio-technical school (eg. the work of the Tavistock Institute of Human Relations soon after the end of the Second World War) and by Leavitt (1965). Leavitt's so-called "diamond" reminds us that any change in process, for example, is likely to have an impact elsewhere in the socio-technical system concept that can be used to describe an organization. An amendment to the original framework proposed by Leavitt which takes into account the cultural issues brought to our attention by proponents of the *systemic* school of strategic thinking (eg. Granovetter, 1985; Whitley, 1991) is provided as Figure 10.2.

   What this analysis suggests is that BPR should be seen as but one aspect of the socio-technical approach implied by the early work of Leavitt (1965). Our focus should not be on process alone, neither should it depend solely on the opportunities provided by new technology. The assessment should certainly take these into account, but in addition, should understand the cultural context in which strategy is being formulated and change is to be implemented. It also needs to take into account the art of the possible ... and this understanding will come in part from an assessment of the implications for organizational structure and the attitudes and beliefs of all relevant stakeholders, both internal to the firm and outside it.

A SOCIO-TECHNICAL APPROACH TO BPR

Given the above analysis, a socio-technical approach to business strategy formation and organizational change, which incorporates IS considerations and aspects of the BPR philosophy, but does not place IT centre stage, nor assumes that change will be necessarily radical and processual, would seem to hold out some promise. The approach is summarised as Figure 10.3.

While the approach might at first sight be placed towards the deliberate half of the horizontal spectrum of Figure 10.1, it nevertheless attempts to incorporate emergent thinking in addition. In the context of the vertical spectrum, it is located towards the pluralistic pole rather than meekly assuming that the outcome is purely about profit maximization.

The approach also incorporates the kind of thinking championed by de Gues (1988) among others in that it views the strategy formation and implementation process as being concerned with learning (as a result of a review of both the intended and unintended impacts of previous actions—planned and unplanned). It also uses the creation of scenarios as a means of considering alternative actions, and reviewing taken-for-granted assumptions about the business and its environment (see also Schnaars, 1987; Galliers, 1993).

Based on the work of Checkland (1981), the approach described below also takes into account Lewin's (1951) analysis that a period of change requires creation of a favourable climate in which change *can* take place ("unfreezing"), followed by a period in which the required change is set in place ("freezing"). A number of feedback loops have been incorporated into the process in order to indicate that it is essentially an iterative one which builds upon past experiences and an evaluation of both intended and unintended consequences of the changes that are being implemented, and the changing nature of the business (and technological) environment in which the organization is operating. The iterative nature of the approach assists the recognition that strategy is, to some extent at least, emergent (*cf.*, Figure 10.1). As a result, the process is designed to aid the kind of organizational learning advocated by Argyris and Schön (1978).

As we have seen, key stakeholders have to be favourably disposed to change for change strategies to have any real chance of success. There is a tendency in much of the BPR literature to view BPR as a process instigated by senior executives and often orchestrated by external consultants. This is not the only mode of operation, nor is it always likely to lead to a motivated workforce should the change include—as it often does—downsizing and forced redundancy. Indeed, we should be aware that in many firms, the anticipated economic and organizational benefits of downsizing have failed to materialize and that any "reductions in headcount need to be viewed as part of a process of continuous improvement that includes organizational redesign, along with broad, systemic changes designed to eliminate [redundant processes], waste, and inefficiency" (Cascio, 1993, p.95). Downsizing as a

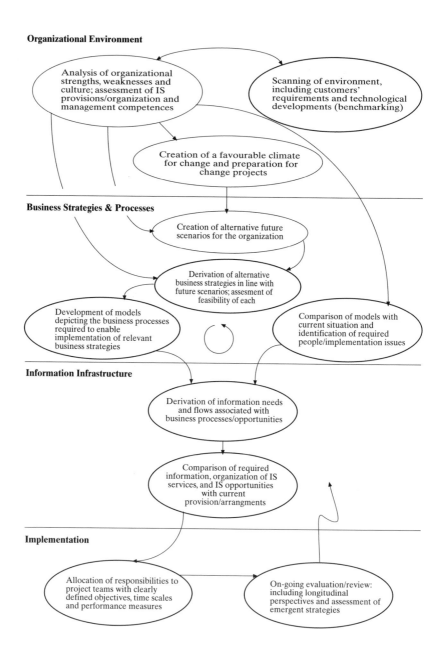

Organizational Environment

Analysis of organizational strengths, weaknesses and culture; assessment of IS provisions/organization and management competences

Scanning of environment, including customers' requirements and technological developments (benchmarking)

Creation of a favourable climate for change and preparation for change projects

Business Strategies & Processes

Creation of alternative future scenarios for the organization

Derivation of alternative business strategies in line with future scenarios; assesment of feasibility of each

Development of models depicting the business processes required to enable implementation of relevant business strategies

Comparison of models with current situation and identification of required people/implementation issues

Information Infrastructure

Derivation of information needs and flows associated with business processes/opportunities

Comparison of required information, organization of IS services, and IS opportunities with current provision/arrangments

Implementation

Allocation of responsibilities to project teams with clearly defined objectives, time scales and performance measures

On-going evaluation/review: including longitudinal perspectives and assessment of emergent strategies

Figure 10.3   *A Socio-Technical approach to business and IS strategy formation and the management of organizational transformation (source: amended from Galliers, 1993, p.206; 1994, p.6)*

sole objective of BPR is likely to be unsuccessful.

The approach being advocated herein has been used to good effect as part of a series of workshops rather than relying on individual interviews. The benefits to be gained from workshops of this kind are well documented (see, for example, Hardaker & Ward, 1987 and Galliers, et al, 1994), and include the opportunity to debate contrasting views as an integral part of the process of gaining a shared vision, i.e. rather than waiting to raise points of debate as an outcome. In the latter instance, such issues remain as obstacles to implementation. In the former, attitudes may well change, and even if they do not, implementation issues can be identified as part of the very process of strategy formulation.

Nevertheless, it is as well to prepare for these workshops in terms of clarifying the nature of such roles as project champion, project manager and facilitator; carefully selecting a team from a range of functional backgrounds, and deciding on the membership of a steering committee (see, for example, Ward, 1990).

A climate in which change is eagerly anticipated is likely to be achieved by a realization that all is not well, for example, that competitors are making inroads into one's markets, that key customers are becoming increasingly discontented with one's products and/or services, and that personnel are becoming increasingly frustrated with the way business is conducted. This perceived need for action can be reinforced and harnessed by the process advocated herein. The very analysis of organizational strengths and weaknesses and environmental opportunities and threats, when undertaken by key executives and with the involvement of personnel who are responsible for key day-to-day operational activities, can often lead to concerted action and, properly handled, an enthusiastic response to ways and means of dealing with the problems that have thereby been uncovered.

The analysis of the internal and external environments can usefully utilize such tried and tested techniques as SWOT (analysis of strengths, weaknesses, opportunities and threats), PEST (analysis of political, economic, social and technical environments), Porter's (1980; 1985) five forces and value chain analysis, and the like. In addition, however, it is worthwhile, especially in the context of understanding the nature of the IS/IT agenda in all of this, to take stock of the quality of IS provision and the full range of issues associated with the management of IS services.

The extent to which an organization is dependent on IS can be estimated by the application of McFarlan's (1984) so-called strategic grid, as depicted in Figure 10.4. In addition, an assessment of the appropriateness of an aggressive competitive strategy with respect to

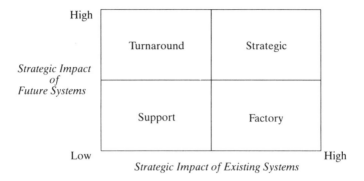

Figure 10.4   *IT strategic grid*
Reprinted by permission of *Harvard Business Review*. From *Information Technology Changes the Way You Compete* by F.W. McFarlan, 62(3), May–June, 98–103. Copyright © 1984 by the President and Fellows of Harvard College; all rights reserved.

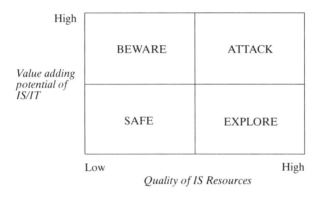

Figure 10.5   *Choosing an appropriate IT-based business strategy (McLaughlin, et al, 1983)*

the utilization of IS/IT can be made using a similar grid developed by McLaughlin, et al (1983), as shown in Figure 10.5.

As indicated by Figure 10.4, having undertaken the kind of analysis advocated by Porter & Millar (1985), for example, it is possible to estimate the value adding potential to the firm of IS/IT. An assessment of the quality of IS resources also needs to be undertaken, however. Organizations with sound IS resources and good business opportunities from the application of IS/IT are clearly in a position to adopt an aggressive stance. Those that have identified only limited opportunities are likely to be relatively safe from attack by competitors even if their IS resources are weak. Conversely, those in a similar position but with sound IS resources may wish quietly to explore the situation further as the business/technological environment changes and/or they uncover a previously hidden opportunity. Should a firm identify considerable value adding potential from IS/IT, but have relatively poor resources, there is a requirement to act with due urgency. Such an enterprise is currently in a "Catch 22" situation, being damned if they do and damned if they don't. An aggressive strategy is likely to become unstuck since they are likely to lack the capacity—both in technological and human terms—to see it through to a successful conclusion. Inaction is likely to lead to the firm coming under attack from the competition.

How then can a firm make an assessment of the quality of its IS resources and decide what urgent action it should take? This is not simply an assessment of the strategic impact of IS as in McFarlan's (1984) analysis. A broader evaluation is required and this can be achieved by a development on the well known "stages of growth" concept (Gibson & Nolan, 1974; Nolan, 1979) which incorporates the so-called "7S" analysis pioneered by McKinsey & Co. (see, eg, Pascale & Athos, 1981). This broader stages of growth model is described in detail in Galliers & Sutherland (1991) and lessons from its application are recounted in Galliers (1991). It is illustrated in outline in Figure 10.6.

As with other aspects of the approach, we have found that the revised model is best used in a workshop environment where key stakeholders can debate their different perceptions about the current state of affairs since there almost certainly will be different perceptions expressed! It is almost always the case that certain elements of the 7S framework will be at different stages of growth. The resultant profile will help to identify where particular urgent action is required[4]. In addition, it is almost bound to be the case that different parts of the organization (eg., functions, SBUs, sites) will find themselves at different stages of growth and this may well point to differing solutions/initiatives in different parts of the enterprise.

Placing the current company profile in relation to the profile that existed, say, five years, three years and one year ago can be particularly

---

[4] For example, in a large multinational chemical company, it was apparent that its current situation could best be described as passing between stages 3 and 4 of the model—except for the fact that a Board level IT Director had recently been appointed. In the discussion which ensued, it became clear that his Board colleagues had assumed that his appointment was practically all that was needed to move the company rapidly ahead in terms of its strategic use of IT, and to deal with the residual relationship problems between the IS/IT function and the business units typical of stage 3. As a result of the workshop, expectations of the new IT Director were revised downwards, and a joint approach, with other members of the Board taking responsibility for a number of initiatives, was agreed. The CEO confided later that, had the model not been discussed in the workshop, it would have been highly likely that very little would have been achieved and that the IT Director's career would have been in jeopardy within a matter of months! The joint approach that resulted led to a series of initiatives that have already borne fruit.

Stage\nElement	I	II	III	IV	V	VI
Strategy	Acquisition of IT (Services)	Audit of IT Provision	Top-Down Analysis	Integration, Coordination	Stategy Linkage	Interactive Planning, Collaboration
Structure	Informal	Finance Controlled	Centralised IS Dept	Information Centre(s)	Departmental Coalitions	Coordinated Coalitions
Systems	Ad Hoc. Operational Accounting	Gaps/ Duplication; Large Back-log; Heavy Maintenance	Uncontrolled End-user Computing Versus Centralised Systems	Decentralised Approach, Some Executive Information Systems	Coordinated: Centralised & Decentralised IS; some stategic IS	Inter-organizational Systems; IS/IT-based Products & Services
Staff	Programmers, Contractors	Systems Analysts, DP Manager	IS Planners, IS Manager, Database Specialists	Business Analysts, Information Resource Manager	Business & IS Planners Integrated	IS/IT Director (Board Level)
Style	Unaware	"Don't bother me – (I'm too busy)"	Abrogation Delegation	Partnerships and Benefits Management	Individual Product Champions	Multidisciplinary teams for key themes
Skills	Individual; Technical: Low level	Systems Development Methodology; Cost-benefit Analysis	IS awareness; Project Management	IS/Business Awareness	Entrepreneurial Marketing	Lateral Thinking re. IT/IS potential
Shared Values	Obfuscation	Confusion	Senior Management Concern, DP Defence	Cooperation	Opportunistic	Strategy Making & Implementation

Figure 10.6   *Assessing the Quality of an Organization's Information Systems Management: A Revised "Stages of Growth" Model (amended from Galliers & Sutherland, 1991, p.111)*

insightful, as this gives an indication of the rate of progress that has been made, if any. This is an important point. There is no God-given right for firms to move towards the later stages of growth as implied by earlier models. Indeed, it can often be the case that firms may revert to earlier stages. Discussion on the reasons for lack of progress or reversion to earlier stages is particularly enlightening.

Having taken stock of the current (and recent past) situation, it is useful then to consider possible future scenarios (Schnaars, 1987; de Gues, 1988) for the organization as a precursor to considering alternative business strategies that appear to be appropriate in these different contexts. A helpful technique in this aspect of the approach is one developed by the SEMA Group. This considers the future in terms of "facts" (those elements that are considered to be relatively stable within the planning period); "heavy trends" (those trends that are thought very likely to continue during the planning period); and "issues" (those elements over which there is disagreement or considerable doubt). By building up alternative scenarios by altering the "issues" while keeping the "facts" constant and making minor alterations to the "trends", it is possible to consider alternative strategies in the light of the differing "futures" thus constructed. It also proves useful to include a counter-intuitive "future" (i.e., altering key "facts"), to identify what the firm might do in such unforeseen circumstances.

Having agreed on a small number of scenarios following discussion of a range of alternatives (three or four is fairly normal), one can begin to consider an appropriate business strategy in each context and the potential role that IS/IT might play in each. Questioning the key assumptions on which these strategies are based is an important route to the identification of strategic information.

A comparison of the processes that go to make up such models, and their interrelationships, especially when the potential of IS/IT is being considered at the same time, often leads to the realization that some of the current business processes which until this time were considered to be key to business success, can actually be streamlined or even omitted altogether. Conversely, processes that are crucial may not be in place or may be undertaken poorly.

It is important to remember that the models are based on *required* processes and do not relate to existing organizational arrangements nor to current functional boundaries. An information architecture based on key information needs and *flows as these relate to required, not existing, processes*, is a natural outcome of this kind of thinking. Key information can be identified by using such techniques as the critical success factor (CSF) approach (Rockart, 1979), augmented by its corollary, critical *failure* factors (Galliers, 1993) and the critical *assumptions* upon which the strategies are based. On-going assessment of the impact of change projects is assisted by the collection of information of this kind.

CONCLUDING REMARKS

This chapter has attempted to answer the question as to where BPR fits into our thinking and practice regarding business/IS strategy formulation and implementation, and what role IT might play in organizational change. It has cast doubt on the novelty of the BPR approach, classifying it with the more traditional strategic approaches that were popularized in the 1960s. Having said that, it has not dismissed it out of hand but has attempted to incorporate some of its more useful features into current thinking on business strategy and the management of change. What is more, the chapter identifies a common omission in much of the BPR literature, i.e. the lack of guidance regarding how one might go about implementing the conclusions drawn from the analysis. In other words, it provides a means by which the kind of discontinuous thinking advocated by Hammer (1990) can actually be achieved.

The comparison of what is needed in the context of alternative future scenarios may lead to a decision that radical change is required—and, just as likely, that it may not! Discontinuous thinking and radical change may well not be synonymous. Incremental change may well be more appropriate, for example, during a period following rapid change (cf., "freezing") or where the analysis suggests radical change is either unnecessary or foolhardy.

IT can often be a catalyst in this process and IT opportunities for new or enhanced products and services should certainly not be overlooked. Having said that, an aggressive competitive strategy with IT at its heart is only likely to yield benefits when the firm's IS resources (human as well as infological and technological) are sound. Organizations should be wary of the hyperbole surrounding the topic of competitive advantage arising from IT, especially those without a sound IT and IS management track record.

The approach that has been described above gives equal weight to internal as well as external concerns. Customer—potential as well as current—requirements are highlighted, as is the changing competitive, political, economic and technological environment. A fresh review of what might otherwise be seen as essential internal business processes is also at the heart of the analysis. Above all, however, concern needs to be focused—as part of the process itself—on the propensity of key stakeholders for change and on the implementation issues. A more balanced, socio-technical perspective is what seems to be necessary.

A word of caution on the process is that it is meant to be applied flexibly and on an ongoing basis so that it contributes to organizational learning and ensures stakeholder participation. The techniques that have been incorporated into it in this chapter, for the purposes of ensuring greater understanding, are meant to be illustrative rather than prescriptive. While they have been found to be extremely helpful in a range of organizational change projects, it is more than likely that other techniques can be applied as successfully. The approach described in this chapter should not be applied rigidly—rigid application leads to rigid thinking and that is certainly *not* what is required!

Finally, it is perhaps worth reflecting on the following:

> "To most business people in the United States, re-engineering has become a word that stands for restructuring, lay-offs, and too often failed change programmes ... the re-engineering fever has broken ... companies that embraced it as the silver bullet are now looking for ways to rebuild the organisation's torn fabric."

I could not have put it better myself! It is surely difficult to argue against such compelling evidence—the more so as the words are those of one of BPR's founding fathers—Thomas Davenport (1996; p.70)!

REFERENCES

Argyris, C. and Schön, D., 1978, *Organizational Learning*, Addison-Wesley, Reading, MA.

Cascio, W., 1993, Downsizing: What Do We Know? What Have We Learned? *Academy of Management Executive*, 7(1), 95–104.

Checkland, P.B., 1981, *Systems Thinking, Systems Practice*, Wiley, Chichester.

Clemons, E.K., 1986, Information Systems for Sustainable Competitive Advantage, *Information & Management*, November, 131–136.

Davenport, T.H., 1993, *Process Innovation. Re-engineering Work through Information Technology*, Harvard Business School Press, Boston, MA.

Davenport, T.H., 1996, Why Re-engineering Failed: The Fad that Forgot People, *Fast Company*, Premier Issue, 70–74.

Davis, G.B. and Olson, M.H., 1984, *Management Information Systems: Conceptual Foundations, Structure and Development*, (2nd edition), McGraw Hill, New York, NY.

de Gues, A., 1988, Planning as Learning, *Harvard Business Review*, 66(2), March-April, 70–74.

Galliers, R.D., 1991, Strategic Information Systems Planning: Myths, Reality and Guidelines for Successful Implementation, *European Journal of Information Systems*, 1(1), 55–64.

Galliers, R.D., 1993, Towards a Flexible Information Architecture: Integrating Business Strategies, Information Systems Strategies and Business Process Redesign, *Journal of Information Systems*, 3(3), 199–213.

Galliers, R.D., 1994, Information Systems, Operational Research and Business Re-engineering, *International Transactions on Operational Research*, 1(2), 1–9.

Galliers, R.D., Pattison, E.M. and Reponen, T., 1994, Strategic Information Systems Planning Workshops: Lessons from Three Cases, *International Journal of Information Management*, 14(1), February, 51–66.

Galliers, R.D. and Sutherland, A.R., 1991, Information Systems Management and Strategy Formulation: The "Stages of Growth" Model Revisited, *Journal of Information Systems*, 1(2), 89–114.

Gibson, C. and Nolan, R.L., 1974, Managing the Four Stages of EDP Growth, *Harvard Business Review*, 52(1), January-February, 76–88.

Granovetter, M., 1985, Economic Action and Social Structure: The Problem of Embeddedness, *American Journal of Sociology*, 91(3), 481–510.

Hammer, M., 1990, Re-engineering Work: Don't Automate, Obliterate, *Harvard Business Review*, July-August, 68(4), 104–112.

Hardaker, M. and Ward, B.K., 1987, How to Make a Team Work, *Harvard Business Review*, 65(6), November-December, 112–120.

Leavitt, H.J., 1965, Applying Organizational Change in Industry: Structural, Technological and Humanistic Approaches, in J.G. March (ed.), *Handbook of Organizations*, Rand McNally, Chicago, IL.

Lewin, K., 1951, *Field Theory in Social Science*, Harper & Row, New York, NY.

McFarlan, F.W., 1984, Information Technology Changes the Way You Compete, *Harvard Business Review*, 62(3), May-June, 98–103.

McLaughlin, M., Howe, R. and Cash, Jr., J.I., 1983, Changing Competitive Ground Rules—The Impact of Computers and Communications in the 1980s, Unpublished working paper, Graduate School of Business Administration, Harvard University, Boston, MA.

Maruca, R.F., 1994, The Right Way to Go Global: An Interview with Whirlpool CEO David Whitwam, *Harvard Business Review*, 72(2), March-April, 135–145.

Nolan, R.L., 1979, Managing the Crises in Data Processing, *Harvard Business Review*, 57(2), March-April.

Pascale, R.T. and Athos, A.G., 1981, *The Art of Japanese Management*, Penguin, Harmondsworth.

Pettigrew, A.M., 1985, *The Awakening Giant: Continuity and Change in ICI*, Basil Blackwell, Oxford.

Porter, M.E., 1980, *Competitive Strategy: Techniques for Analyzing Industries and Competitors*, The Free Press, New York, NY.

Porter, M.E., 1985, *Competitive Advantage: Creating and Sustaining Superior Performance*, The Free Press, New York, NY.

Porter, M.E. and Millar, V.E., 1985, How Information Gives You Competitive Advantage, *Harvard Business Review*, 63(2), March-April, 149–160.

Quinn, J.B., 1980, *Strategies for Change. Logical Incrementalism*, Richard D Irwin, Homewood, IL.

Rockart, J.F., 1979, Chief Executives Define Their Own Data Needs, *Harvard Business Review*, 57(2), March-April, 81–93.

Schnaars, S.P., 1987, How to Develop and Use Scenarios, *Long Range Planning*, 20(1), 105–114. Reprinted in R.G. Dyson (ed.), 1990, *Strategic Planning: Models and Analytical Techniques*, Wiley, Chichester, 153–167.

Senn, J.A., 1992, The Myths of Strategic Information Systems: What Defines True Competitive Advantage? *Journal of Information Systems Management*, Summer, 7–12.

Ward, B.K., 1990, Planning for Profit. in T, Lincoln (ed.), *Managing Information Systems for Profit*, Wiley, Chichester.

Watts, J., 1993, The Future of Business Process Re-engineering, *Business Change & Re-engineering*, 1(3), Winter, 4–5.

Whitley, R.D., 1991, The Social Construction of Business Systems in East Asia, *Organization Studies*, 12(1), 1–28.

Whittington, R., 1993, *What is Strategy—and Does it Matter?* Routledge, London.

11
The Role of Information Technology in Organizational Transformation

JON A. TURNER
Stern School of Business, New York University, USA

Re-engineering and business process redesign (BPR) both seek to transform organizations. Whilst it is generally acknowledged that information technology (IT) plays an important role in organization change, there is little agreement on what that role is, the key technologies that could be used, and how they might be applied. This chapter seeks to reaffirm the message given in Chapter 10 that our purpose is not to dismiss BPR out of hand, but to treat the subject seriously. IT and organizational change is a complex business. Here we consider ways that IT can be used in organizational transformation, with specific technologies being identified along with areas of application. We conclude with a discussion of the role information systems staff may play in this process.

INTRODUCTION

It is increasingly apparent that many firms are finding it difficult to compete in today's business environment. Not only has competition increased and become more global, but its nature has changed—often fundamentally.

Information Technology and Organizational Transformation. Edited by R.D. Galliers and W.R.J. Baets. © 1998 John Wiley & Sons Ltd

In the past, being a low cost producer, or maintaining one's market share was often sufficient as a business strategy. Today, such approaches seem inadequate. More important is the ability to respond quickly to opportunities and threats, to reduce time-to-market, to improve customer service, and to enhance the quality of products and services. Firms are striving now to deliver superior product quality and customer service by leveraging their knowledge and human resources (Hammer, 1990). Clearly, competing on this basis requires different business practices and skills than does competing on size or cost.

When these inadequacies in a firm's strategies, structure and processes become recognized, attention turns, quite reasonably, to remedies—how a firm can be "transformed", or changed. Few notions of organizational transformation have captured the fancy of researchers and practitioners as have those of *re-engineering* organizations (Hammer, 1990; Hammer & Champy, 1993) and *business process redesign* (Davenport, 1993; Davenport & Short, 1990). In these activities, managers are urged to rethink, radically, the business they are in—their business processes, their firm's structure, their value adding activities—and how these take place. Increasingly, information technology (IT) is being promoted both as the primary material out of which new organizations will be fashioned, as well as the driving force in bringing these transformations about.

However, system designers have always used times of new system implementations as opportunities to make substantial organizational and operational change. Often information flows and procedures are completely rethought and jobs reconstituted before an information system is implemented. And job design, including issues of specialization, workflow and division of labour, has been a major theme of industrial organization for the past 50 years. What do these terms "re-engineering" and "business process redesign" mean in this context? And where does, and how should, IT fit in? What does IT enable you to do in organizations that cannot be done without it, and which specific technologies have the greatest potential for application? Finally, what role do and should the information systems staff play in organizational transformation? We consider these issues in the following sections.

CONCEPT DESCRIPTION

While there is little agreement as to what re-engineering and business process redesign really mean, the clearest descriptions of them have been given by Hammer (1990), Hammer & Champy (1993), Davenport & Short (1990), and Davenport (1993).

Re-engineering:

> "strives to break away from the old rules about how we organize and conduct business. It involves recognizing and rejecting some of them and finding imaginative new ways of accomplishing work" (Hammer, 1990, pp.104–105).

Business process redesign is:

> "the analysis and design of workflows and processes within and between organizations ... Business activities should be viewed as more than a collection of individual or even functional tasks; they should be broken down into processes that can be designed for maximum effectiveness, in both manufacturing and service environments" (Davenport & Short, 1990, pp.11–12).

Thus, both re-engineering and BPR are similar in that they desire to *break away* from current work practices and replace them with redesigned ones. Both accomplish this *by identifying* critical business processes that (may) *cut across* normal functional and organizational boundaries, *analyzing* these processes, and *redesigning* them for substantial improvement in performance.

For this process to succeed, Hammer has the following to say:

> "The extent of these changes suggests one factor that is necessary for re-engineering to succeed: executive leadership with real vision. No one in an organization wants re-engineering. It is confusing and disruptive and affects everything people have grown accustomed to. Only if top-level managers back the effort and outlast the company cynics will people take re-engineering seriously ... Re-engineering cannot be planned meticulously and accomplished in small cautious steps. It's an all-or-nothing proposition with an uncertain result" (Hammer, 1990, pp.105, 112).

Re-engineering is not incremental change. Rather it is *radical transformation*, or what Tushman, et al, (1986) have referred to as "frame-breaking" change. Radical change of this nature is risky[1]. Consistent with the high risk nature of re-engineering, consultants estimate that upwards of 70% of re-engineering efforts fail (Hammer & Champy, 1993). And, few firms undertake it unless they are in grave difficulty (I/S Analyzer, 1993).

---

[1] Frame breaking change implies a variety of extreme measures, such as the wholesale replacement of top management, which are not articulated in the literature on re-engineering and business process redesign (c.f. Tushman et al, 1986). This omission in the re-engineering and BPR literature is a major conceptual flaw.

ROLE OF TECHNOLOGY

There are several views of the role of IT in re-engineering which can be classified as "central," usually advanced by promoters and advocates, and "peripheral", often put forward by more detached observers. The central view of technology's role in re-engineering is represented by Hammer, who states re-engineering should "use the power of modern technology to radically redesign our business processes in order to achieve dramatic improvements in their performance [with IT being used] not to automate an existing process but to enable a new one" (Hammer, 1990, p. 108). Davenport & Short (1990, p.12) concur and suggest that in BPR, IT "should be viewed as more than an automating or mechanizing force; it can fundamentally reshape the way business is done".

Thus, in both approaches, IT is viewed as an enabler and driver; it provides new opportunities for the redesign of work, for example, in co-ordinating activities, in relaxing constraints on where work is performed and who performs it, and in making information and knowledge more readily available to workers; and in the way that firms are structured. Technology, in this view, is an *essential* element of the transformation. Note, however, that the converse is not necessarily true. Investing heavily in technology does not automatically bring about organizational transformation.

Hammer (1990) provides a set of principles[2] for using technology in re-engineered jobs:

- Organize around outcomes rather than tasks.
- Have those who use the output of a process perform the process.
- Subsume information processing work into the real work that produces the information.
- Treat geographically dispersed resources as if they were centralized using IT to co-ordinate activities.
- Link parallel activities instead of integrating their results.
- Put the decision point where the work is performed.
- Put control into the process.
- Capture information once at the source.

In this view IT can, by improving the exchange of information among workers, remove constraints of where they are located, thus promoting

---

[2] These principles apply to a single worker, whole job, which is the primary focus in re-engineering.

geographically dispersed workgroups. Capturing data once, at its source, and having the person performing a task also make the decisions concerning it, permits redundant steps in a process to be removed and it reduces hand-off errors. Rather than attempting to synchronize work at completion, IT can be used to link work together while it is being accomplished, leading to better integration. Information is delivered to workers when they need it and where they need it, and it is integrated into task accomplishment, rather than being obtained as separate process.

From this perspective, IT is central to performing re-engineering and accomplishing business process redesign. I/S Analyzer observed that "everyone agrees that information systems play a critical role in business re-engineering" (1993, p.l). Hammer & Champy (1993) consider information systems as the key or "essential" enabler of these radical process changes. The literature is not specific, however, as to *which technologies* have the greatest potential to influence the redesign of work or *how* they might be applied. We will consider these issues in the following section.

In contrast to this IT-centered view, less technology-involved observers tend to underplay the potential role of IT in BPR. For example, the organizational change literature pays little attention to technology in describing the functioning of new organizational forms, or in the process of bringing about planned organizational change. Drucker (1988) suggests that knowledge intensive organizations will become flatter as information flows among individuals, presumably through some sort of technology, and will replace the information handling activities of middle management, although he is not specific about how these flows will take place. Beer et al (1990) and Charan (1991)—authors involved heavily in organizational change—do not even consider technology in their discussion of approaches to change. Walton (1989) acknowledges the importance of IT, but is quiet on which information technologies might be used and how they might be applied.

OPPORTUNITIES PRESENTED BY INFORMATION TECHNOLOGY

While we conclude there is no "technological" imperative in re-engineering, technology can be used to significant advantage in restructuring operational activities and in improving worker co-ordination. We consider now the specific technologies that can enable improved worker performance and provide support for new organizational forms.

Technology Infrastructure

When workers are highly interconnected by IT, they can send messages and work products to each other and share information without concern for where the other worker is physically located. This permits work to be structured around services, products and clients instead of around functions. In a highly interconnected work environment, single worker whole jobs with a strong customer service focus can reduce greatly errors due to co-ordination failures and discontinuities in work processes (Hammer, 1990). Under these conditions, hierarchical flows of information are partially replaced by lateral ones to the person best able to provide useful information or assistance, rather than to a supervisor who has to then seek out the proper remedial action.

This interconnection of workers usually takes place using a local area network (LAN), where each worker has access to a workstation on his or her desk. In environments where workers move frequently around, such as in sales or where there is extensive field work, a laptop computer and a docking station can be substituted for a desk-top workstation, thus allowing one computer to support both field and desk work. Print and file services are provided on the LAN, permitting these resources to be shared among workers on the network instead of requiring each of them to have large capacity disk storage and a printer.

LANs are constructed by assembling off-the-shelf components such as routers, hubs, bridges, interface cards, connectors, and cabling. They usually support a group of workers who are located in proximity, for example, on a floor of a building or in a small building and they, usually, require a separate LAN operating system which resides both on a file server and on the workstation in addition to the normal workstation operating system, (except for the Apple Macintosh and Microsoft Windows 95/NT which have network support integrated into their workstation operating systems). When there is more than one such group that is relatively close to each other, for example in the same building, the LANs would be interconnected through bridges.

When there are groups working together who are located at a distance greater than can be connected using a LAN, the individual LANs are interconnected through leased lines obtained from a common carrier service provider, or by purchasing packet switched services from a wide area network (WAN) provider. This network of interconnected LANs would have some common services, such as authenticating users of the network for security purposes, a name service so that programs and data could be located independent of what machine they may reside on, and a phone book or address server to locate the address of workers on the network. In this network, or cluster of interconnected LANs, there would be a connection, or gateway, to an X400 service provider so that messages can be sent and received from people external to the firm's network and possibly to the Internet.

Such a configuration permits:

- Messages to be sent to and received from anyone within the firm (cluster of interconnected LANs).
- Documents (in their original form) to be sent to or received from anyone within the firm.
- Sharing of programs and firm specific applications.
- Sharing of data.
- Sharing of special purpose hardware resources, such as printers and computational engines.
- If authorized, sending and receiving of messages and documents from people external to the firm, such as customers or suppliers (through an external gateway).
- If authorized, sharing of data and programming resources with people external to the firm.

In a highly interconnected environment, technically facilitated communication can replace the hierarchy as the primary method of transmitting information within a firm. Data captured once can be used wherever the worker using it is located. This removes the need for replication, although some of it may be needed for performance and reliability purposes, should some of the communications links fail. The decision as to what data should be maintained locally and what should be obtained remotely is a complicated one. Data can be delivered in a manner that makes it appear as if it is coming from one repository although it is actually obtained remotely from many.

Such distributed work environments are consistent with the current trends of distributed processing (client/server) and object oriented application design. In contrast to traditional application systems, where all of the resources necessary to run an application—that is, its data, subroutines, peripheral equipment, and application system code—reside on one machine, distributed processing architectures permit portions of applications to run independently, in a co-ordinated manner, on different machines connected by a network. Conceptually, a client, specific to a particular application and workstation type, runs on a local workstation and communicates over the network, using a standard protocol, with a server located elsewhere.

In most applications, data and the procedures that operate on them are separate. One consequence of this is that almost all applications need to be custom written. Object oriented application design combines procedures, called *methods*, and the data the procedures operate on together in a module, called an *object*. Objects communicate by passing messages to each other. Each object knows what messages it can understand. Objects are grouped into classes in a way that subordinate objects can inherit properties from their superior. This hierarchical partitioning permits a natural decomposition of a system into parts that can be shared, thereby reducing the amount of custom code that needs to be written for each new application. Commonly used objects are packaged together in libraries and sold by software developers. In this manner, a certain degree of programming code reusability is achieved. Object oriented systems are attractive because the clean interface among objects permits modules to be shared and to be replaced without disturbing the remainder of the system.

With such a technology infrastructure, a firm can create shared repositories of best practice for use in preparing proposals and for training. Workers on a common project need not be co-located; they can share work products using special tools or Groupware (see following section on computer support for cooperative work).

A major issue in such an environment is information overload. The flow of messages just becomes too great for individuals to handle. Members of a workgroup may need to establish e-mail filters to inspect the incoming stream of messages in order to separate the consequential from the inconsequential. Sproull & Kiesler (1993) provide an excellent description of the issues involved in working in a highly interconnected organization.

External clients of a firm can be given access to these internal repositories, permitting them to investigate options on their own (making use of the firm's data) thus off-loading some of the firm's service personnel from these activities. Linking external clients directly to a firm's information resources and services opens up new avenues in relationship management. For example, mutual dependencies can be created and the opportunities for collaborative work increase. In such an environment, extreme care must be taken with security. An adequate barrier, or "firewall" must be built to prevent unauthorized access to the firm's data and resources.

Easy scripting languages can allow professionals, or *knowledge workers* in Harry Scarbrough's terms (see Chapter 1), to build computer support for their own work routines. Linking protocols, such as Microsoft's OLE2 and Apple's Open Doc, permit work products in different applications to be synchronized, in a manner that allows the functionality of one system to be available in another. *Publishing* and *subscribe* features allow information to be shared with a number of users on a discretionary basis so that changes in one application are available in another.

Using public domain software, such as *Listserver* and *Gopher*, a firm can create a bulletin board service on a particular topic area, for example, Business Process Redesign, as has been done by Delft University in The Netherlands (BPR-L). With a Listserver, subscribers can decide whether to receive messages from the Listserver when they are received, or to be sent a periodic digest of them. Gopher servers (a menu driven, linked repository with navigation features) can be used to provide information access, and data transfer to workers and clients at their instigation. Using these tools, called an Intranet, a firm can create information repositories, for example, a discussion group that can be shared, or an on-line catalogue of courses, without paying the high price of proprietary software, such as Lotus Notes. Individual workers can have their own contact files, schedules and their key knowledge resources on their workstation, and even take these into the field with them if their workstation undocks. Schedule and client data can then be shared among workers.

In this environment, it is not necessary to agree on one standard office tool, for example, a common spreadsheet or word processor. Most word processors and spreadsheets are able to accept input in foreign formats and the most popular ones run on a number of different types of workstations. Highly integrated environments, such as the Microsoft, Claris, or Lotus office suites, in which applications lose their individual identity, are available now.

Traditional application systems are organized around *transactions*— particular types of business actions, such as adding a purchase to a customer's account. An application may contain the processing for 50 or 100 transaction types. *Workflow* systems are organized around the flow of work. They take an overall business process, such as the processing of a purchase order, and execute the actual tasks that need to be performed, or schedule a task for a human operator, in the proper sequence. Workflow systems can maintain the schedule of overall work activity, assuring both that the job is performed by a certain deadline and that facilities executing tasks maintain desired loading. These systems provide a promising technology for the implementation of re-engineered business processes.

Distributed processing environments are more difficult to manage than centralized ones. It is always hard to time equipment and software acquisition properly; obtaining the equipment early enough to reap economic benefits of long technology life, but not so early that unreliable operation is encountered. Because of the dynamics of the computer equipment business, where for a constant price, performance doubles approximately every 18 months, it is often difficult to recognize long term players. In a distributed environment, it is unlikely that all a firm's equipment can be replaced at the same time. Consequently, a firm is likely to have a heterogeneous equipment environment, increasing the risk of interoperability problems.

Performance becomes more problematic in a distributed environment. Operational monitoring is harder with the result that bottlenecks may not be recognized until after performance degrades. The performance of LANs is traffic dependent and they tend to deteriorate quickly after some point as traffic builds up. Network resolution of name and remote procedure calls can make reliable, distributed application operation harder (there are no easy mechanisms for assuring that end-to-end continuity exists in an application).

In distributed environments, there is a tension between providing enough support to foster innovation on the part of users who may have only rudimentary technical skills, and the control needed to establish standards and to co-ordinate equipment acquisition. It is difficult to justify investments in a distributed technology on the basis of hard cost/benefit analysis[3]. Infrastructure investment costs are substantial and there are few cost displacements, such as the substitution of machine processing for labor. In general, management must be prepared to accept soft benefits that result from improved communication, the easy exchange of documents, and improved access to information. This is the reason that technology infrastructure projects are usually funded centrally.

Computer Support for Cooperative Work (CSCW)

A second technology area that shows promise for enabling BPR and new organizational forms is support for people working together, as in CSCW (cf Chapter 2). If one considers three dimensions of work: where it is performed; who performs it; and whether work is performed at the same or different times; several interesting combinations occur. One class, *intelligent e-mail systems*, supports people in different locations working at different times. A second category, *remote group support systems*, adds shared distributed database features to intelligent e-mail for distributed groups working at different times. A third class, *electronic meeting support systems* (EMS), provides support for groups

---

[3] This is not the case, however, when distributed environments replace centralized ones.

working together in the same place at the same time (i.e. in a meeting) in performing activities, such as idea generation and decision making, using various computer based tools.

The *Information Lens*, developed by Tom Malone at MIT (Lai, Malone, & Yu, 1988) illustrates the class of intelligent e-mail systems. It consists of an object oriented database where an object consists of a collection of fields and values. Objects are arranged in a hierarchy of increasingly specialized object types where an object inherits data, actions and other properties from parents. Relationships among objects are represented by hypertext links. The system uses a template based user interface that resembles forms.

Display formats are tailorable and permit selected fields to be shown and default values to be specified. Semi-autonomous rule based agents that are object specific can be triggered by events and used to classify incoming messages and to retrieve data. Customizable folders can be used to store groups of messages or other objects.

Lotus Notes (Lotus, 1993) illustrates the class of remote group support systems. It consists of a flat (rather than a relational) distributed database of form images that can include text, tables and graphics. Sharing of data takes place by remote users downloading a replicated copy of the databases they are authorized to work with from a Notes database server. Notes provides facilities for organizing data, such as indexing and finding particular documents. The system includes an electronic mail facility. Notes allows extensive customization of output screens and it contains facilities for building special applications, for example, a shared client contact database. Notes has security features and requires considerable administrative support.

Encoding of a Firm's Knowledge

Another technology that supports BPR is the encoding of a portion of a firm's business knowledge or expertise in a form that is machine accessible. These systems, called *expert* or *knowledge base* systems, are used to capture the expertise of outstanding workers and to put it in a form that can be shared among others in a firm. For example, one large accountancy firm in the US has developed an expert system to provide advice to accountants on the latest changes in the tax code. In another case, American Express uses an expert system to authorize credit card charges made by customers because these must be quickly done and because by using the best credit authorizers as models the rate of bad charges can be reduced.

These systems consist of a knowledge base containing narrow domain knowledge unique to a firm, an inference engine to manipulate the knowledge base, and an interface subsystem that allows data to be entered into the system and a dialogue with the operator of the system.

A knowledge base system is constructed by observing an expert performing a task and representing those activities that constitute the task (goals, information, reasoning and conclusions) in the system in one of several formalisms, such as production rules (if A and B are true, then conclude C), or semantic networks. This process is called *knowledge acquisition*. A prototype of the system is then built and real work problems are submitted to it for the purpose of validating its reasoning. When improper reasoning is detected, the knowledge base is modified to incorporate revised logic or new data. This iterative design, construction and evaluation process is repeated until a robust system that performs as well as or better than the subject expert results.

These systems are difficult to build in practice for a variety of reasons, including: real world problems tend to consist of knowledge from multiple domains; a difficult to determine amount of common sense (data) needs to be explicitly represented in the knowledge base; the necessary knowledge may not converge (it keeps growing); or the system may scale poorly.

Knowledge base systems have the potential of significantly altering the content of work and the division of labour between people and machines. For example, as part of a BPR analysis, pockets of expertise may be recognized which when properly encoded and shared may permit lower skilled representatives to service customers. Or, making diagnostic data and repair instructions (gathered from expert service staff) available over a firm's network may allow equipment to be maintained in geographically dispersed sites by operators without the need of resident maintenance personnel.

Interorganizational Systems

Finally, *interorganizational* systems, or systems that link, electronically, two firms together have significant potential to support BPR. A good example of this is Electronic Data Interchange (EDI), or the computer-to-computer exchange of structured business transactions among firms (O'Callaghan & Turner, 1995), as discussed in Chapter 8.

The *sponsor* of an EDI system is the firm that conceives of the system, decides what it is to do, obtains a fee for its use, and establishes the standards (structured business transactions) of the system. The *participants* subscribe to the system for a fee, using it to transfer transactions among themselves or between themselves and the sponsor.

One advantage of EDI is that it reduces the per-unit cost of processing transactions by about a factor of ten and it greatly speeds up the exchange of information by circumventing many manual steps in both the firm generating and receiving the transaction. Reduced errors from less manual handling of transactions eliminate the need for costly error correction. These benefits usually accrue to participants. However, as with many IT investments, real savings come with increased transaction volume as incremental costs approach zero, providing potentially high margins, over time, as demonstrated by Johannes Pennings in Chapter 7.

Over and beyond cost and time savings, EDI makes it easy for participants to exchange transactions so they tend to do more of it— both in volume and in the range of transactions handled. This can result in improved relationships with customers and increased switching costs. The sponsor sees an increasing revenue stream for little additional cost. Also, the improvement in quality and range of data that accompanies interorganizational systems results in an improved knowledge of customers and the market allowing faster response to changes. A good example of this is the way operators of airline reservation systems were able to adjust their pricing and schedules in order to maintain profitability under increased competition when air travel was deregulated in the US.

In BPR studies, interorganizational systems expand the range of organizational alternatives by making it easier to outsource various activities over a network. The combination of faster, higher quality, and lower cost business transitions that EDI promotes along with better market knowledge can result in both lower production and co-ordination costs, providing significant advantages.

If technology is to be used in BPR initiatives, information systems staff must be a key part of the process and we now turn to this much overlooked issue: what role might information systems staff play in bringing about organizational change?

THE ROLE OF INFORMATION SYSTEMS STAFF

While there is some general agreement that technology is central to BPR, especially in providing new options for the redesign of work, it is much less clear what role information systems staff should and do play in this process. Bashein suggests that there are three ways that information systems professionals can participate in re-engineering efforts (Bashein, et al, 1993).

They can lead the re-engineering project since they possess the problem-solving skills and have had past experience of implementing the types of systems that are required to bring about significant organizational change.

Another possibility is for IS staff to initiate the re-engineering effort, but not lead it. The rationale for this position is that the internal IS group often lacks sufficient esteem and power within an organization to run and be responsible for a re-engineering effort. Someone closer to the core activities of the firm needs to lead it.

A third alternative is for the IS group to participate as workers and supporters of the project, but not to instigate it. The logic behind this is that since IS does not own the work processes being redesigned, they are in no position either to lead or initiate significant change efforts. Bashein recommends that IS staff seek opportunities to re-engineer business processes and to sponsor these efforts, that they participate enthusiastically, that they facilitate technical innovation, and use the opportunity to learn more about the business and develop change process skills, but not to lead such projects.

I/S Analyzer notes that within BPR work teams, IS staff often play the role of an advisor rather than leader or driver of the team. They reinforce the point that IS, as a group, lacks the holistic vision to lead a major change effort and that IS often does not have the political weight to move a firm in the dramatic manner that is required for radical change (I/S Analyzer, 1993).

The rather weak position the IS staff already play in many BPR activities is at odds with the pronouncements, made by Davenport and Hammer, of the importance of IT to this change activity. One should guard against being evangelistic and overselling in major change projects, as has been argued in Chapter 10. The more critical literature supports the notion that neither IT *per se* nor IS staff should be the primary force driving organizational transformation. Studies of the impact of IT (e.g. Björn-Andersen, et al, 1986; Kraut, et al, 1989; Turner, 1984), have typically shown relatively marginal effects on organizational structure and performance. Similarly, the number of instances where IT has been used successfully as the driving force behind large scale organizational change are few. The current interest in re-engineering and BPR provides a much needed chance to subject current operations to scrutiny. Consistent with notions of continuous improvement, this review should be ongoing rather than a one-time exercise. IT provides many opportunities to redesign basic operations and unnecessary activities can be removed; tasks can be redesigned with fewer hand-offs and in ways that make effective use of the skills and abilities of individual workers. As the cost of IT decreases and firm-wide technology infrastructures improve, it should be possible to deliver relevant information to individual workers wherever they are located.

Removing barriers to effective work and enabling and empowering workers is the new organizational challenge.

ACKNOWLEDGEMENT

I am indebted to my colleagues Professors Niels Bjørn-Andersen and M. Lynne Markus for many discussions on this topic.

REFERENCES

Bashein, B., Markus, M. and Riley, P., 1993, Business Process Re-engineering: Roles for Information Technology and Information Systems Professionals, Working Paper, The Claremont Graduate School.

Beer, M., Eisenstat, R. and Spector, B., 1990, Why Change Programs don't Produce Change, *Harvard Business Review*, November-December, 158–166.

Bjørn-Andersen, N., Eason, K. and Robey, D., 1986, *Managing Computer Impact*, New Jersey: Ablex.

Charan, R., 1991, How Networks Reshape Organizations—for Results, *Harvard Business Review*, September-October, 104–115.

Davenport, T., 1993, *Process Innovation: Re-engineering Work Through Information Technology*, Boston: Harvard Business School Press.

Davenport, T. and Short, J., 1990, The New Industrial Engineering: Information Technology and Business Process Redesign, *Sloan Management Review*, 31(4), 11–27.

Drucker, P., 1988, The Coming of the New Organization, *Harvard Business Review*, January-February, 45–53.

Hammer, M., 1990, Re-engineering Work: Don't Automate, Obliterate, *Harvard Business Review*, July-August, 104–111.

Hammer, M. and Champy, J., 1993, *Re-engineering Work: A Manifesto for Business Revolution*, New York: Times Warner.

I/S Analyzer, 1993, The role of IT in Business Re-engineering, *I/S Analyzer*, 31(8), August, 1–16.

Kraut, R., Dumais, S. and Koch, S., 1989, Computerization, Productivity and Quality of Work-Life, *Communications of the ACM*, 32(2), 220–238.

Lai, K., Malone, T. and Yu, K., 1988, Object Lens: A Spreadsheet for Cooperative Work, *ACM Transactions on Office Information Systems*, October.

Lotus, 1993, *A Quick Tour of Lotus Notes*, Cambridge MA: Lotus Development Corporation.

O'Callaghan, R. and Turner, J., 1995, Electronic Data Interchange: Concepts and Issues in Krcmar, H., Björn-Andersen, N. and O'Callaghan, R. (eds.), *EDI in Europe*, Chichester: Wiley.

Sproull, L. and Kiesler, S., 1993, *Connections: New Ways of Working in the Networked Organization*, Cambridge MA: MIT Press.

Turner, J., 1984, Computer Mediated Work: The Interplay between Technology and Structured Jobs, *Communications of the ACM*, 27(12), 1210–1217.

Tushman, M.L., Newman, W.H. and Romanelli, E., 1986, Convergence and Upheaval: Managing the Unsteady Pace of Organizational Evolution, *California Management Review*, 29(1), 1–16.

Walton, R.E., 1989, *Up and Running: Integrating Information Technology and the Organization*, Boston, MA: Harvard Business School Press.

12
LUCIA Accelerates Service Delivery: A case study of Business Process Re-engineering

PETER C. MEESTER AND JAN POST
International Business Engineers, PTT Telecom BV, The Netherlands

INTRODUCTION

The LUCIA case is part of a large change programme. For PTT Telecom it was the first Business Process Re-engineering (BPR) programme attempted. In the meantime, much has been said and written about BPR. Initially, the expectations of BPR as a radical change instrument were high but now we see a certain reluctance towards its application, given that the chances of failure are high, and the consequential drawbacks in terms of money and motivation can be serious.

The trend now, is to change the business processes in a less radical way. Usually, this is done by implementing workflow tools. Clever marketeers sell these products as a new development in BPR, but in fact it is a way of mechanising an existing process without radically changing it. The original message of BPR is still valid however: in a competitive market it may be the only way to increase performance drastically. The challenge, however, is the capacity to manage change. A good understanding of IT can help, and is often necessary, but the first requirement is to have the necessary power and will to change the

Information Technology and Organizational Transformation. Edited by R.D. Galliers and W.R.J. Baets. © 1998 John Wiley & Sons Ltd

business in all its complexity. This includes processes and IT, of course, but also the organization itself and its culture. We have learned that no simple formula exists to achieve this. However, there are some lessons that emerge. These include:

- The drive for change must come top-down. Throughout, top management must be concerned in stimulating and backing the programme.
- The vision must be clear, with programme management being the "owner" of this vision.
- In implementing change, involvement must be bottom-up. Users and middle management must be involved in piloting, customising, training and "selling" the programme.
- Communication is vital.

The LUCIA case investigates an example of BPR "avant la lettre". It provides a clear example of a business process change project, which happened to take place in Dutch Telecom.

BACKGROUND

PTT Telecom BV was formerly state-owned but is now partially traded on the Amsterdam stock exchange. It serves about six million telephone subscribers with some seven million lines. Since The Netherlands has about 15 million inhabitants, this translates into approximately half the population. To operate this infrastructure PTT Telecom employs 30 000 staff members. Some 3000 of them are concerned with all the aspects of the provisioning of telephone connections. The number of customer orders is about 1.4 million a year. The total income of PTT Telecom is approximately $6 billion per annum.

In 1989, PTT Telecom was privatized. This privatization catalysed a re-thinking of the services Telecom delivers. Although Telecom still held the monopoly regarding the infrastructure, it had no guarantee whatsoever for holding that monopoly after 1995. Its market share, therefore, had to be earned. As a result, the board had specified a number of goals in order to attain better performance, with one of their goals being to redesign their customer processes. This focus is, of course, totally in line with the BPR approach. An additional criterion, however, was that management had to be determined to initiate change and be prepared to re-think its policy.

The Board of PTT Telecom had to decide what performance standards should be applied. The Chairman of the Board, Mr. Ben Verwaayen, stated that Dutch Telecom should be amongst the best telecommunication operators in the world. We benchmarked ourselves against the Bell Operating Companies which had standards of delivery of telephone connections of about two days and planned to install connections instantly within a few years. We decided, therefore, that Telecom should aim to reach the target of two days in 1995. This we succeeded in doing by 1993.

To enable the company to deliver connections instantly, a system was in place to link automatically the administrative data system for local loops and numbers with the different "technical" systems by which the exchanges are serviced. This application is called SOPHIA (Service Order Processing Intermediate Application) and links connections in and out of service automatically.

BUSINESS PROCESS RE-ENGINEERING

Three aspects of the business had to be changed to ensure improved performance: the procedures, the IT and the organization itself had to be overhauled but in an integrated fashion, not separately.

One of the vital aspects of BPR is that the number of handovers has to be reduced to nearly zero. In most conventional processing, no matter whether it is automated or not, tasks are specialized. Henceforth every product or service is supported by a chain of activities which is undertaken by several employees. Most of the supply time accumulates from waiting intervals as a result of the actual activities of employees involved.

Many IT specialists, and others, seem to think BPR is almost the same as system re-engineering. In our experience, this is a misunderstanding which is likely to lead to failure in a change process. It is vital that initially process, procedures and tasks are restructured and data purifying is carried out. Firstly one should get rid of the Taylorist notion of task specialization. As many of the activities as possible should be combined and brought to the front office as one or two tasks. Re-engineering comes into play when it is clear how the process should look. Focusing on information systems as a starting point will do the company and its profit indicators no good at all.

After choosing the "high impact approach" it was decided to have the bulk process, i.e. telephone connections, re-engineered first. An internal group of consultants was assigned to achieve this particular goal, by delivering regular telephone connections to the residential and small business market within two days. Moreover, it was agreed that customers should be given a fixed date and time their phone would be delivered and activated at their first and, hopefully, only contact with the outlet. An outlet in the Netherlands is a Telephone shop or a special toll free number. Additionally, it was decided to give customers a printed contract on that occasion or, in the case of ordering by phone, to send them one on the day that the order was requested.

After completing this task successfully, PTT Telecom founded a consulting company, (at first Delta Business Engineers, later International Business Engineers or IBE). IBE is now a special branch of PTT Telecom. This offers BPR to the market, in particular Telecom providers and IT companies, as IBE considered that their expertise might well be highly marketable, given the fact that many companies world-wide have mass customer service processes which were likely to be amenable to re-engineering.

The Process Itself

The re-engineering of telephone line provisioning was started by re-evaluating the provisioning concerning the possibilities of modern telephone switch techniques and IT. In the Netherlands practically every address is preconnected by cables from the telephone local loop network. 95% of all households possess a subscription. Sufficient infrastructural capacity is available to meet the forecast expansion. Nearly 100% of the exchange capacity is computer-controlled. New connections and removal of connections were carried out in two or more weeks. PTT Telecom uses full electronic data processing for customer handling, information about local loops, numbers, the telephone directory service and billing.

In many respects, in fact, telephone connections are stock items and not specialities to be made by order as they were regarded in the early days of telephony. It is possible to activate or deactivate them remotely. All relevant data is electronically stored. These three aspects provide the possibility for immediate delivery of a connection when the customer asks for it. So it was decided to re-engineer processes and procedures accordingly.

Most of the activities of the former process were transferred to the front office, and hence many of the activities for a customer order now had to be executed by a single person. This necessitated an increase in front office staff and accurate data handling became vital. A massive data purification programme was undertaken. A dedicated user-friendly interface was introduced to facilitate efficient customer servicing. In the back office, staff numbers were reduced substantially.

Pilot Project

After designing the new process, a provisional shell system was installed and a pilot was started in one area where a small group of employees tested the methods. In close cooperation with them, the precise procedures were worked out. After the pilot everything was painstakingly recorded and written down in an implementation handbook, along with process flows and instructions.

Based on the information in the handbook, a massive operation was carried out in which the developed process was installed throughout the country, leaving the old organizational structure intact at first. After the process was implemented and carefully audited, the organization was changed. The implementation was carried out by means of regional project organizations which consisted of a project manager and several project groups. These groups were specialised in such aspects as data purifying, teleshop adaptation, training, network building and communication.

A New Organizational Structure

In accordance with the above, the new organization was developed, and informed by the process. Calculations were made about the numbers of employees needed in the new situation resulting in a 30% reduction. Fewer engineers were needed because connection is carried out by software. With this system, front office personnel benefited from a reduction of 30% in complaint handling and changes of appointment because of the short time between sales and delivery. Back office activities were substantially reduced because administrative preparations no longer had to be completed before regular line delivery could occur. What remained were the 10% complex connections, and quality improved even more, as these received more focused attention.

The decision was made to make the whole process uniform all over the country: to make "one-stop shopping" possible. In other words, a customer could request in Utrecht, for example, the discontinuation of a connection from Amsterdam to be reconnected in a location in Rotterdam. In other words, the client was able to obtain assistance for service in any region and in any city.

Before the BPR project, processing and IT was not uniform. Telecom had good, or at least functional, procedures and systems but they were different all over the country. The country is divided into 13 telephone districts which were rather autonomous entities, so every district had its own systems, especially for customer data handling. The problems with this set-up were obvious to all and this is why the company began—and succeeded in—rectifying the situation in January 1993.

Quality of the Data and Supporting Systems

If a company decides to make appointments about the deliverables on first contact, the employees of the outlet must have access to relevant and *correct* data. If not, complaints will follow. In this respect, the conventional approach is "Thank you for your order, you will hear from us later", which is acceptable. However, contrary to what managers believed, the data were not always correct. It is possible to get the data right, but the problem is one of maintaining validity. The new process allows for leaving the loop physically intact, so that when a customer moves house the new occupant of that dwelling has an intact loop.

The customer data are stored in Automatic Work Order (AWO) processing which operates on a DEC machine. The loop and number administration is processed by a Unisys system, called KANVAS. NOTARIS registers install base data on a DEC platform and black-listed customers are registered in the DBI system on the DEC as well.

Previously four systems were used, which meant, theoretically, that an employee dealing with these issues would require four workstations on his or her desk and would clearly be unable to give sufficient attention to a customer's requests. He or she would also be required to enter data such as name and address or results of actions in the different systems more than once. This increased the risk of incorrect data handling as well as slowing down the process. To prevent this situation a single screen device called Schil (or Shell in English) was developed. It enabled the employee to use one PC for entering the four applications. It is a kind of "Winking Windows" system which allows for the transferral of relevant data from one application to another. Functionally, we were satisfied with it, and it is used today on about 800 workstations.

Lucia

Unfortunately, however, the Shell concept had three drawbacks. Firstly, it was based on screen communication. Full screens were transported over the line and this was expensive in terms of data communication. Secondly, it was prone to screen alterations of the four applications. Thirdly, the screens of the different applications were quite different as were the key conventions.

As no system sophisticated enough to solve these problems existed on the market, several computer suppliers and software houses were consulted on the basis of detailed specifications provided by the IBE people. Unisys was the firm which provided the chosen solution, in the form of LUCIA which is an acronym in Dutch for "Nationwide Uniform Service Order Entry". The system was piloted successfully and installed in 1993.

The system is based on message communication which is a means of data transfer which involves less data communication than screen communication does. It is maintained by a central management system. When, for instance, the AWO system has to be changed, one can change the LUCIA system, and all the workstations will work according to the new version of AWO.

The screens are dedicated to this use, and have proved to be very economical. They are of standard layout and when the system is approached much of the communication is hidden for the user. The key conventions are homogenised and independent of the actual key conventions of the applications in the background.

CONCLUSIONS

PTT Telecom BV managed to re-engineer its process of telephone line delivery successfully, achieved its goal of delivery within two days and made the concept of "one-stop shopping" possible. Procedures were aggregated so that a single person was sufficient to handle an order completely. Accurate data are an absolute necessity for this procedure. While a sophisticated Service Order Entry system has yet to be developed, the revised process works very well and is appreciated by both staff and customers.

Based on our experience, it seems that the BPR concept can be applied to good effect if an organization suffers from one or more of the following symptoms:

- Providing services or products to the market takes far too much time.
- A significant proportion of the elapsed time goes into "waiting for the next activity".
- Too many people are involved.
- Personnel multiply small mistakes creating major problems, leading to a good proportion of the workforce being required to re-work and re-enter data.

Facing competition often demands drastic measures and BPR certainly can be one such. BPR can be no less than a revolution in the company leading to, at the very least, reduced cycle times and in many cases reductions in head count. In the LUCIA case, for example, the reductions were:

- just two to three handoffs from the order to the billing (from 10 to 20)
- a 10 times reduction in delivery time
- a 10 times reduction in faults
- 33% reduction in staff.

While the case provides a good example of a successful re-engineering process by giving an indication of the magnitude of changes involved, the management of these changes is critical and not without difficulty. In our experience a highly "empowered" programme management is crucial and without this highly skilled management then success is likely to be elusive. This problem is exacerbated by the fact that companies tend to allocate their most skilled and effective managers to day-to-day aspects of the business, not to project management and change projects, and it is most often the case that project managers are paid less than line management.

A company's ability to react quickly to the market is an important survival issue these days. A lesson to be drawn from our experience is that a greater part of the (human) resources needs to be allocated to those parts of the organization with a change mission or imperative.

Part 5
AFTERWORD

This book has been about Information Technology and Organizational Transformation. Having said that, our treatment of the topic has been at pains to delve deeper into this complex subject than the all-too-common books in this area that extol the virtues of IT and suggest that by simply harnessing IT and focusing on key business processes, step-function changes in business fortunes can be obtained.

We attempt to reinforce this message by the final chapter in the book. Written by Andrew Pettigrew, the chapter focuses on key messages emanating from research into corporate transformation initiatives. Purposely, IT hardly rates a mention: there is much more to this topic than that. Nevertheless, key messages emerge as a result of Professor Pettigrew's analysis and synthesis of the key factors. This helps to explain why it is that some change programmes succeed while others fail.

13
Success and Failure in Corporate Transformation Initiatives*

ANDREW M PETTIGREW
Centre for Corporate Strategy and Change, Warwick
Business School, UK

INTRODUCTION

As never before, our language is covered by a varnish of managerialism. The ideas and techniques of management are now a global industry led by international consulting firms, gurus, a select number of high profile chief executive officers, business mass-media publications and business schools. Recent research by the Institute of Management and Bain & Co. (1996) indicates that in spite of clear differences in business institutions and culture around the world, the same number and type of management tools are used in North America, Europe and Asia. These tools include the familiar litany of mission and vision statements, customer satisfaction measurement, business process re-engineering, core competencies and benchmarking. Behind these ideas and their associated analytical methods and techniques is a pervasive concern for changing organizations to deliver, at most, sustained competitive advantage, or at least, organizational survival. Competitiveness is no longer just a matter of competitive positioning, but is now an innovation contest where the bureaucratic, the non-

---

*This chapter was published in Dutch as an article in *Nijenrode Management Review*, March/April, 1997, 49–60, under the title "Slagen en falen bij transformatie van ondernemingen".

Information Technology and Organizational Transformation. Edited by R.D. Galliers and W.R.J. Baets. © 1998 John Wiley & Sons Ltd

progressive and the inflexible will lose out in the race for business success.

But innovation has many faces—harmful, volatile and transient as well as beneficial. And there is always the question of beneficial for whom? Many change processes deliver variations which are seen by some as small scale and incremental, yet for others they represent bruising encounters with the devil. There are winners and losers in many changes and the balance of advantage may not be clear at the outset of the process, never mind further down the journey. Quests for transformational change may deliver quantity of change, but through such a pace and quality of change process that the prospect of further related change is written out of the script for the survivors. Much change in organizations is therefore episodic. It appears to the recipients as initiativitis, unfocused meddling—churning not changing.

However, for the initiators and facilitators of change, a different story may be observable or interpretable. The sense of excitement about finally focusing on a problem of substance; of consciousness raising to build others into the process of tackling the problem, and the exhilaration of completing a difficult task and moving the organization on to the next step in its development. Progress and progression are the elixir for those who lead major change episodes.

Faced with these competing versions of reality, it is understandable if both the participants and observers of major transformational processes are taking a more considered and critical stance to these processes. In a range of carefully argued papers, Abrahamson (1991); (1996) uses the language of fads, fashions and bandwagons to characterize management techniques as fashion commodities. Unlike many aesthetic and cultural forms, Abrahamson argues management techniques emerge and are justified through a combination of rational efficiency (sound means to achieve important ends) and progressive (new as well as improved relative to older management techniques). He cites the rise and eclipse of quality circles in the United States in the 1980s as a contemporary example, but also draws on historical data to show that management fashions about, for example, employee stock ownership schemes, have gained and lost popularity since the turn of the century. Crucially, Abrahamson also argues that management fashions are not cosmetic and trivial. They have shaped and continue to shape the behaviour of managers all over the world and can have massive, sometimes helpful, but also questionable impacts on organizations and their people.

This chapter examines some of the evidence for the strengths and weaknesses of management techniques designed to deliver change in organizations. These techniques have been described as programmatic change strategies. A change programme is here defined as a focused, often high investment attempt to create system-wide change using pre-packaged products and technologies. Business Process Re-engineering (BPR)—as we saw in Chapter 10—is the latest in a long line of change management programmes utilized by the private and public sectors. Since the 1960s, these programmes have included: Management by Objectives (MBO); Organizational Development (OD); and Total Quality Management (TQM).

Such programmes share a number of common characteristics. They frequently originate from US-based consultancy firms and/or management gurus and are sold as products, first of all into the North American market and then onward into Europe and Asia. There is often a high profile management text which links the programme to a series of current management problems, lays out the framework of analysis and method and extols the virtues and distinctiveness of the approach by noting the experiences of using the method in a number of named high prestige business clients. These prestige clients represent high profile early adopters of the programme and are used constantly as exemplars to create a bandwagon effect. Later adopters are drawn into the bandwagon because of the sheer number of organizations that have already adopted the programme. Decisions to adopt may be made for one or other of a variety of reasons—fear of being different, concern over loss of potential competitive advantage, genuine belief in the technical efficiency of the new method. Such upward cycles of adoption may in turn be followed by cycles of rejection as evidence accumulates about the lack of effectiveness of the programme (Abrahamson, 1996). These cycles of upward and downward adoption occur through time and space. As the product life cycle begins to peak in North America, the product may be beginning to accelerate in Europe. In the UK a similar pattern is observable with these programmes being first adopted in the private sector and then sold into the public sector as the former market is saturated or begins to turn sour. The bandwagon is fuelled not only by an accumulation of clients but also by an increasing number of programme providers, who dip into the bow wave of enthusiasm created by the success of the first generation of gurus. The original prophet guru can only economically exploit the potential of the innovation by creating an international cadre of disciples who often are even truer believers than the original prophet. Other secondary imitators then pile into the bandwagon. Throughout this process learning takes place and some modification to the programme message and method occurs, faced by an increasingly aware client set who may seek to customise the programme to reflect their national business, sector or organizational culture.

Commentators on programmes such as TQM and BPR frequently refer to the ambiguities of content, method and process surrounding these approaches (Reed, et al, 1996; Ascari, et al, 1995). These ambiguities may be beneficial in implementation as they create opportunities for customisation at local levels. However, they also place further pressures on early adopters who struggle concurrently to justify the programmes and communicate a coherent and consistent view of what they are and how they can be fashioned to meet local needs. Even given their ambiguities of content and method, these programmes are often construed as single issue "off the shelf" interventions which compete for resources and attention in complex multi-issue organizations. They may progress from being seen as solutions to being seen as problems in their own right (Downs, 1972). There is now ample evidence that if such programmes are unable to attract sustained support over a considerable period, rapid regression may set in as energy and momentum drains away. They are vulnerable to turnover at the top as key patrons move, when, for example, sudden crises or panics divert management attention to hotter issues elsewhere. They may also be vulnerable to progressive adaptation and relabelling as they move through the organization (Pettigrew, 1985; Beer, et al, 1990).

Thus the natural history of development of the programme bandwagon is duplicated at each organization location where the programme is implemented. Wilkinson et al (1992), drawing on their research on TQM implementation in the UK, refer to four phases of development. Following a first phase of high profile adoption, they characterize the next two phases as hope, followed by disappointment and disillusion. The fourth phase they describe as what now? With success or failure there is still the question of what comes next. Sustainability is a constant and recurrent challenge for change programmes.

But do all change programmes fail and fade away? Is there evidence of variation in the impact of programmes between organizations and even between different parts of the same organization exposed to the same intervention? Before the bandwagon recedes can an astute management exploit the new approach quickly enough, and institutionalize some of the new techniques and ideas into the organizational bloodstream, in order to deliver some early successes and at the same time improve the firm's capability to manage subsequent change?

This chapter offers a synthesis and review of the key factors which explain differential success rates in implementing change programmes. The chapter is in three parts. In part one use is made of an extended metaphor to explore in symbolic form some of the key characters and process issues which occur in implementing change initiatives. Change journeys are metaphorically portrayed as wagon trains full of optimistic settlers heading (in the classic US tradition) towards the promised land of California. With some of the key dynamics thus explored, part two returns to a more conventional analytic format and considers some of the weaknesses of programmatic change strategies. In the third and final part of the chapter a synoptic account is made of the factors which in combination help to explain why and how some change programmes succeed.

Although the bulk of the research evidence points to either the outright failure or ambivalent success of such change journeys, there is also evidence that, with appropriate management, change programmes can be encouraged towards successful outcomes.

CHANGE JOURNEYS AS WAGON TRAINS

Metaphors can have a valued place in communicating ideas. In extended story form they supply a simplified, value laden imagery which can capture the attention of the reader and assist in the process of identification with the ideas sprinkled in the story. Metaphors can provide the comfort of identification, but they can be used to confront and challenge taken-for-granted assumptions and to explore contradictions and hypocrisy in the interpretations we have of life around us.

What is the traditional story of the 19th Century US wagon train heading westward to California from the relative safety and security of the eastern seaboard? As portrayed in the mass culture offerings of 1950s and 1960s Hollywood, it is a drama of pioneers, of enthusiastic settlers heading for the newly promised land. The saga involves a mixed bag of settlers, driven by a variety of motives, encountering multiple hardships along the way, being coached by hard driving wagon masters and relentlessly courageous scouts and facing the ever present dangers of hostile Native Americans and unpredictably punishing environments. As the journey proceeds there is a sense of emotional relief as landmarks are reached. But there are ups and downs of energy as obstacles are rounded and blind canyons and other deadlocks encountered. For some (the lost and bewildered) there is journey's end, but not where anticipated. For the fortunate there is the prospect of a new life in California now that this particular journey in life's longer journey has come to a successful end.

There are four main characters in the wagon train story: the *enthusiasts* who join and persuade others to join the wagon train; the *power system* that provides the financial and political support to resource the wagon train; the *scouts* who act as guides and transition managers on the long journey; and the cast of thousands, the innocent and not-so-innocent *bystanders*, who observe this next wave of enthusiasts but mostly choose not to participate in the journey themselves. Metaphorically the wagon train journey and the trials and tribulations of its participants mirror many of the reported accounts of transformational change journeys in organizational settings.

Four varieties of enthusiast have been observed on the route to California. The *idealists* or long term day dreamers join because the end point of the journey signifies some venerable place or promised land. This is a value quest, where the motto for the idealist is "Life's better in California".

The *adventurers* join for more mundane reasons. The transformational journey for them is a source of variety and excitement. The adventurers' motto is "Life's better anywhere but here". As such the adventurers are likely to be receptive to the missionaries and *zealots* with their staring eyes, implacable beliefs and unquenchable energy. It is the zealots' task to communicate the virtues of joining the wagon train. This they do with a combination of rhetorical excitement, manic belief and value laden language. Above all, the compulsive focusing of the missionaries and zealots acts as an attention director to draw the easily led and the unsure into the process. This narrow focusing of the zealots in the end becomes their undoing as they concentrate more and more on the wagon train (the means) and begin to lose sight of the end of the journey—reaching California. Their continuing stridency in the absence of tangible successes means in the end the zealots are sacrificed to the impatience of the disappointed fellow travellers, who hear only rhetoric when they are looking for progressive stepping stones on the way to California. The failure to manage and then realize expectations is a trap for all revolutionaries. The failure to manage expectations leads inexorably to a stage of management of disappointment. At this point in the process many zealots are removed from the wagon train.

The fourth group who join the wagon train are the *career opportunists*. As ever they are quietly observing life and note (in the safety of the eastern stockade) that the power system is gathering to proclaim the coming of a new issue (customer satisfaction) and the simultaneous arrival of a new solution (TQM). The assembled masses are being told that virtue lies in a journey to California where quality standards can be realized to match even those being delivered in Japan. Noticing the rhetoric being newly proclaimed by the power system (for some time the zealots have been largely ignored articulating a similar message), the career opportunists conclude there is a rising value in the system and that survival and/or advancement now warrant an agile jump onto the wagon train.

Between them these four groups of settlers provide much of the early energy and commitment to drive the wagon train forward on its journey. By this stage the four groups of primary enthusiasts will also have attracted onto the transformational process sets of individuals with lesser degrees of attachment to the journey and its stated destination. Mixed motives they may have for the journey, but for the time being a veneer of consensus holds them all together on the long journey to their California.

Wagon trains need not only enthusiastic settlers, they also require tangible resources to sustain the travellers on their way. Transformational journeys have to receive the blessing of the power system and merit its financial and political support. Product champions for the journey normally have to emerge on or near the top of the organization. Their role is to promote and ideally sustain the innovation for long enough for it to reach its destination.

But singular product champions often prove to be fickle friends. They move on or get promoted out of the system. This may create a power vacuum and endanger the wagon train's political and financial support. The newcomer patron may not be so committed as his or her predecessor and may confuse the travellers by suggesting they change their route or even their destination. Meanwhile crises and panics can occur at the wagon train's home base and the now distant, committed and yet possibly threatened travellers may find themselves "out of sight and out of mind". New priorities and problems have emerged at home base with their associated wagon train solutions. The urgent has yet again driven the important out of the vision of the power system. Some of the more astute and flexible settlers begin to drift away from the wagon train and head back to the safety of the eastern stockade.

The scouts at the front of the wagon train will have seen it all before. Their job is to look forwards not backwards. They have little time for the doubters and the fainthearted as they sweep gallantly forward. The scouts on the corporate transformational journeys are, of course, the external and internal consultants. In the past their motto was, "we are the transition managers, you are safe with us! we've just returned (safely) from the XYZ wagon train to California. The clients arrived safe, if a little battered. But they learnt a great deal and many now wish to follow them. We can help you too—at a price!".

Clients are now more mature and circumspect. They are likely to wish to be reassured that, if Robert Redford or John Wayne (both senior partners in Scouts Inc) sell the virtues of having a scout, it is they who will accompany the wagon train and not the intelligent and plausible newcomer just out of scouting school. The clients may also be reassured by the scouts' new rhetoric of seeing the journey through to implementation rather than cutting and running after the analysis and planning stage—or worse still the first sign of trouble from the power system. The clients also have their own new rhetoric, "We are in charge of the process not the scouts. We must project manage the scouts so they don't take over and lure us into an unnecessarily long, complex and expensive journey". Meanwhile, it is on record that some big BPR interventions in UK corporations have allowed up to 55 scouts to accompany their wagon train—and for several weeks and months at a time!

The final group in our transformational story is the innocent and not-so-innocent bystanders. This group represents many shades of opinion towards the change journey and its destination. It may contain opponents, doubters, cynics and sceptics. What unites them is their lack of involvement in the process and their decision to avoid joining the wagon train for as long as it is humanly and politically possible to do so. In this mixed group two sub-groups are vocal and therefore visible; they are the cynics and sceptics.

Cynics are an unattractive breed but they can be found at the periphery of most groups of enthusiastic innovators. Their incessant cry is "we've seen it all before, and we've seen them (the missionaries, zealots and idealists) all before too". In the distance the cynics can also be heard muttering, "it will all end in tears"—"don't believe these snake oil merchants"—"the power system won't stick any longer with BPR than they did with TQM; don't get over-involved and certainly don't get on that wagon train". "You may think this journey is going to be career enhancing, but I'm telling you it will be career limiting—it's all going to end in tears . . .".

The *sceptics*, if genuine, can be a misunderstood group. They are likely to be observing the gathering of the wagons and horses and puzzling over, to them, real practical problems. But well intentioned advice from the sceptic to the wagon master zealot that there was a design fault with his wagons is not always greeted with acclaim. At this early stage in the process, enthusiasm for a rapid start means that it is all too easy for the genuine sceptic to be swept aside and marginalized with the cutting remark—"I can't stand these professional sceptics, Smith is getting in the way of change again". The fact that Smith may have been one of the few survivors from a previous wagon train is worth little in credibility. In times of constant change it is dangerous to be a sceptic—you need a licence to be a sceptic in order to survive. Meanwhile the zealots are blissfully ignoring cries about design faults on wagons with only three wheels, and are stridently proclaiming that they personally will drag the wagons to California—if necessary!

The wagon train metaphor, like most stories, is capable of multiple interpretations. It is a story that has never happened. Nobody has witnessed it, yet many can identify with its characterizations and core theme. Change programmes attract zealots and idealists, need product champions from the power system, often start with great enthusiasm and optimism, are linked to consultancy products and invariably are guided and facilitated by consultant scouts. Change programmes also experience loss of energy and enthusiasm and create regressive spirals where organizations go backwards on an issue rather than forwards. Their use also illustrates that most fundamental issue in managing change—how to sustain pressure for and involvement in change process over a long period.

Metaphors have their value but also their limitations. The story line can help us to identify. The angular ironic challenge may assist us to question, but metaphors are no substitute for analysis. The metaphor may also have its own built-in logic which restricts the form of questioning and analysis. The hole in the wagon train metaphor is the assumption that change journeys have fixed destinations. In the complex and ever changing situation of business today it is very unlikely that any fixed standards of customer satisfaction, quality, efficiency or competitiveness are likely themselves to be sustainable for long. Hence the dictum that changes represent journeys and not destinations.

In the final two parts of this chapter a brief analytical synthesis is offered around the two core questions—why do change programmes fail and why and how can they be managed to increase the possibilities of success?

WEAKNESSES OF PROGRAMMATIC CHANGE STRATEGIES

Research on the use of programmatic change strategies reveals some very consistent findings about failure. Beer et al (1990) report on programmes of organizational renewal driven from the uncertain legitimacy of the human resource management function. Often such programmes represented impositions from the top and centre of the firm; they appeared to doubters as off the shelf standardized solutions, and their public failure led to cynicism and a reduced capacity to handle change in the future. Pettigrew (1985), reporting on OD interventions in ICI, noted that failure was linked to the highly normative, exclusive and over-zealous rhetoric of the OD consultants, and the failure to link their programmes to local business needs and political interests. Change programmes focusing on quality or process redesign are simultaneously endangered for some by their single issue status and for others their all-embracing transformational character. Wilkinson et al (1992), reporting findings on the variable impact of TQM interventions, emphasize the narrowly conceived and "bolt on" character of such programmes and their short term orientation. Results were sought in a relatively immediate fashion with little preparedness to invest for the long term to build a deeper consciousness of quality which could then sustain a quality culture. More recently, Reed et al, (1996) have amassed an argument and some limited evidence to suggest that failures result from managers spending too much time on the processes, procedures and mechanisms of quality programmes and not enough time shaping the content of the programme to meet business and competitive requirements.

Explanations for the failure or success of complex human activities are rarely unidimensional. There are nearly always a set of interrelated factors which reinforce one another and precipitate downward spirals of energy in the case of low impact interventions and the opposite in the case of the relatively successful programmes. Although change programmes often appear to be focused one-issue interventions dealing with initiatives in quality or process re-engineering, those programmes also have an indefinite character. They may start with a global and long term issue such as culture and quality change which grapples with intangibles such as changing people's attitudes and behaviour. This apparent clarity of focus, and often because of consultant involvement method, appears to be in contradiction with the long term and intangible nature of the outcomes and benefits of the initiative. In these ambiguities breed a further set of uncertainties and complexities. There may be a history in the organization of cynicism and scepticism about previous failed interventions. The initiative may become an arena where different political interests in the organization play out their thinly concealed antagonisms. The programme itself may be seen by some organizational participants as a solution or method in search of a problem. So change programmes may be endangered practically at birth by the heavy hand of the past, the fact that they are seen to have multiple purposes and be driven by mixed motives. The very fact that TQM and BPR are themselves ambiguous notions further opens up the possibility that they represent different things to different people. And when it becomes difficult convincingly to articulate what is the connection between the change programme and the short term critical path of the business, so major doubts are likely to exist about the justification for having the programme at all. People take a very personal view of change. Why is this happening here? Why is it happening now? Why is it happening to me? Failure to deal with these fundamental questions can disable a change programme at birth.

These early cycles and spirals of uncertainty breeding further uncertainty and complexity put a tremendous strain on the leadership system seeking to build coherence and commitment around the fledging initiative. For a leadership system with policies but not processes, the demands of consciousness raising, communicating, involvement and commitment building can all be overwhelmed by corresponding forces of inertia and indifference.

In this context, the educational and training methods wheeled out to educate and involve often have a limited impact. Groups of managers may be sent off on two or three day workshops to hear the new message about quality and culture change, discover the method of implementation and meet the external and internal consultants appointed to drive the programme through the organization. Such educational and training methods can have a value in communication and consciousness raising but they can also have unexpected liabilities. They may create unrealistic expectations about what is possible on return to work. They may also just encourage representational learning through language rather than behavioural learning through doing. So "buzz words" are acquired—the new language associated with the programme—but people can still see that the old attitudes and behaviours are retained. This gap between what people say and what they continue to do provides a receptive context for the doubters and cynics, and further draws momentum and energy out of the change programme.

A further weakness of change programmes can arise from the use of exclusive project teams. There is a long history of the use of task forces and project teams to facilitate innovation processes. The issue here is not the team's presence but the highly exclusive way it may begin to operate and the effect that exclusivity has on further weakening the change process. Most change programmes have an accompanying structure to support the development and implementation of the initiative. Hammer & Champy (1993), for example, recommend a complex, multi-layered structure involving the five key roles of senior executive-leader, process owners, the re-engineering team, a steering committee and a re-engineering Czar. Within less complex arrangements, it is common for a group of specialists to emerge, perhaps linking the programme leader at senior executive level to middle and operational levels of management. There are well documented examples (Pettigrew, 1985) of such teams drawing themselves into an exclusive posture rather than acting as an inclusive bridge with the rest of the organization. There are many variants of the process which sometimes consciously and other times unconsciously create this exclusive effect. The group members are initially separated out from management by special roles and titles and awarded full-time responsibility for the programme. They quickly become immersed in the esoteric language and method of the programme and are captured by their own focused excitement for the task and the special pleading of the attendant external consultants. For a time the novelty of the new team and its message may attract some converts, but others may be repelled by the relentless persistence and zealotry of the new group. Faced with mixed results, the exclusive group try still harder to capture converts, but rather than exciting others they find potential allies drifting away. By this stage in the process the exclusive group has taken over the problem, driven others away from it and retreats itself into collective self-doubt. Being substantially marginalized in their own culture, the group members look outside for support and get drawn into the role of professional conference attendees or even minor gurus on whatever bandwagon they may now be externally linked to. There may now be a review by their power system of progress on the change programme and some assessment of the exclusive group's impact on that progress. If doubts are evident about the programme, the now isolated exclusive group is an easy target as scapegoat. It is just a matter of time before disbandment of the exclusive group occurs. For the individuals concerned, the perils of the innovation process are now painfully clear.

It is rare for change programmes of scale to emerge from anywhere but the top and centre of large organizations. These are high profile activities which require considerable political and financial investment even to launch, never mind sustain. If the change programme is driven out of the top and centre towards decentralized divisions, units or branches it can fall foul of the recurrent tensions which exist in systems ever moving between centralization and decentralization. One of the dilemmas in the perennial tensions between centre and periphery is when to standardize and by how much, and when to permit customization by the periphery, and by how much. For the centre standardization is a complexity reducer, for the periphery it may create an opposite dynamic. Given what has been argued in this chapter about cycles of process complexity at the launch stage of change programmes, there is a natural inclination for the centre to favour the simplifying possibilities of standardization. With standardization comes the possibility of coherence, control and cost minimization. Coherence and control are offered through one central purpose, one core leadership team, a common language and communication system, and possibly one set of consultants using one change methodology. The whole organization is thereby expected to head for California on the same wagon train. This approach may also have financial advantages by reducing the direct and indirect costs associated with the use of multiple change technologies and a proliferating set of investments and learning curves.

The problem with standardization in change processes is that uniformity produces context insensitive targets, methods and processes. There is now ample empirical research evidence (Pettigrew, 1985; Pettigrew & Whipp, 1991; Pettigrew, et al, 1992; Ferlie, et al, 1996) demonstrating that change processes are highly contextually embedded. Implementation failure and patchy success are heavily associated with the imposition of standard processes and solutions on units who are variously likely to proclaim, "we're different", "we're at a different starting point in this process from those at the centre", "we're already half way there and don't need their help!" and more defensively "it wasn't invented here, it can't be any good!". The reluctance or refusal of the top and centre to countenance some variation on the standard package thereby fuels a policy of rebellion, indifference, or nominal acquiescence, by the periphery. Tensions between the centre and periphery thus drain further energy out of the faltering change programme. The other route of encouraging some controlled customization by the periphery (a strategy much associated with more successful change processes) is probably by this stage too late. The periphery does not have enough belief or confidence in the change journey to wish to customize.

GETTING TO CALIFORNIA...

What is known about the interrelated set of factors which contribute to the success of change programmes? Indeed what is success in the management of change? Definitions of success can include notions of quantity, quality and pace of change. There may well be trade offs between those three, with quantity and pace taken at the price of quality of the process. A poor quality process can deliver change in a particular episode but at the expense of reducing the capability and willingness of that part of the organization to contemplate further change in the future. If the goal is sustainable change the notional success can in reality be a failure. Success may only be realistically addressed against self-proclaimed targets. But what target? Some of the wilder transformational targets for BPR may have been attainable had they been more modestly expressed as process improvement and simplification.

Judgements about success are also likely to be conditional on who is doing the assessment and when the judgement is made (Pettigrew, 1985; 1990). Most change processes do not attract universal acclaim. There is likely to be a mixed bag of supporters, doubters and opponents, and individuals may move between these groups over time.

A further difficulty in assessing what is known about the success of change initiatives is the now voluminous literature on this subject. A great deal of the most accessible literature is written by practitioners and consultants, who are hardly disinterested observers of the processes they describe and proclaim. The academic literature on change also has its limitations. Few academic researchers studying change processes collect time series data and many do not include an outcome variable such as success or failure, or impact or performance. These two limitations constrain what we can conclude from research studies about success factors in using programmatic change methods.

In a recent review of the published literature on BPR implementation Ascari et al (1995) draw out a range of factors linkable to successful BPR development. The Ascari et al list includes factors such as building preparedness for change before the launch of the initiative; articulating clear change goals and a company mission that emphasizes customer focus; top management understanding and commitment; the availability of a clear and respected change leader; managing an appropriate pace of change by the use of high learning–high impact pilot projects; and ensuring business objectives drive the change process and not vice versa. These statements of BPR success have, of course, to be placed alongside consultant estimates that around 70% of BPR interventions do not meet expectations (Bashien, et al, 1994).

The theme of persistent and consistent top level support permeates much of the literature on change. The withdrawal of a key product champion and shallow commitment from a fragmented and therefore incoherent top management team will rapidly destabilize change efforts (Pettigrew & Whipp, 1991). Paradoxically, zones of relative continuity and comfort are necessary to manage change effectively. For the top this means developing a coherent and sustainable direction for the business, and holding key executives in post for long enough to see major change initiatives through. It may also require the top to clarify and communicate what is not going to change (for the time being), whilst the current change programme is in process.

All change processes are influence processes. All influence processes require awareness of, if not action in, the political processes of the organizations. Change and politics are inexorably linked (Pettigrew, 1973; 1975). This observation and principle should inform the perspective and action of all levels of management in major change processes. For the product champions at the top, middle and lower reaches of the organization this means that campaigning, lobbying, coalition-building and the sharing of information, rewards and recognition are all fateful for change through all the various unpredictable stages and loops of the programme journey (Pettigrew, 1985).

Leading change is not just about individual leadership. Neither is it just about building a coherent team at the top and pressuring the levels below. Pressure from the top is essential to break any bounds of inertia, and crises are often constructed as attention directors to build a climate for change (*ibid.*). But the top get weary pushing for change if there is no reciprocal and reinforcing pressure from below. Leadership is also about followership. Important linkage mechanisms between leaders and potential followers arise from leaders creating opportunities for a marriage between top-down pressure and bottom-up concerns. Top-down pressure seems to deliver more where that pressure is selectively and astutely orchestrated at local level and linked in a coherent and sensitive fashion to bottom-up concerns (Pettigrew, et al, 1992). The content of change programmes requires customization at lower tiers in order to match local circumstances and thereby script in local commit-ment and psychic energy.

Customization is a key strategy for linking strategic and operational change. Its use has risks attached to it—it may initially slow the process down because learning and adaptation have to occur in many localities. It may cost more and bring dangers of incoherence as standardized templates and methods are altered to reflect operational circumstances. Without a clear purpose and strategic framework for the change pro-gramme it may also precipitate sub-optimal grabs for autonomy at the periphery. This is particularly evident where there is a climate of low trust and poor communication between the centre and the periphery. However, customization is a key factor in linking strategic and opera-tional change and for many has been a risk worth allowing and taking to build in local identification and commitment to central purposes.

The global, long term and intangible nature of many change pro-grammes implies these are long journeys which require persistence and patience and an investment rather than a cost view of people at work (Pettigrew & Whipp, 1991). In a survey of TQM in the West and Japan, *The Economist* (1992) noted that unlike their Japanese comparators, many Western firms had abandoned TQM after two years. Major Japanese firms had been investing in quality programmes for 30 years or more. In the absence of such quality consciousness and behaviour, many Western firms have sought ways of compromising between short-termism and long-termism. One route to this end is to create and publicise intermediate successes or "islands of progress" along these change journeys. Such stepping stones require as a precursor real thought being given to operationalizing the intangibles of, for example, quality and culture change, and then using such operational indicators to assess progress over time. Change programmes can appear to many as all input and process and no output. Without the successes involved in achieving intermediate outcomes, even the most committed travellers get weary on what begin to appear interminable journeys.

Thus far the argument about success has linked together the complementary effects of persistent and consistent top level support; skill in leading change and linking strategic and operational change; drawing in the commitment and psychic energy of operational levels through customization; and the need to assess operational indicators of progress in order to create and publicize intermediate successes. Evidence also indicates that a range of other factors may additively have a role to play in sustaining change programmes long enough to harvest real benefits. Beer et al (1990) and many others have drawn attention to linking the change initiatives to the critical path of the business as a necessary but not sufficient condition for success. Pettigrew (1985) has produced some research evidence of the virtues of inclusive project team management in allowing change teams to bridge with key people and problems. To change the world one must live with it, is the motto of the inclusive change team as it seeks to keep one foot in the present as it coaches and challenges the organization into the future.

The 1985 Pettigrew study of OD in ICI also found that inclusive change groups who operated as a voluntary association rather than as a semi permanent department were able to institutionalize OD skills and knowledge into ICI much more deeply than their more exclusive and formally structured counterparts. The adroit use of reward and recognition systems can also play their part in deepening people's commitment to new attitudes and behaviour. Governments have long since recognized the value of incentives and disincentives in encouraging us to change our behaviour. Faced with the objective of persuading motorists in the UK to change their habit of buying leaded petrol and to move to the unleaded pumps, the Government did not spend millions of pounds on communication programmes. Rather, it prepared the ground by triggering a debate on the issues at other people's expense in the media, and then encouraged us all to drive up to the green pumps by creating a large enough price differential between the two types of fuel.

Reward and recognition systems can be an equally powerful lever to pull in corporate settings but all too often it is a lever pulled too little and too late. Organizations moving from a quantity to a quality culture are unlikely to be persuaded just by rhetorical statements at the top. Unless and until the old quantity based reward and recognition system is itself changed and begins to reflect the quality culture, it is very unlikely that the bulk of the organization—and certainly its most ambitious members—will walk easily into this new future.

There are two final success factors which can play their part in sustaining change programmes. These are: episodic versus continuous process views of changing, and coherence in the management of the overall process of change in the organization. Recent research on the cognitive aspects of organizations has drawn our attention to the way individual and collective thought processes can shape the way managers respond to problems (Huff, 1990; Hodgkinson & Johnson, 1994). One example of such cognitive structuring is the tendency for managers to think (unwittingly) of problems and then act on them as projects or episodes. Thus major change issues which clearly have a continuous rather than an episodic presence are conceived of as substantially time limited events. The effect of this is twofold. Firstly, the project mode implies the intervention has a clear beginning and a finite end. Thus, for example, the quality issue could have been dealt with between 1988 and 1991 and our processes transformed between 1994 and 1996. Secondly, this way of breaking up change interventions has the effect of limiting any possibility of constructing a continuous process view of changing in the organization. This in itself can limit the success potential of any programmatic change strategy which has deeper and longer term ambitions. Breaking this episodic view of management can, however, be extremely difficult indeed, and especially in engineering and retail dominated firms where there is often a deep culture of project and operational management.

The final success factor relates to coherence in the management of overall processes of change. Research in the US and UK private sectors by Kanter (1983) and Pettigrew & Whipp (1991) has clearly linked segmentation and incoherence to organizational inertia, and integration and coherence to change capability. Coherence has many facets and challenges some of which have already been acknowledged in this chapter, and elsewhere within the book. There is purposive coherence—the placing of any change programme in the context of the longer directional path of the firm; business coherence—linking the change initiative to the short term critical path of the business; and political and policy coherence—emanating from a well chosen and interpersonally effective top management team, and crucially, the trust and understanding which can flow from a firm where there are sound mechanisms for linking strategic and operational change.

In today's business world the pressures for change are such that there is no longer the luxury of handling changes sequentially. Most organizations are in the business of managing change concurrently—tackling a simultaneous change agenda on a moving stage. This kind of complexity raises real challenges for firms who struggle to maintain direction, coherence and operational effectiveness under the strains of such a multi-faceted change agenda (Pettigrew & Whipp, 1991). A key aspect of coherence is skill and will to focus this multifaceted change agenda onto a sub-set of issues that are profoundly important and not merely urgent or politically expedient. Within this limited sub-set may lie a number of change initiatives, the boundaries between which require careful and constant monitoring and adjustment if the purposes, methods and success criteria of one are not to get in the way of others. These big issues of coherence represent the meta-level change management task which can be overseen only by the highest level of management in the firm. The isolation and management of this task is a key factor in those firms where the management of change is properly treated as a means to building and sustaining competitive performance.

REFERENCES

Abrahamson, E., 1991, Managerial Fads and Fashions: the Diffusion and Rejection of Innovations, *Academy of Management Review*, 16, 586–612.

Abrahamson, E., 1996, Management Fashion, *Academy of Management Review*, 21, 1, 254–285.

Ascari, A., Rock, M. and Dutta, S., 1995, Re-engineering and Organizational Change: Lessons from a Comparative Analysis of Company Experiences, *European Management Journal*, 13, 1, 1–30.

Bashein, B., Markus, M.L. and Riley, P., 1994, Business Process Re-engineering: Preconditions for Success and Failure, *Information Systems Management*, 11, Spring, 7–13.

Beer, M., Eisenstadt, R.A. and Spector, B., 1990, *The Critical Path to Corporate Renewal*, Boston: Harvard Business School Press.

Downs, A., 1972, Up and Down With Ecology: The Issue Attention Cycle, *The Public Interest*, 28, 38–50.

Economist, 1992, The Cracks in Quality, *The Economist*, April 18, 67–68.

Ferlie, E., Ashburner, L., FitzGerald, L. and Pettigrew A.M., 1996, *The New Public Management in Action*, Oxford: Oxford University Press.

Hammer, M. and Champy, J., 1993, *Re-engineering the Corporation: A Manifesto for Revolution*, London, Nicholas Brearley Publishing.

Hodgkinson, G. and Johnson, G., 1994, Exploring the Mental Modes of Competitive Strategists, *Journal of Management Studies*, 31, 4, 525–551.

Huff, A. (ed.), 1990, *Mapping Strategic Thought*, Chichester: Wiley.

Institute of Management and Bain and Co., 1996, *Managing the Management Tools*, London: Institute of Management.

Kanter, R., 1983, *The Change Masters: Corporate Entrepreneurs at Work*, New York: Counterpoint.

Pettigrew, A.M., 1973, *The Politics of Organizational Decision Making*, London: Tavistock.

Pettigrew, A.M., 1975, Towards a Political Theory of Organizational Intervention, *Human Relations*, 28, 191–208.

Pettigrew, A.M., 1985, *The Awakening Giant: Continuity and Change in ICI*, Oxford: Blackwell.

Pettigrew, A.M., 1990, Longitudinal Field Research on Change: Theory and Practice, *Organizational Science*, 1, 3, 267–292.

Pettigrew, A.M. and Whipp, R., 1991, *Managing Change for Competitive Success*, Oxford: Blackwell.

Pettigrew, A.M., Ferlie, E. and McKee, L., 1992, *Shaping Strategic Change: The Case of the NHS*, London: Sage.

Reed, R., Lemak, D.J. and Montgomery, J.C., 1996, Beyond Process: TQM Content and Firm Performance, *Academy of Management Review*, 21, 1, 173–202.

Wilkinson, A., Marchington, M., Goodman J. and Ackers, P., 1992, Total Quality Management and Employee Involvement, *Human Resource Management Journal*, 2, 4, 1–20.

Postscript

We have come along way—to use Andrew Pettigrew's metaphor—in our journey to the promised land of transformed organizations, utilizing the power of modern information technologies. We hope that we have helped to provide some useful learning on the way. While demonstrating, through serious analysis of the various literatures and through case study material, the complexity of corporate transformation initiatives, we trust that nevertheless the journey has not been presented as too overwhelmingly difficult to contemplate or comprehend. We need more settlers, more pioneers, but we hope that they are drawn from a range of communities and backgrounds so as to provide a transdisciplinary approach in tackling the difficult road ahead. While we undoubtedly need the technology—the wagon train—to assist us in our journey, there are other features to our quest that are equally as important. While, to quote Davenport, BPR may have been "the fad that forgot people", we trust that our treatment of the topic of Information Technology and Organizational Transformation will be seen neither as faddish nor as lacking in the human dimension. Let us set out on our challenging journey armed with the technology, yes, but also with the necessary knowledge and commitment to see it through.

Good luck in your travels!

Bob Galliers and
Walter Baets
April 1997

Index

7S framework 180, 235
accountants 21–2, 255
Achmea Holding 216–20
action research 138–9
activity systems 50–1
advanced information management
	system 72–3
AHS Corporation 96–7, 102–3
air traffic controllers 48
airline industry 102–3, 257
Alcatel Bell Telephone 185–92
algorithms 114–15, 125, 186
American Express 255
Andersen Consulting 73, 78
Apple Mackintosh 250, 252–3
Arizona, University of 207
artificial intelligence 8–9, 115, 200
artificial neural networks 4, 8, 86, 107,
	115–28, 198, 212–14, 216
artificial neurones 120
ASAP 96–7, 102
augmented business teams 39
automatic teller machines 31, 103, 163–4
automatic work order processing 266–7

Bain & Co. 271
banking 26–33, 98, 102–3, 110, 118, 153–4,
	158, 160–1, 163–75, 213, 216
bargaining 6
Baxter Healthcare see AHS Corporation
Bell Operating Companies 263
benchmarking 198, 263
Boeing 202
Boston Consulting Group 161

BritBank 28–9
building societies 25
Burr-Brown Corporation 207
business process redesign/re-engineering
	3–4, 11–13, 39, 53, 107–9, 117, 135,
	137, 145, 151, 223–41, 243, 245–6,
	248–9, 253, 256, 273–4, 280, 283–4
	and artificial neural networks 122
	and computer supported collaborative
		working 43, 46–7, 254
	and IS personnel 257–8
	definition of terms 247
	LUCIA 12, 261–8
	Oticon 10, 65–6, 74–7, 82
	socio-technical approach 230–8
	UK corporations 278
business systems planning 32

CAD/CAM 159
Caledonian Phonebank 26, 28–9
Canon 204
capabilities see core capabilities/
	competencies
CaptureLab 206
case based reasoning systems 100, 127–8,
	198, 202–3, 212, 214, 216
Case Point 202
CBR Express 202
change
	failures 279–83
	successes 283–8
	wagon train metaphor 275–9, 282
	see also organizations
chaos theory 115, 218

chemical industry 123–4, 235n
chief executive officers 223
Claris 253
CLAVIER 202
COCOMAP 211
cognition 45
cognitive mapping systems 125, 127–8, 198, 208–11, 214, 216
cognitive psychology 3, 8, 138
Cognitive Systems and Inference Corp. 202
COLAB 206–7
collaborative computing 39
communication theory 5
communities of practice 50
compact disks 159
Compaq 202
competencies *see* core capabilities/competencies
complexity theory 115
computer aided design 43
computer aided software engineering 43
computer integrated manufacturing 43
computer supported collaborative working 17, 37–63, 65–7, 79, 82, 243, 254–5
concretization 52
connectionist models 8
Consensus Builder 206
consultants 277, 279–82 *see also under name*
consumer behaviour 159
co-operative systems design 52
co-operative work support 12, 17, 39
Coopers & Lybrand 204
co-ordination technology 39
COPE 211
core capabilities/competencies 3, 10, 85, 88–104, 108–9, 111
  inimitability 103
  sharing 100–1
core process redesign 74
corporate maps 10–11
corporate mind set 10, 23, 107–31
corporate transformation initiatives 13
credit cards 26–7, 255 *see also* banking
critical success factor 237
customization 282, 285–6

databases 66, 72–3, 254–5
Davenport, T. H. 224–6, 239
decision making 144

decision support systems 101, 116
Delft University 253
Delta Business Engineers *see* International Business Engineers
developmental work research 50–1
Digital Equipment Corporation 202, 204, 266
document storage and retrieval 73, 80
DOS 2, 72
downsizing 231–3
Dutch Telecom *see* PTT Telecom BV

EC COST CO-Tech Work Programme 59–60
EDS Corp. 206
educational sociology 138
electronic brainstorming 100
electronic data interchange (EDI) 4, 6, 11–12, 151, 179–93, 243, 256–7
  and the individual 183–4
electronic funds transfer at point of sale 29
electronic meeting support systems 254–5
e-mail 5, 100, 214, 252, 254–5
employees
  commitment 76–7
  flexibility 70
  mobility 79
  participation 77
  skill enhancement 76
  stock ownership schemes 272
  training 77–8
Engeström, Yrjö 50
entrepreneurs 155
ESTEEM 202
ethnographic approach 48–9, 51–2, 59
EU ESPRIT COMIC Basic Research Action 60
experience 110–12
expert systems 127, 198, 203, 213, 255
ExperTax 204
ExploreNet 213
Explorer Neuralworks 213

Federal Express COSMOS system 102
financial sector 19, 23–36, 153, 161, 164, 168, 176, 216
Finland 145
first mover advantage 2
Ford 158–9
Frame Agreements 186–90
frameworks, impact 180–4, 191

Future Workshops 42

General Motors 158
Gopher 253
group decision support systems 39, 43,
    45, 74, 127, 198, 204–7, 214
group processes 11
Group Systems V 74
Groupware 4–6, 39–41, 43, 45, 54, 100,
    125, 206, 252
GTE 202

handovers 263
hardware 144, 174
HCI 45
'Heathrow School of Management' 2
Hewlett Packard 72–3, 78
Highland Insurance 26, 29, 31–3
hospitals 96–7 *see also* medical centres
human factors 43–6, 49, 142, 144

IBM 24, 207
ICI 279, 286
industrial revolution 154–5
inflation 168
information 141–2
    overload 252
Information Lens 255
information systems 3
    advanced information management
        system 72–3
    and learning 10–11
    and organizational change 12
    evolution model for information
        systems strategy 140–3
    management information systems 26,
        29, 31–3
    office 43, 49
    personnel 146, 257–8
    planning 11, 133–49
    quality 236
    strategic 7, 9–11, 88, 96, 104, 133–49
information technology
    and competitive advantage 13
    architectures 6, 9, 11–12, 55, 126, 143,
        152, 195–222, 237, 251
    cost-benefit 30–1, 35, 154, 254
    infrastructural patterns 23
    investment in 141, 153, 174, 257
    outsourcing 35, 257
    research 14
    role in organizational change 12, 27–8

strategy 7
symbolic value 27–8
tools 8, 40, 196, 214, 216, 253
    see also under name
Informix 73
innovation 11, 24, 151–222
    administrative 153–4, 157–9, 161–6, 168,
        170, 172, 175
    and performance 160–77, 181–2
    distribution 220
    IT 166–8, 172, 175
    marketing 154, 156, 166, 171
    process 157–66, 174
    product 153–4, 156–66, 170–2, 174–5,
        220
    research 165–72
    time windows 154, 168, 170
    types 157–9
    variables 166–8
Institute of Management 271
institutional isomorphism 164
insurance industry 216–17
International Business Engineers 264, 266
Internet 4, 6, 251
intranet 4
invention 156–7

Japan 204, 217, 276, 285
J. C. Penney 101
job design 246
joint ventures 198

KANVAS 266
knowledge 10, 109–11
    constructs 197
    encoding 12, 255–6
    management 8
    trading between competitors 25
    see also learning
knowledge based systems 128, 202–4, 214,
    216, 255–6
Kolind, Lars 67–8, 70–2, 74–8, 80n, 81
Kuutti, K. 50

labour, division of 48
LanManager network 73
leadership 285
learning 51, 111–17
    basic processes (core capabilities/
        competencies) 96
    by using 174
    capability loop 92–5, 99–100, 102

conceptual 101
double loop 5, 112–14
dynamic 211–13
individual 112, 208–11
integrated intelligent support system
    214–15
interactive 138–9
interorganizational 198, 201–2
IS strategy 138–40, 142, 144
networks 122
OADI-cycle 112–13
operational 101
participative strategy formation 204
path dependent 89–90
radical 95
routinization loop 92–5, 99–100, 102
single loop 5, 113
situated 88
specificity degree 90
strategic loop 93–5, 101–2
system construction and use 146
see also knowledge; organizations
Leavitt's diamond 230
Leont'ev 50
libraries 160, 162
Listserver 253
Lockheed 202
logistics 151, 191
Lotus Notes 55–6, 253, 255
LUCIA 12, 244, 261–8

Malone, Tom 255
management
    by objectives 273
    coherence 287–8
    information systems 26, 29, 31–3
    quality 123–5 *see also* total quality
management
    scientific 115
    techniques 272
    tools 271
'Management in the 1990s' framework
    180
managers
    cognitive structuring 287
    hybrid 20
    middle 249
    senior 19–20, 28
    training 281
manufacturing industries 154–5, 160, 164,
    174, 176

marketing 21–2, 69
markets 21–2, 110
Marx, Karl 155
medical centres 160 *see also* hospitals
mental models 110–14, 123, 125, 127, 142,
    208
Microsoft 2, 252–3
MIND 209
mindfulness 146
MIT 180, 255
Mrs Field's Cookies 97–8

National Bank 26–7, 29–31, 33
NEC Corporation 202
Netherlands 261–8
networking 174–5
networks 5–6, 43
    branch 26, 29–30
    inter-sectoral 24
    learning 122
    local area 250–1, 254
    physical 4–5
    public 12
    social 4–5, 8
    wide area 214, 250
    see also artificial neural networks; *and*
        under name
Neuroshell 213
New Wave 72–3
Nippon Steel 202
NOTARIS 266

objects (software) 252, 255
offices 49, 55
    automation 43–4, 48–9 *see also* Oticon
    design 71
    information systems 43, 49
    paperless 65–6, 71–4, 78
OLE2 252–3
one-stop shopping 265, 267
Open Doc 252–3
operations research 116
organizational development 273, 279, 286
organizations
    and trading partners 190–1
    behaviour 3, 8
    classical theory 20–1, 227–9
    competition 25, 34–5, 80, 87–8, 91, 93–4,
        97, 101–4, 108, 115, 134–5, 142, 156,
        172, 228, 233–5, 245–6, 271–2
    critical path 286–7
    culture 78, 217, 262, 280, 286–7

departments 69
distributed environments 253–4
evolutionary theory 227–9
external environment 20–1, 109, 228, 231, 238, 252
forms 5
frame breaking change 247
growth 235–7
hierarchical 65–8, 78
inertia 95, 97, 102, 287
innovative control philosophy 70
internal politics 20, 27, 29, 41, 280, 284, 287–8
interorganizational systems 151, 179–80, 256–7
knowledge and learning 5–6, 8, 10–11, 29–33, 38–9, 59, 85–149, 154, 162, 195–216, 231, 239, 243
managing expertise 9–10, 17, 19–36, 51
metamorphosis 75–82
mission 93, 95, 102
performance 11, 160–77, 181–2
power and empowerment 6, 21, 27, 34, 41, 57
processual theory 21, 227–9
radical/incremental change 225–7, 238
resource based view 87–90, 102, 104
routines 89–90, 97–8, 100, 114, 163
sectoral factors 19, 23–5
security 252
size 172
social constructionist theory 21–3, 34
social groups 21–3, 29
spaghetti metaphor 65, 68, 75, 79, 82
strategy 2–3, 7–10, 17, 19–36, 151, 182–3, 198, 211–12, 225, 227–38, 246
systemic theory 227–30
virtual 174–5
vision 75, 126, 138
ORGEN 203
Orlikowski, Wanda 55
Orr, J. 56–7
ORSYS 203
Oticon 10, 17, 65–83

Participative Design 51–2, 58
PC operating systems 2
PDP Research Group 111
PEST 233
petrol, leaded 286
Plex Center 207

positive feed forward mechanisms 2
private sector 287
process engineering 58
process innovation 74
process modelling 53
procurement *see* purchasing
production outsourcing 71–2
productivity 57, 174
programming codes 252
project groups see workgroups
PTT Telecom BV 244, 261–8
purchasing 101, 185–90

QDES 202
quality circles 272

radios, portable 57
Rank Xerox 202
redundancy *see* downsizing
REMIND 202
remote group support systems 254–5
research and development 156, 172, 176, 187, 197
Russia *see* Soviet Union

Sachs, Pat 51, 55
Santa Fe Institute 115
Scandinavia 51–2
Schil single screen device 266
Schumpeter 155
ScotBank Group 26–9
screen communication 266–7
SEMA Group 237
service industries 153–7, 159–61, 164, 174, 176
Shell 198, 211
SMART 202
Smith, Adam 228
SODA 211
soft systems methodology 116, 226
software 54, 144, 174
    credit cards 26–7
    research and development 41
    see also under name or type
SOPHIA 263
Soviet Union 50
spreadsheets 253
SQUAD 202
stakeholders 116, 123–5, 127, 231, 235, 238–9
standardization 282–3
static efficiency concept 92–4

STELLA 211
strategic grid 233–4
strategic information systems 7, 9–11, 88, 96, 104, 133–49
Suchman, Lucy 53
SWOT 233
system re-engineering 263
systems design 42, 52
systems dynamics 115

task forces *see* workgroups
Tavistock Institute of Human Relations 230
Taylor, F. W. 46, 263
technological lag 173
technology infrastructure 12
TEDIS II programme 185
telecommunications industry 185, 262
total quality management 3, 273–4, 276, 278, 280, 285
Trouble Ticketing System 56

Unisys 266–7
United Kingdom 273–4, 278, 286–7
United States 163–75, 239, 272–3, 287
UNIX 73

Vectra 386 PC 73

Verwaayen, Ben 263
videos 101, 214
VIPS 203
Vogue/Voguepac 26–7
voice mail 214
Volvo Corporation 213
Vygotsky 50

Wall Charting 42
Whitwam, David 223–4
Windows 2, 72–3, 266
word processors 253
work 43
    activity orientated 51
    practices 91–2, 99–100
    processes 10, 38–40, 44, 46–59, 237–8, 253
    projects 69–70, 77
    see also business process redesign/re-engineering
workflows 46, 53, 55, 253, 261
workgroups 39, 41, 57, 74, 77, 184, 204, 249, 252, 265, 281–2
workshops 233, 235, 281
work-to-rule 49

X400 service provider 251
Xerox Parc 206